Theology as if
Jesus Matters

The Living Issues Discussion Series

*T*HE LIVING ISSUES DISCUSSION SERIES is edited by Michael A. King and published by Cascadia Publishing House (earlier by Pandora Press U.S.) as well as sometimes copublished with Herald Press. Cascadia Publishing House, in consultation with its Editorial Council as well as volume editors and authors, is primarily responsible for content of these studies. Tpically through a main text followed by materials providing affirming and critical reactions from respondents, these volumes address "living issues" likely to benefit from lively and serious discussion.

1. To Continue the Dialogue:
   Biblical Interpretation and Homosexuality
   Edited by C. Norman Kraus, 2001

2. What Does the Bible Really Say About Hell?
   Wrestling with the Traditional View
   By Randy Klassen, 2001

3. Reflecting on Faith in a Post-Christian Time (a revised and expanded edition of Theology in Postliberal Perspective, first published by SCM Press and Trinity Press International)
   By Daniel Liechty, 2003

4. Stumbling Toward a Genuine Conversation on Homosexuality
   Edited by Michael A. King, 2007

5. Theology As If Jesus Matters:
   An Introduction to Christianity's Main Themes
   By Ted Grimsrud, 2009

Theology as if
Jesus Matters

An Introduction to
Christianity's Main Convictions

Ted Grimsrud

Responses by
Douglas Harink, Brenda Martin Hurst, David
Neville, and Duane Friesen

Cascadia
Publishing House
Telford, Pennsylvania

copublished with
Herald Press
Scottdale, Pennsylvania

Cascadia Publishing House LLC orders, information, reprint permissions:
contact@cascadiapublishinghouse.com
1-215-723-9125
126 Klingerman Road, Telford PA 18969
www.CascadiaPublishingHouse.com

Library of Congress Cataloguing-in-Publication Data
Grimsrud, Ted, 1954-
 Theology as if Jesus matters : an introduction to Christianity's main con-
victions / Ted Grimsrud.
  p. cm. -- (Living issues discussion series ; v. 5)
 Includes bibliographical references.
 Summary: "What would Christian theology be like if it consistently took
Jesus' central command to love God and neighbor as the most important
consideration? This book engages that question"--Provided by publisher.
 ISBN-13: 978-1-931038-67-6 (trade pbk. : alk. paper)
 ISBN-10: 1-931038-67-8 (trade pbk. : alk. paper)
 1. Theology, Doctrinal. I. Title. II. Series.

BT78.G76 2009
230--dc22

2009032033

16 15 13 12 11 10 09   10 9 8 7 6 5 4 3 2 1

To my friends at Shalom Mennonite Congregation
Harrisonburg, Virginia

Contents

Series Editor's Preface 9
Author's Preface 11

1 What Do We Do with Theology? [Introduction] • 15
2 Who Is That Guy? [The Person of Christ] • 30
3 News of God [God] • 45
4 God's Spirit—And Ours [The Holy Spirit] • 60
5 This is God's World: So What? [Creation] • 75
6 How Does God Communicate? [Revelation] • 90
7 Humanness: A Blessing or a Curse? [Humanity] • 106
8 Salvation: Healing Our Damage [The Work of Christ] • 120
9 The Church: Why Bother? [Christian Community] • 136
10 Evoking the Presence of God [The Sacraments] • 151
11 Bless All the Families of the Earth [The Religions] • 166
12 The End Times are Now [Eschatology] • 182
13. Do This and Live [The Christian Life] • 197

Responses   208
Notes   219
Bibliography   226
The Author   230

Series Editor's Preface

*T*TED GRIMSRUD AIMS TO INTRODUCE Christianity's "main convictions." His is no generic introduction, however; rather, Grimsrud wants to theologize "as if Jesus matters." Suppose instead he theologized "as if Paul matters." Or using, say, such earlier church formulations as the Apostles' or Nicene creeds. Such starting points would have generated a different book. I believe each book could have been a Christian one, illuminating some Christian understandings while shadowing others. The fact that such different books could have been written suggests that the starting point we choose for Christian theologizing is a "living issue" deserving serious discussion and an examination of various ways Christians may view such agenda.

This is what makes Grimsrud's book fit the Living Issues Discussion Series. To set the conversation in motion, typically books in the series include a vigorous statement of position regarding an issue or set of issues sometimes controversial in faith circles. Then, after a book's main text, a Responses chapter provides affirming and critical commentary.

The result in this case is a fruitful one. Grimsrud shows us what theologizing as if Jesus matters can look like. Then Brenda Martin Hurst, Douglas Harink, David Neville, and Duane Friesen help us envision Grimsrud's contributions as part of a mutually enriching discussion in which Grimsrud at times challenges their views and vice-versa yet the five of them together generate an exciting foundation for further thought and discernment regarding—precisely—how Jesus matters.

—*Michael A. King, Living Issues Discussion Series Editor*

Author's Preface

SINCE THE FALL OF 1996, I HAVE TAUGHT Introduction to Theology at Eastern Mennonite University, a class for lower-level undergrads. At the beginning of the semester, when I go over the course goals, I tell the students that by successfully completing the class, they will discover that theology is interesting, fun, and important.

I have not done a survey of students who took the class to see if indeed the class did achieve the predicted outcome, but I am happy to make the same claim for any who successfully complete reading this book!

My sources for the chapters that follow, along with years of reading theological writing, come from two places. The dozen or so times I have taught Introduction to Theology and dozens of sermons over the years on theological themes. Most immediately, with this book in mind, I preached thirteen sermons at Shalom Mennonite Congregation in Harrisonburg, Virginia. Reflecting this "sermonic" agenda, I seek in this book mostly to encourage readers toward themselves embodying Jesus' way—more than simply supplying academic information.

I am grateful to my friends who are part of Shalom both for the opportunity to take on this experiment of constructing doctrinal theology in the pulpit and for the follow-up discussions after the sermons that pushed, prodded, and affirmed.

I am also grateful to the couple of hundred college students who, in my Introduction to Theology classes, also pushed, prodded, and (occasionally) affirmed.

My most important theological influence continues to be John Howard Yoder. One Yoder theme that looms large in what follows is his understanding of "tradition." As I seek to do, Yoder wrote as an Anabaptist theologian—one who orients all elements of Christian theology and ethics in relation to the Jesus Christ of the Gospels.

Yoder proposed that we best understand tradition not so much like "an ongoing growth like a tree" but more like a vine: "a story of constant interruption of organic growth in favor of pruning and a new chance for the roots." This "pruning" is a kind of "looping back," "a glance over the shoulder to enable a midcourse correction, a rediscovery of something from the past whose pertinence was not seen before, because only a new question or challenge enables us to see it speaking to us" ("The Authority of Tradition," in *The Priestly Kingdom: Social Ethics as Gospel*, University of Notre Dame Press, 1984, p. 69).

I understand the story of Jesus to be the "root" for Christian theology, and I attempt to use it as a basis for criticism and ongoing evaluation for present-day faith convictions. This approach leads to a kind of relativizing of post-biblical creeds, confession, and "orthodoxies." This relativizing is not a move toward a general relativism born out of modernist or "liberal" sensitivities. To the contrary, it is a profoundly *conservative* interpretive move in the sense of placing priority on the originating vision of our faith. And it stems from a confession of Jesus' divinity, his identity as God incarnate—that is, God manifest in this flesh-and-blood life. (Here again I follow Yoder. See especially his classic text built on this link between the content of Jesus' life and teaching and our confession of his divinity, *The Politics of Jesus*, 2nd. ed., Eerdmans, 1994).

To relativize post-biblical creeds, confessions, and "orthodoxies" is not to reject them. It is simply to insist that they be evaluated in light of the founding revelation in Jesus. The roots are not grown away from as the "tradition as tree-like" image suggests. Rather, they retain a living presence meant to enhance our continuing theological reflection and our lived convictions.

Christian theology, of course, emerges as a communal enterprise. Along with my several congregations and college classes, I also have gained immeasurably from conversations, short and lengthy, relaxed and heated, over many years with friends. Most directly related to this book, I want to thank EMU colleagues such as Ray Gingerich, Christian Early, Nancy Heisey, Earl Zimmerman, and Mark Thiessen Nation for all the great talk.

Even more, I want to thank former EMU colleague and Shalom congregant, David Kratz Mathies, not only for great talk but also for reading through my manuscript and offering innumerable perceptive comments.

And most of all, as always, I want to thank my partner in so many things, Kathleen Temple, for great talk and everything else.

—*Ted Grimsrud*
 Harrisonburg, Virginia

Theology as if
Jesus Matters

1

What Do We Do with Theology?

[Introduction]

*D*O YOU THINK OF YOURSELF AS A THEOLOGIAN? If you're like my students, you'd probably say no. Every spring I teach a class aimed at first- and second-year college students called "Introduction to Theology." Few have taken a theology class before. In our first session, when we do introductions, I ask students to tell the rest of us what theological issues most interest them. Every time, most students say, "Well, I guess I don't really have an issue."

For their first reading assignment, I give them an essay that suggests that all Christians actually are "theologians," since we all think and talk about what we believe. After reading that essay, many students who had said they had no "theological issue" they were interested in come back to say, "I hadn't thought about it that way before, but maybe I am a theologian. I do have life issues I am interested in, and I do care about my faith and how it relates to life."

Usually we go on then to have numerous stimulating conversations over the semester about "theological issues." The students come to realize that when they think and write and talk about "faith issues" and "life priorities issues" and "coming to terms with my parents and grandparents issues," they usually are dealing with *theological* issues. It takes them a while to figure this out, though, because of negative associations they have with what they think "theology" has to do with.

What do you associate with the term *theology*? When I do word association discussions in my classroom or congregation, often terms such as *boring, self-satisfied, otherworldly, heavy,* and *irrelevant* come up. And these are people going to church or attending a church-related college! Theology has an image problem.

This book seeks to help rehabilitate theology. Or, at least, I hope to help you see how theology may actually be fascinating, important, and even potentially life changing.

WHAT IS THEOLOGY?

Beyond rapid-fire word association, what do we mean by *theology*? These are some possibilities, most of which may reinforce the negative feelings many Christians have about this term and what they think it stands for:

Theology is an academic discipline. One takes classes in theology. One gets degrees in theology. We have theology departments. To be a theologian one must have specialized, graduate school training and be able to use technical, insiders-only language (with terms such as *soteriology, ontological trinity,* and *hypostatic union*).

Or, theology is a collection of formal written statements of doctrinal belief issued by various Christian bodies—creeds, confessions, statements of faith. If you want to know what, say, Mennonite theology is, you read the 1995 *Confession of Faith in a Mennonite Perspective* formally adopted by the Mennonite Church General Assembly. If you want to know what Presbyterian theology is, you read the Westminster Confession of Faith.

Or, theology is the basis for determining boundary lines, an elaboration of official beliefs for an organized religious group that serves as the basis for determining which beliefs are acceptable and which are heretical, who may be considered inside the circle of membership and who is to be outside.

Or, theology could be defined as the study of what theologians have written. This would be parallel to how Robert Pirsig describes philosophy in his book *Zen and the Art of Motor-*

cycle Maintenance. He coined the term *philosophology–*
phy as the study of what philosophers write.[1] Maybe v
say "theologology," theology as the study of what theo
write. To study theology one must be well educated, a
understand a lot of technical language. One must be able to
sustain intense levels of concentration with highly abstract and
often speculative formulations that compare and critique other
highly abstract and often speculative formulations from
thinkers recognized as theologians.

All of these definitions may be valid, perhaps—at least as
descriptions of how the term *theology* is used in actual practice.
However, I have something different in mind when I write
about theology in this book.

I believe that our "theology" is made up of the convictions
that matter the most to us. We each have a hierarchy of values
and commitments, things that we see as most important in our
lives. At the very top of this hierarchy is our God or gods. The
term *theology* does literally mean "the study of God"—*theos*
being the Greek word for God. (My first name, Theodore means
"gift of God.")

For right now, let's say that the term *God* signifies what we
believe is ultimate or supreme. This ultimacy may or may not
be associated with a "supreme being," as in Yahweh or Allah.
To understand the actual theology we live by, we should be
asking first of all about how we order our lives. What in practice are the priorities in our lives that reflect what we truly accept as ultimate? What priorities are reflected in the actual
ways we live? These priorities tell us what our *actual* God or
gods are.

So, first of all, theology describes our priorities, our most
fundamental beliefs and values. Theology deals with the convictions and commitments we order our lives around and devote our best energies toward.

We *do* theology when we reflect on and describe these values. Theology is about communication. To express our own
convictions to others, we must find ways to communicate. This
process of learning to communicate about our most basic values and commitments may be defined as "doing theology."

Let me give an example. My mom's hierarchy of values
could be seen in her commitments to love her children, as a

teacher to help her fourth-graders feel acceptance and an excitement about the world of which they were part, and to create beauty through her music, her painting, and her crafts. These values revealed what she truly believed about God and life and our place in the world.

My mother didn't put this theology into words very often. When she did, however, she talked about the importance of unconditional love toward her children (both biological and in school) and how this stemmed both from her sense of her own mother's love (and her father's love) and her understanding of God being a God of love.

So, my mom's "theology" had to do with how she lived her life, her highest priorities, the matters that led her to make the choices she made of how to spend her time and energy. She operated as a "theologian" when she tried to say where these values came from and why they mattered to her.

My mom's lived theology had little to do with official church statements or the writings for formal theologians, as is true of most people, even the most devout Christians. However, when we are attentive we will probably find ways that theology in the more traditional sense of that term does influence our lived theology.

DISHONEST THEOLOGY

Defining theology in terms of our actual values, I suggest that if we talk about bad theology or false theology, we might mean mostly *dishonest* theology. Theology is dishonest when one's *stated* beliefs and values are quite a bit different from the values that actually determine what one does.

This proclivity for dishonest theology should push us to be more self-conscious about our true convictions, more self-aware of how we actually do or don't implement ultimate convictions. Certainly the problem of hypocrisy—obvious contradiction between stated convictions and actions (or we could say, contradiction between stated convictions and true convictions as evidenced in the actual way we live)—takes a terrible toll on the witness of communities of faith. Working to be self-conscious about our theology should help us to live more closely in line with the ideals we sincerely hold.

Certainly none of us lives with full honesty or in total harmony with our deepest values. However, the *goal* of integrity remains central for authentic theology. Most of us can think of people whose lives inspire and encourage us. In most cases we are likely thinking of people of integrity—those whose belief and practice hang together. I think of two of my friends who during the 1960s believed the war in Vietnam was immoral. To express their opposition, they joined a development and relief organization and actually put their own lives on the line living in Vietnam and helping those whose lives were disrupted by that war. In the years since, they have continued to live lives of integrity that encourage those who know them.

In seeking to do Christian theology, we should want to discern the factors that make it difficult to integrate our beliefs about Jesus with our actual lives. Our surrounding culture imposes a kind of theology on us on most of us. Walter Wink suggests that the predominant "religion" in our world today is "the myth of redemptive violence," the belief that violence is necessary and effective and worth untold amounts of time, money, and natural resources.[2]

Now I imagine few Christians in North America would overtly affirm this theology that makes its *highest* priorities the redemptive power of violence. However, look at the message our national government gives with its budget priorities. Those of us who pay taxes spend over half of those taxes on military related items. The highest presidential approval ratings almost always occur at the moment when our nation is about to go to war or is in the midst of battle.

We are challenged to be self-conscious and name our deepest convictions. Then we may find ourselves in our actual lives simply living by the priorities and values with which our wider society inundates us (such as the myth of redemptive violence).

BRINGING OUR TRUE
CONVICTIONS TO THE SURFACE

How do we work at bringing our true convictions closer to the surface? How do we work at conforming our lives to the vision we truly do want to affirm? How do we resist living by a theology we do not really want to embrace?

The first step may be simply starting to reflect on where our beliefs about ultimate things come from. This process of self-reflection itself will move us closer to being able to exert some self-determination on what we believe and how we live.

All of us grow up internalizing beliefs and commitments passed on to us by our families and communities. We may call this our "embedded theology"[3]—a set of values we have maybe before we can even talk, mostly beliefs that seep into our hearts with no self-awareness at all.

I had a friend once who told me that her strongest concern growing up as a Mennonite was "What will other people think?" This ranked about at the top of her hierarchy of values. But it was certainly not a value she chose. It was deeply embedded long before she was self-aware.

All of us may have similar examples. Think back to your earliest memories. Then, try to flesh how you saw the world then. What did you value? How did you want to spend you time? Who mattered to you the most? What would you have said was most meaningful, most important in your life?

How most of us answer these questions probably tells us a great deal about our embedded theology. What we valued the most when we were five years old came from our environments, our parents, our siblings, our friends, maybe our exposure to television and movies. These values reflected the theology we had embedded in our hearts and minds. This "embedded" theology did not come to us through our own choices, our own quest for answers. It was given to us; we inherited it.

We take the various elements of our embedded theology with us our entire lives. They are part of who we are. For some people, embedded theology is all that is ever needed. They stay in the same communities and live around the same people all their lives and face few threatening questions or traumas.

For most of us, though, our embedded theologies are not enough. When we face a world bigger and more diverse than we experienced in younger years. When we suffer, when we face questions and struggles that shake us up, when we are asked by someone else who does not share our background what we believe and why, then we will be pushed to move from embedded to what we could call *deliberative* theology. Then we think and apply and expand and understand and articulate.

I think of myself as an eighteen-year-old, packing up and leaving home for the first time. It wasn't as if Oregon College of Education was the city that never sleeps or populated by many people not from small-town Oregon. However, after living my whole life in a village of 150 people fifty miles from the nearest movie theater, I wasn't exactly sophisticated. I did find this new place scary. I had to ask, What do I really believe? How can I make sense of what I am hearing from these Vietnam War vets, these kids who grew up in Portland, my dorm neighbor smoking those funny-smelling cigarettes?

As is typical of new college students, I had to be more self-conscious about what I valued and why. I not only had to make choices about how to behave, how to spend my time and money, and who to spend time with—I also had to explain my choices, sometimes to others, always to myself. Why am I doing what I am doing? Being removed from the secure womb of home and childhood community, I couldn't just rely on social convention or assumed values. I had to think, to deliberate, actually to choose among a number of options.

Hopefully, as we grow and become more self-conscious about our theology, we will mostly find that the things we absorbed as children are useful for us. Hopefully, the move from embedded to deliberative theology will mostly be a process of affirmation—but with a sense that we know what and why we make the affirmation. But for just about all of us, there will be things we need to cast aside or at least revise in major ways.

Often, no matter how comfortable and safe our youthful environment was, we will find that quite a bit of our embedded theology needs revision. And sometimes much of the embedded theology needs to be discarded. ☙

Neither of my parents spent much energy openly describing and defending their beliefs to their five children. They taught us more by example than proclamation. One of the lessons they taught that did indeed have theological importance was how closely they linked God and country. Both of my parents were World War II veterans. They regularly flew the American flag at appropriate holidays.

When I left home, I began to encounter a different perspective. Several of my college classmates in the early 1970s were recent returnees from combat in the Vietnam War. They told stories of how this was not a noble war. Many were deeply disillusioned with America and with God. I also studied the history of the war. Then I learned of a stream in the Christian tradition of believers who rejected the close identification of God and country I had grown up with. Learning of the Anabaptist take on Jesus' message led me to a deliberate choice: Would I continue to worship a God who placed a higher priority on the United States than most of the rest of world? Or would I worship a God who, in the John Prine song of that era, "don't like killing, no matter what the reason for"?[4]

My choice marked a decisive move away from my embedded theology that so linked God and country. Yet I have come to understand since that I didn't move from my embedded theology quite as decisively as I thought at the time. I had many other elements in my own embedded theology that *supported* the new vision of Christian faith I embraced when I turned from my God-and-country theology—the priority on love over ideology and the value placed on independent thinking, for example. And I find that I have retained a deep appreciation for and commitment to the ideals of the democratic vision my parents both believed they were serving during World War II.

Our embedded theology gives us our start. It is a mixture of truth and falsehood. We cannot fully transcend it or live as if it never were a part of us. Yet from my own experience I conclude that we generally need self-conscious deliberation to separate what should be affirmed in our embedded theology from what should be jettisoned.

We hopefully do become more self-conscious about our hierarchy of convictions as we are exposed to other people with other theologies. Likely, we will become aware that we have a whole range of things to sort out, many options and choices. William James accurately wrote about life in the modern world being lived amid the "blooming, buzzing, mass of confusion."[5]

Does this cacophony of voices, values, priorities, philosophies, commitments, and opinions that makes up our contemporary world leave us without any sure guidance? Do we have any criteria to guide our deliberation and quest for self-consciousness about our theology? Christians claim that we do. We claim that in Jesus Christ we have God's definitive revelation for shaping our theology.

However, one big problem with many ways of thinking about Christian theology is that they allow us to focus only on beliefs, only on doctrines, only on what we *say* we believe. This is why it has been possible for so many Christians over the years to proclaim our belief in Jesus as savior while at the same time fighting wars, owning slaves, abusing our children, and destroying the earth. Problematic doctrinal beliefs have taken the place of Jesus' own message in the hierarchy of convictions for many Christians. As a consequence, other values and commitments (many of them variations on the myth of redemptive violence) have taken priority over the content of Jesus' own life and words in the hierarchy of Christian theology ("theology" again defined in terms of how people actually live).

THEOLOGY AS IF JESUS MATTERS

Let me suggest that we need fresh attention to Jesus in our theology. In this book, I intend to consider each of the main traditional Christian doctrines. How might they look if pursued consistently in light of Jesus' life and teaching? I will present an alternative to the disjunction between belief and practice that has too often characterized the lives of Christians.

It seems obvious to me that when we talk about *Christian* theology, our ordering point should be Jesus' life and teaching. But as I will suggest, this has *not* typically been characteristic of Christian theology. Still, the path I take in this book does treat Jesus' life and teaching as its ordering point. I will add a second, complementary ordering point—our vision for wholeness in our lives and the lives of all creatures. We look *back* at what Jesus said and did. He shows us God as nothing else does. And we look *forward*. How might we envision being whole?

In the actual history of Christianity, what seems obvious to me today has not usually been obvious for traditional theology. Going clear back to the Apostles' Creed, perhaps first formulated only 100 years after Jesus' death, we see an amazing omission. This is how what matters most about Jesus is concisely stated in the Apostles' Creed: "I believe in Jesus Christ, God's only Son our Lord, who was born of the Holy Spirit and the Virgin Mary, crucified under Pontius Pilate, and buried; the third day he rose from the dead."[6] What's missing?

The Creed jumps from "born of the Virgin Mary" straight to "crucified under Pontius Pilate"—as if what matters theologically are only Jesus' birth, crucifixion, and resurrection. It totally *leaves out* Jesus' words and deeds. No wonder Christians have found it so easy to confess Jesus as Savior while living in ways that contradict how he lived and how he taught his followers to live. No wonder theology became the domain of experts, focused on abstract ideas, and the tool of institutional control and boundary marking.

Such an omission makes it easier to see Christian theology as being about general ideas, abstract doctrines, spiritualized banalities, and hopes for heaven after death. When the actual deeds and words of Jesus are excised from the picture, we lose our main source of concrete guidance about life in the here and now—and the sense that this source links directly to God. As Jesus said in John 14, when we see his life and works we see God—and are challenged to share in those works ourselves as a core aspect of our identity as Jesus' disciples.

I suggest something quite different than that theology is something constructed only by experts. Theology is something all people do. Our theology reflects our commitments that shape how we actually live in the world. *Christian* theology, as a self-conscious task, looks at our values and convictions and actions in light of the life and teaching of Jesus. If we approach theology as I suggest, this is what it may involve:

(1) We engage in self-reflection and conversation that helps each other to clarify our lived values.

(2) We seek to know ourselves better and to discern how closely our lives actually fit with our stated ideals.

(3) We work to find ways to name our true convictions, to hold them to the light of day, to test them, and to revise them accordingly.

(4) We grow in our understanding of what kind of people we truly want to be, how better to become such people, and what hinders us from doing so.

(5) We learn better and better what our gods actually are and how to differentiate the God of Jesus from other, lesser gods.

Insofar as they help us work at such self-reflection and conversation, traditional Christian doctrinal categories may still be useful. At least they will provide the framework for this book. These doctrines (such as Christology—the doctrine of Jesus Christ; ecclesiology—the doctrine of the church; and anthropology—the doctrine of humanity) must not be made into absolutes. The doctrines are not ends in themselves that serve as definitive statements of Truth and become the center of our religion.

o The doctrines are aids. They serve to help us reflect on real life and real practices and real values by pointing beyond themselves to the living God and the model of Jesus. Doctrines are valid when they help us to love God and neighbor.

We run the danger, when we speak of discrete doctrines, of reifying (or absolutizing) them. We too easily think of doctrines as having some kind of static existence rather than being fluid human creations. Doctrines are constructed as guidelines that help us order our thinking and better communicate; they do not transcend human finitude.

o Yet, when they work properly, doctrines help us think about the life of faith more fully. They aid us as we consider the many different aspects of how we live and think and relate to one another. More importantly, doctrines help us consciously to think about our theology (our highest values) in light of Jesus' life and teaching.

This is what I will seek to do in what follows in this book. I will use the life and teaching of Jesus as our key for reading the Bible, for reflecting on Christian tradition *and* understanding, and for adapting what we want to be most important in shaping our lives. Jesus' message and way of life will serve as our basis for evaluating what we find when we read the Bible, when we reflect on the Christian theological tradition, and when we consider present-day experience.

BIBLICAL RESOURCES

With Jesus as our clue, we will find much in the entire Bible to help us clarify what matters most. Let's touch on three representative biblical texts from different parts of the Bible— Psalm 146, Luke 10:25-37, and James 2:1-17. These passages, and many more help us as we shape our sense of what matters the most for Christian theology done as if Jesus matters.

Let me start with some worship literature from the Old Testament. We may characterize the Book of Psalms as Israel being honest before God. In the Psalms, the worshiping community finds words for its hope, doubt, fear, joy, anger, and gratitude.

Psalm 146 captures some of the people's deepest hopes. In this psalm, Israel's aspirations find expression. The hopes in this psalm reflect a theological view of human social life. The psalm contrasts trusting in princes with trusting in the Maker of heaven and earth. The psalmist emphasizes that trust in princes and trust in God are *competing* alternatives; trust in one leads to mistrust of the other.

The Lord is trustworthy for people committed to genuine justice, the psalm proclaims, because the Lord's life continues, unlike human leaders who die. This steadfast God, the creator, sides not with the princes but with the oppressed, the hungry, prisoners, those who can't see, the bowed down, resident aliens, orphans, and widows. This clear statement of God's priorities obviously points ahead to Jesus' own message, as we see clearly in Jesus' opening words in Luke 4.

Psalm 146 puts in the language of worship the ideals that stood behind the Hebrew prophets' critique of the nations around Israel, the great empires such as Egypt, Assyria, and Babylon. More pointedly, though, the sentiments in this psalm critique political life within Israel itself. The prophetic critique of Israel included concern with trust in "princes" rather than God and with disregarding justice for the oppressed. True justice, which is Israel's reason to exist, involves loving God and loving the vulnerable neighbor.

> Praise the Lord! Praise the Lord, O my soul! I will praise the Lord as long as I live; I will sing praises to my God all my life long. Do not put your trust in princes, in mortals, in whom there is no help. When their breath departs, they return to the earth; on that very day their plans perish. Happy are those whose help is the God of Jacob, whose hope is in the Lord their God, who made heaven and earth, the sea, and all that is in them; who keeps faith forever; who exercises justice for the oppressed; who gives food for the hungry. The Lord sets the prisoners free; the Lord opens the eyes of the blind. The Lord lifts up those who are bowed down; the Lord loves the righteous. The

Lord watches over strangers; he upholds the orphan and the widow, but the way of the wicked he brings to ruin. The Lord will reign forever, your God, O Zion, for all generations. Praise the Lord! (Ps. 146)

Jesus himself took several opportunities to name his priorities, the priorities he followed in his own life. Perhaps the most famous moment in his teaching came in an encounter with an expert on the Law (a "lawyer" in the NRSV translation) recorded in Luke 10. The lawyer asks Jesus a theological question of the utmost importance: "What must I do to inherit eternal life?" This question touches on just about every theological issue that matters.

Jesus likely did not know of Socrates, but he follows good Socratic method. He asks the lawyer to answer the question for himself. Jesus affirms the answer the lawyer gives: To inherit eternal life one must love God with one's whole being *and* love one's neighbor as oneself. In Matthew's parallel account, these words are spoken by Jesus himself, who then adds that the command to love God and neighbors sum up the Law and Prophets (Matt. 22:34-40). These few words summarize the message of the Bible.

The lawyer's response emphasizes the connection between love and God and love of neighbor. The true test of love of God is to love the neighbor. Paul, another "expert on the Law," also makes this point when he summarizes the Law as "love your neighbor as yourself" (Rom. 13:8). The lawyer's next question zeroes in on the call to love neighbor. The lawyer recognizes that the most crucial measure of love of God and neighbor is one's love of one's actual neighbors.

So he asks, "Who is my neighbor?" This question leads to a story so powerful it will reappear several times in this book, a tale of a man mugged then left unattended by the in-group members and religious leaders who pass him by, but cared for by a Samaritan, a despised outsider. Jesus then asked which of the men the lawyer thought "was a neighbor to the man who fell into the hand of the robbers?" The lawyer got the point: "The one who showed him mercy." Jesus said to him, "Go and do likewise" (Luke 10:30-37).

Jesus' story makes clear the inextricable link between what we believe and how we live. One's relationship with God has everything to do with one's relationship with others. Jesus' story also radicalizes the nature of neighbor love born out of faith in God. The object of neighbor love should not only be one's friends; it also includes one's enemies. A key background point in relation to this story is that "orthodox" Jews whose worship centered in the Jerusalem temple held powerful antipathy toward Samaritans, who did not accept the Jerusalem temple. Jesus cuts through this antipathy with this story.

Finally, let's consider James 2:1-17. This text condemns church folk who favor wealthy people over those in need. It also asserts that the core of the Law is love of neighbor. James 2 claims that since mercy triumphs over judgmentalism people of faith must practice mercy. Faith without works is dead.

James challenges his readers with their own claims to "believe in our glorious Lord Jesus Christ." He insists that belief and practice must go together. The one who believes in Jesus must show evidence of this belief and imitate Jesus' own way of life. Did Jesus show acts of favoritism, favoring the wealthy and powerful over the poor and socially insignificant? Of course not. Neither, then, can those who claim to believe in him.

> If a person with gold rings and in fine clothes comes into your assembly, and if a poor person in dirty clothes also comes in, and if you take notice of the one wearing the fine clothes and say, "Have a seat here, please," while to the one who is poor you say, "Stand there," or, "Sit at my feet," have you not made distinctions among yourselves, and become judges with evil thoughts? (James 2:2-4)

Just as Jesus taught "blessed are the poor," James echoes: "God has chosen the poor in the world to be rich in faith." Ironically, many of those wealthy people that the churches are prone to fawn over have in fact contradicted Jesus' love command.

> Listen, my beloved brothers and sisters. Has not God chosen the poor in the world to be rich in faith and to be heirs of the kingdom that he has promised to those who love him? But you have dishonored the poor. Is it not the rich who oppress you? Is it not they who drag you into court? Is it not they who blaspheme the excellent name that was invoked over you? (James 2:5-7)

James directly quotes Jesus in stating the Christian hierarchy of values: "You shall love your neighbor as yourself." And like Jesus, James emphasizes that this command summarizes the basic message of Scripture. James insists that belief and action belong inextricably together. If we confess Jesus as Lord, our lives must embody the love command or we prove that our confession is empty.

> What good is it, by brothers and sisters, if you say you have faith but do not have works? Can faith save you? If a brother or sister is naked and lacks daily food, and one of you says to them, "Go in peace; keep warm and eat your fill," and yet you do not supply their bodily needs, what is the good of that? So faith by itself, if it has no works, is dead. (James 2:14-17)

Amen.

Who Is That Guy?

[The Doctrine of the Person of Christ]

*I*N TITLING THIS BOOK *THEOLOGY AS IF JESUS MATTERS*, I have in mind especially "theology" in the sense of *articulating* our central convictions. "As if Jesus matters" signals a desire to orient these convictions in terms of Jesus' life and teaching.

Such an approach to theology requires that the first doctrine we consider be Christology.[1] We start by thinking carefully about Jesus, since he establishes our hierarchy of what matters most. Then, in light of Jesus' message, we look at the other doctrines. We treat each doctrine as if Jesus matters. By doing so we will avoid theologizing that ignores or minimizes the directives Jesus' life and teaching give us for faithful living.

WHO IS THAT GUY?

As I thought about this chapter on Jesus Christ, I remembered one of my favorite movies, "Butch Cassidy and the Sundance Kid," from back when I was a teenager. This movie starred a young Paul Newman and Robert Redford as two lovable and smart-mouthed outlaws who rob trains in the Southwest.

Butch and the Kid are robbing the railroads blind. Finally, the railroad line hires a superstar tracker to get the outlaws. They try to escape through endless mountains and gorges and canyons. They try all the tricks in the book and then some to get away. But they can't shake the tracker. They make one particularly fancy escape move, then look back in the distant hills, and there he is. "Who is that guy?" Butch and Sundance cry time after time.

Who is that guy? That made me think of Jesus. Christians have gone to a lot of trouble to *escape* from the Jesus of the Gospels—and almost have made it. But he remains at the edge of the picture, always "tracking" those who have taken his name. "Who is that guy?" We can't quite get away from him.

We may also think of the famous account in Mark's Gospel (8:27-30), where Jesus travels with his disciples after a time of healing and proclaiming the good news. People are marveling at this great prophet. So are the disciples. Who are people saying I am? Jesus asks the disciples. John the Baptist. Elijah. One of the prophets. Then Jesus ask, "But who do you say that I am?" This remains the big question. Who do *we* say that he is? Who is that guy?

We could answer the question "Who is that guy?" in line with the little boy during a Sunday morning children's story. The pastor has a stuffed animal. She asks, "Does anyone know what this is?" And a little boy says, "It looks like a squirrel but I bet it's Jesus." Who is that guy? A soft, cuddly friend?

Or, we could answer the question more in line with much of Christian tradition. Who is that guy? He is God incarnate. He is the one whose perfect sacrifice saves us from sin—and who was without sin himself. He is all-powerful and mighty. That is, he's anything but human and his actual life has little to do with how we answer this question of who he is. Remember how the Apostles' Creed jumps from "born of the Virgin Mary" straight to "crucified under Pontius Pilate."

One of my first classes as a college professor was on Jesus. I made a comment once about Jesus having to pee. Later, a student told me that that comment really shook him up. In fact, it opened his mind to a whole new way of thinking about Jesus. He said never before had he imagined that Jesus actually peed. As he thought about this, he realized that *his* Jesus actually wasn't a human being at all. Rather, he had seen Jesus as a super-being who never truly touched down in history. He realized he needed to revise his Christology to allow for a human Jesus.

Instead of a warm, cuddly friend, and instead of the super not-actually-a-human-being of much of the Christian tradition, I want to suggest a different answer. Who is that guy? Let me propose this: Jesus Christ was a human being, just as human as we are, who lived among us. In his life, he showed us how God wants all human beings to live.

For Christians, "that guy" *should* be our central guide for discerning our theological convictions. Our "theology" has to do with our hierarchy of values, the things that matter the most to us and are expressed in the way we live our lives. The convictions at the top of our hierarchy are the ones that reveal what our God is like. *Christian* theology, I believe, should identify its highest values in terms of Jesus' way, the convictions Jesus had, *Jesus'* hierarchy of values.

THE DOCTRINE OF JESUS CHRIST

Often the doctrine of Jesus Christ—called Christology—is divided into two parts. First, the "person of Jesus Christ"; second, the "work of Jesus Christ." The doctrine of the *person* of Jesus Christ focuses on his identity—"Who is that guy?" His second name, "Christ," is about his identity. Who is he? He is the Christ, the king, the Messiah.

The doctrine of the *work* of Christ focuses on how Jesus brings salvation—"What did that guy do to reunite us with God?" His first name, "Jesus," is about his work. This name *Jesus* (the Hebrew version is "Joshua") means "God saves" or "God liberates." In this chapter, I want to talk about the person of Jesus Christ, his identity. We'll wait to think more fully about God, creation, the Holy Spirit, and humanity before we take up the work of Christ (or the "doctrine of salvation") below in chapter 8.

In Christian theology, the *order* we discuss the themes or doctrines shapes *how* we discuss those themes. The first theme sets the tone for the others. It provides a point of orientation that impacts how we develop each of the following themes. Certainly, each of the themes relates closely to all of the others. None really makes sense in isolation from the others. Yet we have to start somewhere, and where we start impacts what follows.

I propose that we start with the person of Christ. I propose this because of what we learn about our hierarchy of values from Jesus' life and teachings. Jesus provides our lens for evaluating all of our values and convictions. He helps us understand God. He provides the orienting point for making sense of everything else—including every other theological theme.

What if we understand God *first of all* in terms of Jesus' life and teaching? Then we will likely have quite a different understanding of God than if Christology follows *after* we formulate a doctrine of God based on other materials. All the other core themes (e.g., the Holy Spirit, humanity, the end times, and the church) would also be different if formed *before* Christology.

Of course, our Christology (how we answer "Who is that guy?") itself will be much different when we make Jesus' life and teachings the core content of that doctrine. It matters if we self-consciously think of theology in relation to our hierarchy of values. Then, we start with our revealed model for human life, Jesus Christ in his life 2,000 years ago as interpreted by his first followers.

THE CHRISTOLOGICAL EVASION OF JESUS

When we repeat the name *Christ*, we make a confession about Jesus' identity, about who we think he is. However, we are not always that clear about what we mean by Christ. We may act as if this is just Jesus' last name with no special meaning.

Or, if asked, we may say that by Christ we mean something like Jesus is the Son of God (which is literally what "Christ" can mean)—by which we may actually mean that Jesus is God, that Jesus is divine. And when we think of *Jesus* as divine we may have in mind Jesus as perfect, sinless, and all-powerful. When we think of Jesus in this way, the name *Jesus* may actually disappear and be replaced with only Christ. And often the *life* of the person Jesus tends actually to disappear. What matters is his perfection, god-ness, and perfect sacrifice for sin that makes it possible for God to forgive our sins.

What happens then is what we could call the "christological evasion of Jesus." By this I mean the process whereby Christianity's hierarchy of values ends up being very different from

Jesus' own hierarchy of values. We have Christology but we don't pay much attention to Jesus.

Too many Christians have a "Christ" like the one who led the emperor Constantine's armies into battle. Constantine became the leader of the Roman Empire early in the fourth century after deciding to embrace the Christian God. He ended the Roman Empire's policy of persecuting Christians. After Constantine, the empire espoused a version of Christianity. For its first couple of centuries of existence, the Christian church had called on its members to reject fighting in wars. After Constantine, such pacifism largely disappeared.[2] For Constantine's armies, and many, many armies since, Jesus' cross stood as a call to battle, not a call to love.[3]

Too often Christians focus on *belief* instead of focusing on following Jesus' way of life. Christology then tends to have to do with correct doctrine more than correct discipleship. Too often theology focuses on the idea of Jesus dying and receiving God's wrath that we deserve. Then theology concludes that Jesus took up his cross—so *we don't have to.*

This delinking of Jesus' cross from our discipleship is the opposite of what Jesus actually taught: he told us, indeed, *to* take up our cross and follow him. A key example is Mark 8:34-35, immediately after Peter's confession of Jesus as the "Christ." For Jesus, the cross is not something he frees Christians from; it is what follows from being a Christian. For Jesus, the cross had to do with standing for a love that resists oppression and injustice.[4]

The "christological evasion of Jesus" links with what we could call a "doctrine-first Christology." Doctrine-first Christology focuses on Jesus' god-ness. It makes doctrine and belief central and pays little attention to discipleship. In effect, doctrine-first Christology starts with a doctrine of God that emphasizes God's "attributes" such as omniscience ("all-knowing"), omnipotence ("all-powerful"), impassibility ("non-emotional"), and immutability ("unchangeable"). These attributes focus on God's "perfection" and do so in ways that distance God from our human characteristics.

Such a focus on Jesus' other-than-human attributes as what matters most about Christology shapes how we view God. When we confess Jesus as God Incarnate within the doctrine-first Christology framework, we typically start with God's other-than-human "attributes" as definitive of Jesus' divinity. When we do so, we likely will focus on beliefs *about* Jesus as central and absolute. This may lead us to marginalize or ignore altogether the actual shape of Jesus' life as a human being. Jesus' words and acts will then have little theological relevance. And they ultimately will then have little direct relevance for how we live.

PRACTICE-FIRST CHRISTOLOGY

However, what if we take our cues from the Gospels themselves, and from Jesus himself? Then, we will be compelled to seek instead a "practice-first Christology." A practice-first Christology will focus first on Jesus' actual life and teaching. Confessions we make about Jesus' identity as God Incarnate will be *conclusions* following from his life (coming from "below") rather than *assumptions* following from doctrines about Jesus.

Jesus' first disciples drew their conclusions about his identity from the quality of his life, validated by God raising him from the dead. In his life, we see that Jesus was goodness, mercy, and love incarnated. He fulfilled the true meaning of the Law, and he embodied as no one else the message of the prophets.

The following are only some of the ways Jesus did this. He performed miracles of healing. He taught with authority of the meaning of the kingdom (or reign) of God. He included marginalized people as full members of God's community. He confronted unjust structures, challenging oppressive and exclusive legalism, hierarchical religion, and cynical politics. He practiced nonviolence, even in the face of his own arrest and impending death. He manifested deep trust in God, from the time of his initial temptations in the wilderness down to his execution.

With a practice-first Christology, we will realize that confessing Jesus as "the Christ" comes as the *conclusion* his followers drew based on the quality of his life. It wasn't so much Jesus' sinlessness or his own insisting that he is God that showed him to be "the Christ." The disciples saw that Jesus was the Christ due to his love and compassion, his entering into life with sinners, outcasts, the poor and oppressed. God confirmed Jesus' messianic identity when God vindicated Jesus' way of life by raising him from the dead.

A practice-first Christology starts with the story of Jesus' actual life, the story told (in various ways) by the four Gospel writers. This story emphasizes Jesus' humanity—and his faithfulness in living as a human being who embodied the life God expects from all human beings. Jesus' *faithfulness* and his embodying what a trusting life looks like established his identity as Christ.

Jesus' Christ-ness mattered because it established a pattern for others to follow to be Christians (Christ-followers). The difference between a doctrine-first Christology and a practice-first Christology may be illustrated by two different ways of thinking about Jesus' cross.

For the first view, Jesus' cross is understood more as a necessary sacrifice that allows God to forgive our sins. Jesus' cross is unique and only effective because of his utter sinlessness. Jesus takes up his cross as a substitute, being punished for our transgressions. That is, Jesus takes up the cross so we do not have to.

The second view understands Jesus' cross more as a model for believers. When Jesus called upon his disciples to "take up the cross and follow me" he meant it pretty literally. The "cross" is a consequence of living with open and welcoming mercy in a world that sustains oppressive social structures with domination and violence. The people who take up the cross are those who know that God's love matters more than the systems' dominating ways. They already know God's mercy and take up the cross as a response to this mercy.

In the first view, Jesus' resurrection ends up being peripheral to the cosmic transaction that happens in the events of Jesus' sacrificial death. In the second view, Jesus' resurrection looms large as God's vindication of Jesus' way of life. In the second view, Jesus does not take up the cross so we don't have to; Jesus takes up the cross to show us the kind of life God wants from us all. God vindicates such a life.

For us to confess Jesus as Christ reveals *our* hierarchy of values. When we say, "you are the Christ," we do not simply make a statement about Jesus being divine in the doctrinal sense. More so, we make a statement about Jesus' values standing at the top of our hierarchy of values.

When we say, "you are the Christ" we confess that the kind of life Jesus lived shows us what God values. Jesus' life reflects the core truths of what is means to be authentically human. We also confess that these core values embodied by Jesus led directly to conflict. He bumped up against the Powers that be, the human structures (religious and political) that responded to his authentically human life by putting him to death.

A third aspect of our confession of Jesus as Christ (along with his embodying God's values and his living in conflict with the Powers) is that God underscored God's embrace of Jesus' way by raising him from death, conquering the Powers with persevering love.

Too often, theology, it seems to me, *starts* with a view of God and kings as authoritarian and dominating. So when we call Jesus the Christ, we tend to fit him within that view of kings—almighty, perfect, aligned with wealthy and powerful human beings, the great judge and punisher.

In contrast, I want to suggest we should define Christ by looking first at Jesus' life. What if we were to let Jesus (the actual Jesus of the Gospels) determine our understanding of God? Instead of going from our preconception of kingly God to Jesus, what if we were to go from Jesus to God?

Then we would have Christology as if Jesus matters. We would look at what his life was like. We would confess that this life shows us what God is like. We would say that *Jesus* provides our way of orienting ourselves theologically in relation to everything. Nothing would be as high on our hierarchy as the way of Jesus. Sharing that hierarchy is what it would mean to confess him as the Christ. Jesus' "kingliness" may be seen in his practices of service and nonviolence.

PROBLEMS WITH THE THEOLOGICAL TRADITION

The christological evasion of Jesus has bedeviled Christianity for most of its history. I will mention just a couple of important markers. In the year 325, the leaders of the church in the Roman Empire got together to write what became one of the Christianity's definitive creeds, the Creed of Nicea. This is part of what it says:

> We believe in one Lord Jesus Christ, . . . God from God, Light from Light, true God from true God, begotten not made, of the same essence as the Father . . . ; who for us men and our salvation came down and was incarnate, becoming human. He suffered and the third day he rose and ascended into the heavens.[5]

This statement of faith still shapes Christian theology in powerful ways. According to this core part of the creed, what matters about Jesus Christ? He's God, he was killed, and he rose. What doesn't get mentioned? We don't learn anything about what Jesus actually said. We don't learn anything about how Jesus lived. And we don't learn anything about who killed him and why.

Whatever the contextual issues were that shaped the creed in the fourth century, these issues disappeared from the tradition and the timeless words of the creed remained. And these words set a tone. What matters about Jesus Christ is his divinity per se, his sacrificial death, and his resurrection as a miraculous act rather than as a vindication of a particular way of life. This is doctrine-first Christology par excellence. It simply does not provide any sense of Jesus' life and teaching. It does not speak to lived faithfulness. It does not reflect Jesus' continuity with the story of Israel and the core concerns of Torah.

The important elements (divinity, death, and resurrection) are delinked from their context in Jesus' life—and their meaning is thereby transformed. They become independent events rather than part of a single story that features Jesus' words and deeds.

Many centuries after the Creed of Nicea, the events we now call the Protestant Reformation split the Catholic Church into many parts, triggering a theological revolution. However, the christological evasion of Jesus continued. We can see the evasion in most of the theology of the magisterial Reformation (Lutherans, Reformed, Anglicans). It finds obvious expression in a document formulated as kind of a summation of Reformed theology about 100 years after the ministry of John Calvin. This document, one of the greatest Protestant theological statements, was the Westminster Confession of Faith, written in 1646. The Westminster Confession of Faith has been definitive for Presbyterians and crucial for Congregationalists and Baptists.

This is part of what Westminster says:

> The Son of God, the second person in the Trinity, being very and eternal God, of one substance and equal with the Father, did, when the fullness of time was come, take upon himself man's nature . . . yet without sin. . . . Which person is very God and very man, yet one Christ, the only mediator between God and man.[6]

Again, what matters most here? That Jesus Christ is "very and eternal God" and that he is "the only mediator between God and man" (that is, that he offers the necessary sacrifice to save us from God's wrath). The Westminster Confession says nothing about what Jesus did and said between his virgin birth and his death as a sinless sacrifice.

One key issue we must face in constructing our Christology is how we weigh our various sources. Typically, Christians who affirm creedal statements such as Nicea and Westminster claim that these creeds do not operate with as high a level of authority as Scripture itself. The creeds are given authority as important interpretations of the Bible's message. It is said that this authority *follows from* the accuracy with which the creeds are understood to reflect biblical teaching.

However, we find a significant tension with regard to the role that Jesus' words and deeds play in Christology. The creeds and the Gospels seem clearly to emphasize different themes. Should we see these different emphases as complementary? Or do we actually have a near contradiction between the emphases of these key creeds and the Gospels' account of what mattered most to and about Jesus? Do the creeds *complement* the Gospels' story that focuses on Jesus' mighty deeds, his message of loving enemies, and his challenging religious and political hierarchies? When they assert as their core statement about Jesus that he is "of the same essence as the Father," are they *illuminating* the story of Jesus? Or is this a different kind of assertion altogether that implies that Jesus' words and deeds are peripheral for Christology?

If we do our Christology as if the Jesus we meet in the Gospels matters, we will be bound to side with the gospel accounts should there in fact be incompatibility between the creeds and the Gospels. I suggest that at a very fundamental point, we do in fact find significant tensions.

It would appear that the message we get from the creeds is that what matters most about Jesus is simply his being, his God-ness that is part of who he is by definition. We find little emphasis on a life with concrete acts and words that demonstrate God's ways in the world. The divinity of Jesus is a starting point based simply on who he is, not a conclusion based on how he lived.

Hence, the creeds pay little or no attention to the significance of Jesus' life for our lives. They do not present Jesus as a model for authentic human living. They give no sense of the social-spiritual context of Jesus' struggle with the Powers and his genuine struggle to trust God and live faithfully. The creeds also give little sense of Jesus' connection with the story of Israel. They actually tend to turn the Bible's emphases upside down. They make abstract conclusions about Jesus' divinity central. And they make the actual story of Jesus' message of costly discipleship to his fellow Israelites in the nitty-gritty of first century Palestine peripheral. It is small wonder that most Christians who have made the creeds central for their Christology have not taken Jesus' message of love of enemies as normative.

CHRISTOLOGY BASED ON THE GOSPELS

Based on what the creeds affirm, the titles "Son of God" or "Messiah" or "Christ" at their heart seem to refer to Jesus Christ's divinity, his unity with the transcendent and perfect God of omniscience and omnipotence. However, as these terms appear in the actual story of Jesus, initiated at Jesus' baptism, they convey something different. They seem much more to refer to Jesus' vocation, to the shape of the life and ministry Jesus will embrace as a response to God's call.

God's affirmation, "You are my Son, the Beloved; with you I am well pleased" (Luke 4:22), marks a transition into Jesus' public ministry. Jesus next retreats into the wilderness and en-

counters Satan. In this encounter, Jesus' clarity about his vocation is tested with three powerful temptations concerning what
kind of "Son of God" he would be. His life then repudiates the
visions of "Son of God" that Satan tempts him with. The
specifics of Jesus' life and teaching have everything to do with
his identity as God's Son/Messiah/Christ.

Let's take just one statement from the Gospels that provides Jesus' own take on his identity. We see that he affirms
that this identity could be understood in messianic terms. He
did offer a kind of definition of what *he* meant by "Christ" or
"messiah." This statement is found in Luke 7.

> The disciples of John [the Baptist] reported all [that Jesus
> was saying and doing] to him. So John summoned two of
> his disciples and sent them to the Lord to ask, "Are you
> the one who is to come, or are we to wait for another?"
> When the men had come to [Jesus], they said, "John the
> Baptist has sent us to you to ask, 'Are you the one who is to
> come, or are we to wait for another?'" Jesus had just then
> cured many people of diseases, plagues, and evil spirits,
> and had given sight to many who were blind. And he an-
> swered them, "Go and tell John what you have seen and
> heard: the blind receive their sight, the lame walk, the lep-
> ers are cleansed, the deaf hear, the dead are raised, the
> poor have good news brought to them." (Luke 7:18-22)

John the Baptist had wanted to know—was Jesus the one
who is to come (that is, was Jesus the Messiah)? Jesus replies,
in effect, yes I am the Messiah. You can know that I am the Messiah *because* of what I am doing. Jesus states that bestowing the
title Messiah should be a *conclusion* based on what kind of life
he was living.

Jesus asserts: When you look at my actual deeds and words
you will see that I am healing people and bringing good news
to the poor. I am exercising power over demons and providing
sight to those who could not see. Luke's Gospel has shown already that these very manifestations have messianic connota-
tions, drawn directly from Israel's story.

When Luke tells of the very beginning of Jesus' ministry
in his hometown (Luke 4:16-30), we read of Jesus reading directly from the prophet Isaiah, describing the "favorable year
of the Lord" (the messianic age that reinvigorates the Levitical

Jubilee legislation). Isaiah spoke directly of the very things Jesus tells John the Baptist's followers to report back to their teacher. Jesus asserts that the deeds Isaiah prophesies are being fulfilled in his presence.

The deeds Jesus mentions show us what God is like; these are the kingly (messianic) values. "Son of God" is a *vocation* in the Gospels, a calling Jesus received to live as the Messiah. His confessed identity as God Incarnate follows from the life he lived, his embodiment of what it meant to be the Messiah.

Contrary to the impression we get from the creeds, Jesus' messianic identity included a direct call to his followers to imitate his way. The creeds focus on aspects of Jesus' identity that separate him from humans ("of one essence with the Father") and underscore his uniqueness ("the only mediator between God and man"). According to the Gospels, though, Jesus' identity as Messiah fed into a sense of connection between Jesus and other humans. Jesus as Christ is the definitive human being who shows the rest of us how to live as humans in God's image.

The report Jesus gives for John the Baptist includes actual mighty deeds. The healings Jesus performed are certainly literal. Jesus did minister to people's physical needs. However, I think the healings also operate on a metaphorical level. And the most basic metaphor is bringing sight to the blind.

The more I think about it and study the Bible, the more I'm convinced that *revelation* is at the heart of Jesus' message. Jesus makes visible the true character of God and the true calling of human beings. We need *sight* to perceive God as merciful.

Go back to the story of Eden. Adam and Eve violate God's command and eat the fruit. What we often miss, though, is that *after* this, God still comes into the Garden to hang out with them in the same way God always did. God does not turn against them—but they hide from God. They hide from God because they are afraid. They are blinded to God's mercy. The traumas of human history have followed from that blindness.

The Bible may be read as the story of God's attempt to convince human beings that we don't have to hide from God. God tries to help humans *see* that God offers mercy and healing, that God is worthy of our trust. This story reaches its conclusion by telling how God entered human history, showing us through Jesus' life the reality of this transformative mercy.

According to the gospel of Mark, Jesus' first words when he begins his ministry are, "The kingdom of God is here, turn to God and believe the good news" (Mark 1:15). Jesus brings sight. His actions and his words reveal the true nature of God and God's intentions toward human beings. He does this as one who walks and talks with humanity and models a life that does see God for who God truly is.

Jesus proclaims: See this, the universe bends toward justice and mercy. God is not a punitive God to run away from. God is like the shepherd looking for the lost sheep (the one out of 100) and the woman looking for the lost coin. Both rejoice when they find what was lost—a model for Jesus' welcome of sinners (Luke 15:1-10). All it takes are eyes to see.

This truth about God of which Jesus spoke and that shaped his life, is truth he means to shape his followers lives. "Love your enemies, do good, and lend, expecting nothing in return. Your reward will be great, and you will be children of the Most High; for he is kind to the ungrateful and the wicked. Be merciful, just as your Father is merciful" (Luke 6:35-36).

JESUS AS THE CHRIST

Doing theology as if Jesus matters does include a version of the creedal affirmation of Jesus' identity. Jesus *is* God incarnate. Indeed, Jesus as Messiah is Jesus as God in the flesh. However, when we follow the biblical portrayal of this identity, we will make this confession based on Jesus' life. Our confession will be a *conclusion* based on what we know of how Jesus lived, what he taught, consequences of his way of living (the cross), and God's vindication of Jesus' life through resurrection.

We cannot confess Jesus as Christ without being quite specific both about the content of his life that revealed him to be the Christ and how he insists that his way should define his followers' lives. The problem with the creeds is that they start and finish with the conclusion (Jesus' divinity) as if the content of the life were irrelevant for Christology.

Our affirmation of Jesus' identity as the Christ expresses our commitment to make his hierarchy of values our own. There is no authentic confession of Jesus as Christ without a corresponding confession of his way of life as our norm.

So when we confess Jesus as Christ, we affirm that we want to see God as Jesus does. For Jesus, God is "Abba," an endearment for father. With this expression, Jesus seems especially to be communicating a sense of intimacy and personal trust.

Jesus powerfully portrays a symbol of God as Abba in the story he told about a son who disrespects his father, takes his inheritance, and leaves to live a life of self-indulgence (Luke 15:11-32). When the son runs out of money and "comes to himself," he returns home intended to be a hired servant. However, the father runs out to meet him, embraces him, offers full restoration even before the son can apologize, and throws a big party to celebrate.

When we confess Jesus as Christ, we affirm that we want to stand for what Jesus stands for. We too want to embody radical love in our lives. We too want to value and respect people who are vulnerable, exploited, and disrespected by the great ones in our world and in our churches.

In story after story from the Gospels we see Jesus showing respect to the disrespected and honor to the dishonored. He touches lepers and "unclean" women. He heals children and servants of religious and political leaders. He forgives sinners. He eats with tax collectors. From the beginning of the story (when disreputable characters such as shepherds recognize the significance of his birth) to the end of the story (when he offers forgiveness to the crucified criminal at his side at Golgotha), Jesus models unilateral compassion.

When we confess Jesus as Christ, we affirm that we too want to challenge the powers that be in our world. We want, like Jesus did, to resist the politics of domination. We want, like Jesus, to resist valuing wealth over workers, profits over nature, or possessions over friends.

When we confess Jesus as Christ, we affirm that we too want to order our communities so that the greatest are the servants. We too want to reject imitating the kings of the nations in their authoritarian leadership.

Who is that guy? The one who stands with us as we stand for life.

News of God

[The Doctrine of God]

*F*OR THEOLOGY AS IF JESUS MATTERS, every other theme follows after Christology. We *start* with Jesus, and then from that perspective we reflect on topics such as God, humanity, and the church.

So, in this chapter we think about God *in light of Jesus*. Certainly in a genuine sense God is our most fundamental theme. However, our understanding of God will be decisively shaped by the kinds of questions we ask, by the concern with which we begin. For Christians, these questions and concerns *should* begin with the life and teaching of Jesus.

What might result if we approach our doctrine of God as a news story? I think it might be fruitful to take a "journalistic" approach to this theme.

When I was about twelve, I decided I wanted to be a journalist. But by the time I finished my journalism degree I had decided journalism was not for me. I didn't really like my professors or fellow J-school students. I had the sense that if I wanted to be a journalist I would have to start smoking and be a much pushier kind of person!

About the time I finished college, I discovered theology. I got hooked, and the focus of the rest of my life was pretty well decided. I remember when I told my parents of my decision to pursue church work and theology rather than journalism, my dad (who was a preacher's kid) said, "Sure, we will affirm you in whatever you decide, but you need to be aware that if you go that route you won't make much money." I suppose he knew what he was talking about.

One thing I learned in J-school, though, stuck with me. When you write a news story, you use the "Six Ws"—these provide your basic questions. Who, what, when, where, why, and how (a word that ends with "w").

THEOLOGY AND OUR HIERARCHY OF VALUES

Well, I still have some journalistic impulses. I think doing theology might be a bit like covering a news story. I define theology as reflection on and self-awareness about our central values. How do we order our sense of what matters most? What is our hierarchy of values? And how do the way we live, the choices we make, and the priorities we follow express our hierarchy of values? Our answers to these questions constitute our "theology."

The word *theology* means, literally, the study of God. (The Greek word for God is *theos.*) Seeing our theology as built from our hierarchy of values, we could say that whatever stands at the top of our hierarchy of values and shapes how we actually live our lives is our "God."

When we reflect as Christians on what shapes our lives, traditional doctrines may help clarify our reflections. We then talk about the doctrine of Christ ("Christology"), the doctrine of God ("theology proper"), the doctrine of the Holy Spirit, and so on. I think, though, that we need always to keep our doctrines anchored in real life—viewing them in relation to how we live. I'm not interested in a doctrinalizing of faith that too easily tends toward being abstract, intellectualized, and jargon-laden.[1] Theological reflection should help us understand how we live, why we have the commitments we do, what values matter—and to be more self-aware about our faith and its relation to our lives.

I believe the doctrine of Jesus Christ should be our "master doctrine." As we confess Jesus as the definitive revelation of God, we are saying (or, we *should* be saying) that in Jesus' life and teaching we see our model for ordering our values and convictions. Jesus' faith, convictions, values, and way of living shape the values we want to be our core values.

Because Jesus provides our basic hierarchy of values with his life and teaching, we draw on the general shape of those values in reflecting on the rest of the central themes of Christian theology. Jesus' message should determine how we think of God, the Holy Spirit, the church, and everything else.

QUESTIONS ABOUT GOD

So, we turn to the doctrine of God. Our understanding of God will be very different if we consider God from a Jesus-centered perspective rather than start with a definition of God that doesn't initially pay much attention to Jesus. So, as a would-be journalist, I will approach the doctrine of God as a news story, following questions suggested by the Six Ws.

Who is God? What does God do? When do we see God? Where is God present? Why care about God? How does God work? Seeking to answer these questions might help us get a sense of "news of God."

What would our *news* story about God say? Well, are we looking for good news or bad news? Which kind of news we look for when we think of news of God will shape what we actually see.

Many people *want* a God who is bad news. That is, most likely, they want a God who is bad news to their enemies. Generally, when we hear people arguing for the need to emphasize God's harsh, wrathful side they are thinking that harshness and wrath needs to be expressed toward someone else, someone they do not like.

Once there were two neighboring shopkeepers who were longtime bitter rivals. One night, an angel came to one shopkeeper, hoping to bring some good news into the situation. The angel told the man, "I am here to bless you. I will grant you anything you wish—only, whatever I give you, I will give your neighbor twice as much of the same thing."

The old man thought for a second and exclaimed, "Praise God, I knew he would answer my prayers. This is what I want; strike me blind in one eye!"

A wish from God leads to a desire for his enemy to be blinded, not to be blessed. The God this man wanted was bad news, a God who would smite his enemy.

Throughout history, God has often been associated with human vengeance and retribution. What kinds of values, life priorities, would lead people to construct a view of God centered on bad news? Why would we need a God of wrath? Probably we could find countless possible answers to such questions. One thought that comes to mind links feelings of fear and insecurity with a desire for a God who will punish those we fear.

Remember, though, that we are attempting here to develop theological affirmations in light of Jesus. So we must ask, Does Jesus' portrayal of God (and his embodiment of God's will for human life in his own ministry) base itself on fearfulness and insecurity? Is the God of Jesus a God who would smite Jesus' enemies? Hardly.

According to Jesus, we best imitate God when we *love* our enemies. God is gracious to those who don't deserve it. Jesus tells a story of a father (likely symbolizing God) offering unconditional acceptance to the returning rebellious son with no payback required (the parable of the "Prodigal Son," Luke 15:11-32). He tells another story that follows a close linking of love of God and love of neighbor and makes clear that in Jesus' view, the "neighbor" is embodied in the enemy (the parable of the "Good Samaritan," Luke 10:25-37).

Hand-in-hand with a God of wrath, and just as problematic in relation to the message about God we get directly from Jesus, we also find in the Christian tradition a God distant and above the fray. Some Christian theology has confessed this absolutely "sovereign" God to be without passions, unchangeable, incomprehensible, always the actor, never a re-actor.

Such a notion of God runs into many difficulties. This kind of "sovereign" God all too often has been the God of powerful people who practice precisely the kinds of ethical behavior that Jesus saw as most *problematic*: excluding those considered to be unsuitable for the "pure" community of faith, focusing on legalistic minutia and neglecting the weightier matters of the law such as justice and compassion, lording it over those under their power, remaining aloof from the sufferings and struggles of vulnerable people. Why might so many Christians have felt the need for this kind of separate-from-us God?

The Westminster Confession of Faith says that God

is infinite in being and perfection, a most pure spirit, invisible, without body, or passions, immutable, immense, eternal, incomprehensible, almighty, most wise, most holy, most free, most absolute, working all things according to the counsel of his own immutable and most righteous will, for his own power. (chapter II, article I)[2]

What kind of "news" would we associate with such a God? It could be news that is intimidating, fearful, and impersonal. Why would such news be attractive? It certainly would place less responsibility on human beings to challenge political and religious domination systems. This news would be of a kind of God who reinforces patriarchal social relationships and diminishes movements toward empowering vulnerable people.

Again, this God is not much like Jesus (or Jesus' portrayal of God). Jesus' God, the one he affectionately called "Abba," does not seem to be distant and patriarchal nor to exercise a monopoly on power. Rather, Jesus' Abba is notable for his approachability, his tender care for vulnerable people, and his message of empowerment: "Blessed are the meek, for they will inherit the earth" (Matt. 5:5).

GOD IN LIGHT OF JESUS

So, in light of our commitment to share Jesus' hierarchy of values, what kind of news of God should we be looking for? Where do we expect to hear about God—and what do we expect to hear when we hear about God?

Now, there is a word for "news" in the Bible. It's not "journalism." It's "gospel." The gospel is news—and a certain kind of news, *good* news, glad tidings. This idea of the news about God as *gospel* seems quite different than the bad news about God we have just noticed. Are there limits to the "goodness" of the gospel of God?

If we consider news of God in light of Jesus, we will see why the news is good. Christian theology *should* be theology in light of Jesus. Christian theology should be theology that reflects Jesus' own hierarchy of values. The Christian doctrine of God should echo Jesus' own portrayal of God.

Let's return to our six Ws—though I will only take time to touch on two of them.

Who is God? And, *Where is God present?* What do we learn as we pursue these questions in relation to Jesus?

WHO IS GOD?

Who is God? God is Jesus' Abba. When we hear Jesus say "father" we too easily misunderstand his point. His point is not that God is male. He's not saying God is the great, all-powerful patriarch standing above everyone else. No. When Jesus calls God "Abba" he means to convey that God is like a loving parent. Jesus uses Abba as a term of endearment.

Think of it like this. You are a young child and you see your parent with a hand raised. Do you flinch, expecting a blow of discipline? Or do you reach out your hand to share in the embrace you know is coming? Two very different views of the parent. Two very different views of God. Jesus' Abba is the one who reaches out to embrace.

The great story that shows this is Jesus' parable, "The Prodigal Son." Remember when the wayward son returns home, beaten down by his failures, hoping simply to be hired as a servant to his father. "While he was still far off, his father saw him and was filled with compassion; he ran and put his arms around him and kissed him" (Luke 15:20).

Some of the prophets anticipated Jesus. Probably the most poignant passage may be found in the prophet Hosea. Like his contemporaries Amos and Micah, Hosea offers sharp critiques of the injustices, idolatries, and violence of the people of Israel and Judah. Hosea centers especially on idolatry and its disastrous consequences. To make the point personal, Hosea writes of his own wife's unfaithfulness.

But after the severe warnings and expressions of grief and anguish, Hosea portrays a remarkable resolution within God's own heart. The prophet provides a nutshell account of Israel's history with God, but with a surprising conclusion.

He begins with God's merciful calling of Israel that turns to rebellion and idolatry.

> When Israel was a child, I loved him, and out of Egypt I called my son. The more I called them, the more they went from me; they kept sacrificing to the Baals, and offering incense to idols.

> Yet it was I who taught Ephraim to walk, I took them up in my arms; but they did not know that I healed them. I led them with cords of human kindness, with bands of love. I was to them like those who lift infants to their cheeks. I bent down to them and fed them. (Hos. 11:1-4)

Despite Yahweh's care, the people continue to turn away. So negative consequences inevitably follow. Hosea captures the basic message of the Bible's history books. God's people end up alienated from the land and return to the status they had while living in Egypt before the exodus.

> They shall return to the land of Egypt, and Assyria shall be their king, because they have refused to return to me. The sword rages in their cities, it consumes their oracle priests, and devours because of their scheme. My people are bent on turning away from me. To the Most High they call, but he does not raise them up at all. (Hos. 11:5-7)

To this point, Hosea echoes a common prophetic refrain—God's love, the people's faithlessness, inevitable consequences. But now he comes to his punch line, a theological revolution. God does some soul searching and decides to break the cycle of transgression/punishment.

> How can I give you up, Ephraim? How can I hand you over, O Israel? How can I make you like Admah? How can I treat you like Zeboiim? My heart recoils within me; my compassion grows warm and tender. I will not execute my fierce anger; I will not again destroy Ephraim; for I am God and no mortal, the Holy One in your midst, and I will not come in wrath. (Hos. 11:8-9)

God here leads "with cords of human kindness, with bands of love." Even more "Abba"-like, "I was to them like those who lift infants to their cheeks." Despite God's kindness, Israel turns away. However, the loving Abba's response to this turning away, captured by Jesus in his Prodigal Son story, here also ends in mercy: "My heart recoils within me; my compassion grows warm and tender. I will not execute my fierce anger . . . ; for I am God and no mortal, the Holy One in your midst, and I will not come in wrath."

Who is God? Jesus' loving parent, Hosea's "Holy One" whose holiness leads to healing mercy, not the punishment one may expect from a "Holy God." Hosea and Jesus both redefine holiness. God indeed is holy. However, God's holiness does not destroy human beings who violate it—it enters their world and brings them healing and transformation.

The news of God concerning God's basic disposition toward us may be summarized by the words Jesus quotes from Hosea: "I desire mercy not sacrifice" (Matt. 9:13 and 12:7 quoting Hosea 6:6). These words may be reframed as a description of God: "In my deeds, I express mercy not retribution."

WHERE IS GOD PRESENT?

Our second "W" question is this: *Where is God present?* We answer this question by looking at the story of Jesus. Jesus' life makes clear where God is present in the world.

If Jesus shows us God, we see God present *in* the brokenness, *in* the pain and suffering, *in* the humiliation and shame of vulnerable humanity. God's holiness leads God to bring *healing* to sinners, not condemnation. God does not push imperfect human beings away. Rather, God in Jesus does enter the fray, eating and drinking *with* sinners and lepers and others in need.

As much as any of the accounts of events in Jesus' life, the story of his anointment by the woman "who was a sinner" in Luke 7 illumines how he embodied God's presence. Jesus is invited to eat with one of the Pharisees at the Pharisee's house. While at the table, Jesus is approached by a woman "in the city, who was a sinner." This woman,

> having learned that [Jesus] was eating in the Pharisee's house, brought an alabaster jar of ointment. She stood behind him at his feet, weeping, and began to bathe his feet with her tears and to dry them with her hair. Then she continued kissing his feet and anointing them with the ointment. (Luke 7:37-38)

Jesus' host thought harsh thoughts about his guest. What kind of prophet is this who doesn't realize that this woman he allows to touch him is a sinner? Jesus realizes what is going on and challenges his host. "Listen, Simon, I want to tell you something." Then Jesus tells of two people who have their debts cancelled, one debt is about ten times higher than the other.

Wouldn't the person with the larger debt love their creditor more? Sure, Simon says.

> And Jesus said to him, "You have judged rightly." Then turning toward the woman, he said to Simon, "Do you see this woman? I entered your house; you gave me no water for my feet, but she has bathed my feet with her tears and dried them with her hair. You gave me no kiss, but from the time I came in she has not stopped kissing my feet. You did not anoint my head with oil, but she has anointed my feet with ointment. Therefore, I tell you, her sins, which were many, have been forgiven; hence she has shown great love. But the one to whom little is forgiven, loves little." Then [Jesus] said to her, "Your sins are forgiven." (Luke 7:43-48)

Many of you will have seen Fritz Eichenberg's famous woodcut, "Christ of the breadline." This portrait of Jesus standing with hungry people in a Depression-era breadline became a symbol for the Catholic Worker movement. The Catholic Workers for several generations now have sought to make clear to the world where God is present—with people in need, with the vulnerable, with those excluded by upright society.[3]

We also affirm that God is present wherever new life enters the world—literally when babies are born, more figuratively when one's cold heart is melted, when dead relationships are restored, when hope takes the place of discouragement, when faith is kindled in the ashes of despair. Where there is life there is hope; where there is life there is God.

We saw such a restoration of life and hope in the story from Luke 7 we just read. We see renewed life in many other of the stories of Jesus, when he forgives the woman caught in adultery and shares the water of life with the Samaritan woman at the well, when he brings sight to the blind and freedom to the demon possessed. God as present in such healings continues.

STORIES OF GOD'S PRESENCE

God is present in melted hearts. We find a latter-day manifestation of such presence in this story of transformation.

The late C. P. Ellis was a leader in the Klu Klux Klan in the 1960s who told his story to Studs Terkel. His father had died when Ellis was in the eighth grade. He'd had to quit school to go to work. He married young and had four kids. His family barely hung on. "I will never forget," he said,

> outside of my house was a 265-gallon oil drum, and I never did get enough money to fill up that oil drum. What I would do every night, I would run up to the store and buy five gallons of oil and climb up the ladder and pour it in that drum. I could hear that five gallons when it hits the bottom of that oil drum, splatters, and it sounds like it's nothin' in there. But it would keep the house warm for the night. Next day you'd have to do the same thing.[4]

"I really began to get bitter," he continues. "I didn't know who to blame. I tried to find somebody. I began to blame it on black people. I had to hate somebody. Hatin' America [in general] is hard to do because you can't see it to hate it. You gotta have somethin' to look at to hate." Ellis joined the Klu Klux Klan, finding a sense of power and purpose. "I didn't like blacks. I didn't want to associate with 'em. Blacks, Jews, or Catholics. My father said: 'Don't have anything to do with 'em.' I didn't."

Ellis's entire life changed due to an encounter with Ann Atwater, an African-American woman he served with on a committee formed to deal with problems in the schools. Both Ellis and Atwater, coming from opposite positions, experienced much resistance from their own communities, just for being willing to talk.

They shared their frustrations one night, reporting the many ways their children had come home every day in tears as a result of being made fun of from one end of the political spectrum or the other. "At this point," Ellis reports, "I begin to see, here we are, two people from the far ends of the fence, havin' *identical* problems. From that moment on, I tell ya, that gal and I worked together good. The amazing thing about it, her and I had cussed each other, we hated each other. Up to that point, we *didn't know* each other. We didn't know what we had in common."

The changes continued in Ellis. He hadn't shed all prejudices but was "beginnin' to look at a black person, to shake hands with him, and see him as a human being." He felt like he was "born again," told others of dreaming of stopping wars and fights, and was told in turn that his "impossible dream" made him "sound like Martin Luther King." Now this ex-Klansman even "listened to tapes of Martin Luther King. I listen to it and tears come to my eyes 'cause I know what he's sayin' now. . . ."

A second story of God's presence began in summer 2006—June 30, 5:45 p.m., to be precise. That was when my grandson Elias entered the world. I have to admit, a bit sheepishly, that the joy of parents and grandparents has generally seemed a bit abstract to me. Sure, it's nice when someone else's child is born, but what's the big deal? I kind of forgot how I felt when our son Johan was born. That was a long time ago.

Well, with Elias' birth, that all changed. What a gift, what a sense of the presence of God, what a ray of hope! *Now*, when I think of a child being born, I think of the miracle of creation. I think of the proverb that says rather than cursing the darkness we should light a candle. I feel a lot more invested in the future. It's just amazing to observe the new person—beautiful, fragile, like a sponge soaking in life. Where else could this all come from except God?

I admire Elias's parents, Jill and Johan, so much—and all others who take this step into the future. But what better way to resist the darkness? What better way to discover God's presence in our world? What better way to resist our tendency to settle for comfort and withdrawal? What better way to take on the huge challenges that face us all as we seek to sustain life in a world that seems so bent toward death? Steve Earle's Christmas song, "Nothing But a Child" captures this hope in God's presence as it imagines parents with tears washed away as they gaze with awe at the children giving them another chance.[5]

We see news of God whenever a child is born, whenever human relationships are healed, whenever hearts are melted, whenever nature renews itself and brings forth green and growing things. The news of God basically reports on the enhancement of life, the fulfillment of God's purposes in creation, the reconciling of all things to God (Col. 1:20). The definitive news that helps us discern what news truly is God's *good* news is the gospel of Jesus Christ, the story of Jesus life, teaching, death, and resurrection.

GOD'S CHARACTERISTICS IN LIGHT OF JESUS

This good news of Jesus provides our basis for understanding a hierarchy of values that truly reflects the will of God and should shape our theology. When we start with Jesus as our lens for discerning what we believe about God, we will come to several conclusions about God, conclusions about what convictions help us cohere with Jesus' own convictions.

God is loving. God is Jesus' daddy who loves unconditionally, toward whom we may turn with genuine trust and find genuine security. God initiates healing action toward God's enemies (see Rom. 5), always desiring the best for all God's creation.

God's love does include holiness and justice. As a just God, God desires to heal that which is broken. God's justice seeks wholeness in its response to injustice—*healing* the alienation, not simply punishing it. As a holy God, God desires to clean up that which is dirty. God's holiness does not destroy that which is not holy, but seeks to transform it.

God does not heal or clean up as a means of making people loveable; God initiates the healing and cleaning up because God finds us loveable already (even while we are broken and dirty).

However, human beings who experience brokenness and refuse to respond to love perceive the love as harsh. God's love also includes "wrath." Wrath may be understood as God allowing the consequences of refusal of love to be manifested. These consequences are best understood not so much as punishment but as aspects of God's work to bring long-term healing to creation. The Book of Revelation portrays this work as a process of creation being cleansed of the powers of evil.[6]

God is personal. God has (or, we could say, *is*) personality. God is relational. God cares for specific people, not only people in general. God feels and expresses emotions (especially grief and joy). God is self-conscious and rational. However, God is not a "person" like we are. Because God is not a person, God cannot be reduced to a particular gender. God is both he and she, and God is neither he nor she.

God is powerful, a better term than "omnipotent" (*all*-powerful). God being powerful means that God is able to accomplish God's purposes. God is not defeated by sin and evil. The power of God is the power of love, though, not the power of dominance and control.

God endures over all time and is always present (there is no "sacred"/"secular" split). The best descriptors of God's power are persistence, persuasion, awareness, and consistency. God's power is like the power of water gradually making a path for itself. This understanding of power contrasts with the notions of power as coercive, arbitrary, overwhelming, and like a bulldozer.

God is knowledgeable, a better term than "omniscient" (*all-knowing*). God's knowledge is personal. God knows me and you and all people, our relationships, needs, and sorrows. God's knowledge is not so much knowledge of "facts" as of people. God is more like the wise, deeply loving matriarch in a close-knit community than like an infinite computer.

God hears all and remembers all more than foresees all. God's knowledge does not have to do with God knowing about everything before it happens. It is not the knowledge of facts and figures. God is not the universe's master computer. God's is like the knowledge of lovers and friends, parents and children.

God knows that love wins out but not precisely how. God does not override our freedom and responsibility. To speak of God having a "plan" for our lives is not to say that God has prepared a detailed blueprint for each of us. Rather, it is to believe that God created life in such a way that faithfulness to God leads to happiness, contentment, and joy.

God is steadfast, a better term than "immutable" (*unchanging*). God's will is consistent, dependable, always seeking healing. God *is* responsive and changeable in "tactics" in relation to human beings because human consciousness of God does (must) change. Since God's power is the power of love, it will be responsive to the actions and needs of those who are loved. God's steady love, thus, is inherently dynamic and takes the shape of the new elements of the relationship God has with an ever-changing creation.

God's "plan" has more to do with God's will to love and heal than with God predetermining events and never wavering from a detailed "script." Going back to the story of creation in Genesis and following the twisting path of the human quest for living in relationship with God, we see that God's purposes with creation have to do with loving relationships. Since God's creatures have their own integrity and will, God does not set out to manipulate them like chess pieces to carry out a set-in-stone "game plan." The entire dynamic of the human/divine relationship includes the openness to the future characteristic of love.

God is seen most definitively in Jesus. The central element of a Christian concept of God based on Jesus' message is that God is most clearly revealed in Jesus' life and teaching. Jesus saw God as compassionate, empathetic, forgiving (see the Sermon on the Mount ["be merciful as God is merciful," Matthew 5:48] and the parable of the Prodigal Son), caring, saving, and liberating.

God may be seen in Jesus' way of life—peaceable, indiscriminately loving, subversive of human power structures, and steadfast in the face of resistance.

We may also speak of creation itself as consistent with God as revealed in Jesus. Jesus was with God in creation. As Colossians 1 tells us,

> In [Jesus Christ] all things in heaven and on earth were created, things visible and invisible, whether thrones or dominions or rulers or powers—all things have been created through him and for him. He himself is before all things, and in him all things hold together. (Col. 1:16-17; see also John 1:1-4 and Heb. 1:2-3)

Theologically, we might infer from this affirmation of Jesus' presence in creation itself that the way the world works reflects the same characteristics of God that Jesus' life and teaching reflect. We will reflect more on this possibility in chapter five on creation below.

The final theme about God that we need to consider is the traditional understanding in Christianity that *God is "Trinity."* Although the Trinity is not a direct element of Jesus' own teaching about God, we should try to reflect on the doctrine of the Trinity in relation to Jesus' good news.

Trinitarian doctrine needs to be understood as part of the Christian confession of God as one. This doctrine recognizes that the one God relates to the world in various ways. The "trin-

ity" motif specifies that God specifically relates to the wor
three distinct ways. (1) God relates to the world as its as creator
and sustainer (God, the "father"). (2) God relates to the world
as incarnated in Jesus, who embodied God's will for human
life (God, the "son"). (3) God relates to the world as an imma-
nent, all-pervasive presence (God, the "spirit").

If we understand Jesus to be the basis for our hierarchy of
values, we will understand the doctrine of the Trinity as another way of discussing why Jesus' hierarchy of values should
be seen as normative for Christians. If we understand Jesus as
part of the Trinity, one of the three expressions of the *one* God,
we will have a strong basis for recognizing Jesus' way as God's
way. We will also have a strong basis for discerning the ongoing presence of the Holy Spirit in the world and in our communities of faith. We will recognize the Spirit as confirming the
message of Jesus throughout time and space.

Christian reflections on God as Trinity emphasize both
God's three manifestations and the reality that nonetheless we
believe that God is one ("*mono*theism"). Each expression of God
is all God. There is no differentiation in will or strategy or concern among the three members of the Trinity. God is always the
God of Jesus Christ. The Holy Spirit is always the Spirit of Jesus
Christ—as we will consider in our next chapter and in further
thoughts there on the Trinity.

4

············

God's Spirit—and Ours

[The Doctrine of the Holy Spirit]

CHRISTIAN THEOLOGY HAS ALWAYS MADE its trinitarian affirmation central (God as three-in-one). However, the Holy Spirit as a distinct doctrinal theme (called "pneumatology") has received less attention than Christology and the doctrine of God.

So, we have the possibility of turning to our theology of the Holy Spirit with a bit of freshness. We do not have as many deep-seated theological ruts to struggle free from. What might we come up with if we think about the Spirit *as if Jesus matters*? How should we approach debates about the meaning of the Holy Spirit?

For most of my life I have been an intense sports fan. I've watched *a lot* of sports on TV. I've learned to keep it under control in recent years. However, like a smoker who quit smoking, I have never lost the desire to watch sports. So I have seen many beer commercials. Some of them have been pretty clever, even if pushing a pretty disgusting product. Older people may remember the Miller Lite, tastes great/less filling "debate."

In thinking about *theological* debates, there might be an instructive parallel. Not that theological debates are no more important than whether a beer tastes great or is filling. Theological issues *do* matter. However, the parallel is that in both cases we are talking about the opinions of human beings. All theological debates are debates about *human* opinions. Some opinions are worth more respect than others, but they all remain human opinions. Because they are differences among human perspectives, theological differences should not be a matter of life and death.

THE HOLY SPIRIT AS PART OF THE TRINITY

No *human* theological position is the same as upper-case R "Reality." No human being or group of human beings speaks definitively for God. Certainly, though, theology does matter. It is important. Our theological convictions are not simply a matter of opinion with all views equally valid. Some theological perspectives are better than others. However, theology always remains human work, never authoritative enough or absolute enough or true enough to justify hurting those who have different views.

I think of this point especially when I reflect on the doctrine of the Holy Spirit. I do not perceive that this particular doctrine is in itself so controversial. Among Christians, the doctrine of the Holy Spirit (pneumatology) does not usually actually receive a great deal of direct attention. However, the doctrine of the Holy Spirit by necessity relates closely to theological convictions concerning God (theology proper) and Jesus Christ (Christology). When we include theology and Christology along with pneumatology, we move into a bigger arena than simply pneumatology.

We cannot reflect on pneumatology without reflecting on the doctrine of the Trinity. Many Christians see this doctrine, above all others, as *the* key theological boundary marker. As one Mennonite theologian wrote several years ago, the doctrine of the Trinity is not simply a human idea; it corresponds to Reality.[1] To disagree is to put oneself outside the pale.

I believe that we encounter an important principle here. How literally should we take our language about God? Does our theology transcend our finite humanness? Can *any* human idea about God be more than a metaphor, more than saying "God *is like* this"? Can we say, definitively, that God *is* anything? I think not.

No theological language can ever be more than metaphorical. I would agree that trinitarian thinking, identifying three aspects of God—Creator, Son, and Spirit—is helpful. However, as a biblical Christian, I also insist that I believe in *one* God.

God as seen in creation, God as seen in Jesus, and God as seen in the Holy Spirit, is *one* God with *one* will—not so much a "Triune" God, but simply God.

The danger with trinitarian language is that it too easily lends itself to making distinctions within God, as if God as "Father" is one way (judgmental, harshly holy, punitive) while God in Jesus is different. This opens the door to acceptance of violence in God. Such an acceptance would not be so possible if God's revelation in *Jesus* defined what God most truly is like.

We must respect our differences on such issues. All our views are at most *partly* true. The point of theological reflection is to help us to be better people. "Doing theology" is about conversation and testing our opinions with each other, not staking out truth territory that we must fight for, coercively if need be.

I understand Christian theology to be critical reflection on our convictions, seeking to identify what is most important. As Christians, we do this in light of our commitment to Jesus as our clearest revelation of what God is like and of what matters most. Thinking theologically about the Holy Spirit should happen in terms of what we believe about Jesus.

Our pneumatology should not be simply a sub-point in our trinitarian doctrine. As we reflect on the Holy Spirit theologically in this chapter, we will not focus mainly on how the Holy Spirit functions as a distinct member of the Trinity. Rather, pneumatology as if Jesus matters asks this: How does identifying God's-Presence-as-Spirit as the *Spirit of Jesus* help us live faithfully?

The Holy Spirit is kind of like the end of the rainbow—elusive, *not* stationary and stable, impossible to put your hands on. I have heard it said that we don't commune with the Holy Spirit, the Holy Spirit *is* communion. The Holy Spirit is like fire, like a rainbow, like the air we breath. It's here. It's real. It's crucial to life. But it is not containable, nor even that easy to talk about.

In reflecting on the Holy Spirit biblically, I want to bring together two points. The first point is that the Holy Spirit, the Spirit of God, is the Spirit of life.[2] Wherever there is life, the Spirit is present. The second point is that wherever the Spirit is present, then Jesus is also present. That is, Jesus' hierarchy of what is most important (love the Lord your God with your entire being and love your neighbor as yourself) is reflected in all life. Life is holy. Each person is holy. All life (*each* life) is to be valued and revered.

THE SPIRIT OF LIFE AND CREATION

Genesis 1 and Genesis 2 have become central for my understanding of the Holy Spirit. First, we read:

> In the beginning when God created the heavens and the earth, the earth was a formless void and darkness covered the face of the deep, while the Spirit of God[3] swept over the face of the waters. Then God said, "Let there be light"; and there was light. And God saw that the light was good; and God separated the light from the darkness. God called the light Day, and the darkness he called Night. And there was evening and there was morning, the first day. (Gen. 1:1-5)

"The Spirit of God swept over the face of the waters." Genesis 1:1-2 gives us the picture of God bringing order out of chaos. Many translations have rendered the Hebrew word *ruach* as "wind"—as if God blew a mighty wind to bring order to the universe. However, *ruach* may also be translated "spirit" (or, "Spirit" if we understand *ruach* here to refer to the direct involvement of God). The sense then becomes one of God as Spirit participating in creation. God as Spirit brings order out of chaos, brings peace (*shalom*, wholeness) out of randomness.

If we read Genesis 1:1-2 as referring to the Holy Spirit, we way see here a clear portrayal of God's immediate presence throughout the cosmos. Such a portrayal supports the belief that all of creation in some sense then links with the Spirit of God.

Western civilization has a lot to answer to the universe for, not least our exploitation of creation. One key move toward the profound alienation that has characterized our culture in relation to creation came when the world became mere matter and lost its spirit.

Ironically, it was human beings who created *impersonal* machines. Such entities never occur in nature. As we relied more and more on these machines, we found ourselves more and more alienated from creation. Then the fatal step: Human beings projected from our own creation (impersonal machines) on to nature and claimed that nature is impersonal, that nature is merely matter. As Richard Tarnas writes, "This is the ultimate anthropomorphic projection: a [human]-made machine, something not in fact ever found in nature. From this perspective, it is the modern world's own impersonal soullessness that has been projected from within onto the world."[4]

With the world understood as impersonal and soulless, we then exploit what we believe to be inert matter. We extract fossil fuel and poison the earth both in the extracting and in the burning of this fuel. We treat the soil and the seas and the forests as mere instruments from which we extract what we then use for our utterly unsustainable "modern way of life."

One way to see this problem is to say that by separating the Spirit of God from the material universe, we have planted the seeds of our own destruction—spiritual and physical.

So Genesis 1 provides a crucial basis for our doctrine of the Spirit—though its teaching is reinforced throughout the Bible. It is Godself who infuses the universe as it is shaped from disorder into its goodness and beauty. The Spirit of God is the Spirit of creation.

Numerous Psalms underscore this emphasis on God's direction connection with the created universe. In Psalm 19 we read of how

> the heavens are telling the glory of God; and the firmament proclaims [God's] handiwork. . . . In the heavens [God] has set a tent for the sun, which comes out like a bridegroom from his wedding canopy, and like a strong man runs its course with joy. Its rising is from the end of the heavens, and its circuit to the end of them; and nothing is hid from its heat. (Ps. 19:1-6)

Later in the book of Psalms we find another direct reference to the role of God's Spirit (*ruach*) in the creation of life:

> O Lord, how manifold are your works! In wisdom you made them all; the earth is full of your creatures. Yonder is the sea, great and wide, creeping things innumerable are there, living things both small and great. . . . When you send forth your Spirit[5] they are created; and you renew the face of the ground. (Ps. 104:24-30)

Another possible mention of the Spirit of God comes in Genesis 2—and is also often obscured in English translations.

> In the day that the Lord God made the earth and the heavens, when no plant of the field was yet in the earth and no herb of the field had yet sprung up—for the Lord God had not caused it to rain upon the earth, and there was no one to till the ground; but a stream would rise from the earth, and water the whole face of the ground—then the Lord God formed man from the dust of the ground, and breathed into his nostrils the Spirit[6] of life; and the man became a living being. (Gen. 2:4-7)

The description of creation beginning in Genesis 2:4 focuses on human beings. A key point is made right away. "There was no one to till the ground." A caregiver is needed. So, God forms the first human being out of the "dust of the ground." This dust becomes human when God "breathes into the human's nostrils the Spirit of life; and the human became a living being" (2:7). We are being told here, I believe, that the Spirit of God itself enters the dust of the earth and enlivens it, makes it live, makes it human.

In a sense, this picture repeats what we are told in a different way in Genesis 1. There, the completion of creation is God creating human beings (male and female) in God's own image. And they are immediately given the task of caring for the rest of creation ("have dominion").

I believe that the very essence of life, the mystery of what differentiates living organisms from the dust of the earth, is the Spirit of God. Where there is life, the Spirit is present. In fact, the Spirit is what makes it life. I want to make this claim for all forms of life, but I also want to emphasize the idea that there is indeed something special about human life. We manifest the Spirit of God in an especially profound way.

The special way we manifest the Spirit of God is in our potential (and our responsibility) to *care* for the rest of creation. When we deny the Spirit of God's presence in our physical world by treating the world as an object to exploit, we deface the Spirit of God's presence in our own being. The same Spirit of God that infuses the cosmos and infuses all life of whatever form also infuses human beings created in God's image. This oneness of the Spirit, part of the oneness of God, requires us to acknowledge the sacredness of all life. We should actually acknowledge the sacredness of the inanimate elements of creation as well.

We thus should confess the oneness of God and the unity of creation. We also should recognize that the "specialness" of human beings makes us responsible to God. God calls us to care respectfully for all of God's creation. Such care should stem from our pneumatology, our understanding that the Holy Spirit is the Spirit of life in relation to all creation.

One of my favorite theologians is the Kentucky poet, essayist, and farmer Wendell Berry. He embodies my understanding of what theology should be about—critical reflection on what it is that matters most in life.

In his essay, "Is Life a Miracle?," he puts into words part of what I am trying to get at here. Berry says that amid all the work done on learning about living things and their parts, none of us

> knows much about the *life* of living things. I have seen with my own eyes and felt with my own hands many times the difference between live things and dead ones, and I do not believe that the difference can be so explained as to remove the wonder from it. What is the coherence, the integrity, the consciousness, the intelligence, the spirit, the informing form that leaves a living body when it dies? What was the "green fire" that Aldo Leopold saw going out in the eyes of the dying wolf?

So Berry is convinced that "life is a miracle" and that there is a practical point to this belief: "If I believe it is a miracle, then I cannot believe that I am superior to it, or that I understand it, or that I own it."[7]

If all of life is a miracle, certainly human life is such. If God infuses the creation of each new creature, certainly God infuses the life of each new human being. This link between human life and other creatures is not a diminishment of human life; it recognizes the holiness of all life. We diminish human life when we deny the holiness of any form of life.

So, from Genesis 1 and 2, we get a clear sense of the Spirit as part of the entire created order and, in a special way, as part of each human life. We violate the Spirit when we separate Spirit from matter and alienate ourselves from creation. Perhaps even more, we violate the Spirit when we think of some human beings as less than fully infused with God's Spirit.

The basic danger we face in either case is the same—dividing that which God means to be unified. When we do so, we resist the presence of God's Spirit in all the places that it actually is present. This is why the story of creation in Genesis is so important. It helps us see that God and creation go together through the agency of God's creative Spirit of life. As creator, God's Spirit infuses the entire cosmos.

The Genesis creation story also helps us better understand the human role in the creative processes. Our role involves both our spiritual (infused with the Spirit of God) and material (made from the dust of the earth) realities—together in harmony as part of God's good creation.

Early in the Genesis account we come to the key moment in the alienation of human beings from the Spirit of God. The very first act of blaspheming the Holy Spirit comes in Genesis 4. Cain murders his brother Abel. Almost always, we do violence to other human beings only after denying their full, Spirit-infused humanity. When we deny the full, Spirit-infused humanity of someone else violence in one form or another is almost sure to follow.

THE HOLY SPIRIT AND COMMUNITY SUSTENANCE

God's Spirit works throughout the biblical story with the people Israel. At a particularly crucial moment in the story, we read of the direct involvement of the Spirit in sustaining the community that had gone astray. The prophets told of Israel's departure from the message of Torah, culminating in the destruction of their nation state and temple. However, God did not abandon God's people, as we read in Isaiah 42: "Here is my servant, whom I uphold, my chosen in whom my soul delights; I have put my Spirit[8] upon him; he will bring forth justice to the nations" (Isa. 42:1).

We read of the servant's gentle and faithful doing of justice. At the heart of the work we find perseverance and commitment in bringing the message for which even "the coastlands" wait. God, the creator of the heavens and the earth, calls the servant and those who respond to his justice-making work.

am the Lord, I have called you in righteousness, I have
taken you by the hand and kept you; I have given you as a
covenant to the people, a light to the nations, to open the
eyes that are blind, to bring out the prisoners from the
dungeon, from the prison those who sit in darkness. I am
the Lord, that is my name; my glory I give to no other, nor
my praise to idols. See, the former things have come to
pass, and new things I now declare; before they spring
forth, I tell you of them. (Isa. 42:5-9)

This remarkable passage speaks of God's Spirit sustaining
the life of God's people in their vocation of bringing healing to
all the earth, of being "a light to the nations." God's mercy out-
lasts the brokenness that resulted from the people's disregard
for their covenant with God. This merciful God continues to
call the people of the promise to the vocation of blessing all the
families of the earth, the vocation given originally in the calling of Abraham and Sarah (Gen. 12:3).

The God who sustains this covenant through the presence
of the Holy Spirit is the same God who created the heavens and
earth. This God gave "breath to the people upon it and spirit
to those who walk in it." The healing justice that God's servant
people are still called to express in this broken world takes the
form of opening eyes that are blind and releasing prisoners
from dungeons. The Spirit of life brings healing amid the brokenness of life.

THE HOLY SPIRIT AND JESUS

When we jump ahead in the biblical story to Jesus, we find
these points profoundly reinforced. Remember our confession
of Holy Spirit as the Spirit of Jesus. We see a close connection
between the presence of the Spirit and key moments in the
story of Jesus.

We first read of Jesus when his mother Mary is informed
of her pregnancy. The presence of the Spirit plays a crucial role
in conveying the significance of what the angel Gabriel tells
Mary. This young Galilean woman, not yet married, receives
some amazing news.

"Mary, you have found favor with God. You will conceive
in your womb and bear a son, and you will name him

Jesus. He will be great, and will be called the Son of the Most High, and the Lord God will give to him the throne of his ancestor David. He will reign over the house of Jacob forever, and of his kingdom there will be no end." (Luke 1:30-32)

Mary, of course, finds this hard to believe. How will she give birth to such a wondrous son when she still is a virgin?

"The Holy Spirit will come upon you, and the power of the Most High will overshadow you; therefore the child to be born will be holy; he will be called Son of God." . . . Then Mary said, "Here am I, the servant of the Lord; let it be with me according to your word." Then the angel departed from her. (Luke 1:35-38)

God's Spirit enters human existence through the giving of new life to this young woman, Mary. The power of the Spirit is the power of life. The transformation the Spirit brings to human existence happens through the agency of this young woman's acceptance of her vocation (echoing the vocation given in Gen. 1 and the vocation given to the Servant in Isa. 42).

Then, years later, when Jesus' time of preparation comes to end and he readies to begin his public ministry, he submits to the baptism of John. As this happens, Luke writes, "the heaven was opened, and the Holy Spirit descended upon him in bodily form like a dove. And a voice came from heaven, 'You are my Son, the Beloved; with you I am well pleased'" (3:22).

The Holy Spirit is present in Mary's faithfulness to her vocation and her conception in a powerful way. This presence is then reiterated in Jesus' own step of faithfulness in accepting John's baptism as an act of commissioning. The identity of Jesus as God's Son finds its validation when the Spirit descends on Jesus and God's voice expresses his pleasure with Jesus' action.

Luke tells of two key events that emphasize Jesus' empowerment by the fullness of the Spirit. These events, his temptations and his opening proclamation, make clear the nature of his vocation as God's Son.

Immediately after the baptism, Jesus moves deeper into the wilderness for a time of testing and clarification before beginning to manifest his special vocation: "Jesus, full of the Holy

Spirit, returned from the Jordan and was led by the Spirit in the wilderness, where for forty days he was tempted by the devil" (Luke 4:1-2).

What will Jesus do to express his vocation as God's Son? Given that "Son of God" is likely a term for "the Messiah" and "king," what kind of *king* will Jesus be? The tempter offers options. He offers Jesus ruling authority over "all the kingdoms of the world." He also offers the acclaim of the leadership of the Jerusalem temple through a miraculous angelic rescue. Empowered by the Holy Spirit, Jesus turns down the devil's temptations. The kingship God calls Jesus to embody does not rule with top-down power. The Holy Spirit empowers Jesus to hold fast to his true calling, a much more delicate and difficult expression of "kingly" power expressed through *persevering love*.

After clarifying his vocation through the temptations, Jesus returns to his home territory and begins his public ministry. As he does so, we are told, he is "filled with the power of the Spirit" (Luke 4:14). His teachings and deeds lead to his being "praised by everyone" (4:15). He makes his message clear:

> When he came to Nazareth, where he had been brought up, he went to the synagogue on the Sabbath day, as was his custom. He stood up to read, and the scroll of the prophet Isaiah was given to him. He unrolled the scroll and found the place where it is written: "The Spirit of the Lord is upon me, because he has anointed me to bring good news to the poor. He has sent me to proclaim release to the captives and recovery of sight to the blind, to let the oppressed go free, to proclaim the year of the Lord's favor." And he rolled up the scroll, gave it back to the attendant, and sat down. The eyes of all in the synagogue were fixed on him. Then he began to say to them, "Today this Scripture has been fulfilled in your hearing." (Luke 4:16-21)

"The Spirit of the Lord is upon me," Jesus asserts. And what is the Spirit anointing Jesus to do? We go right back to the affirmation that the Spirit is the Spirit of life and that each human being is infused with God's Spirit. Each human being has infinite value. Each human being deserves all the respect and care and compassion the rest of us can muster.

We see the Spirit as the Spirit of life in Jesus' description of his task as the Son of God. Empowered by the Spirit, Jesus "brings good news to the *poor*, proclaims release to the *captives* and recovery of sight to the *blind*, and lets the *oppressed* go free" (4:18). The poor, captives, blind, oppressed. These are the very people whose humanity is being denied. These are the very people who are treated as objects, as non-humans.

Jesus, the supremely Spirit-infused human being, *centers* his Spirit-directed work on bringing good news, release, recovery, and freedom to those whose human dignity is most at risk. Jesus announces this work at the very beginning here—and the rest of his life is spent putting these commitments into practice.

He suffered a great deal because he did so. The Spirit-*denying* forces of human culture fought him tooth and nail. And killed him. But the Spirit was not to be denied. God raised Jesus and confirmed that the Spirit that animated Jesus was indeed the Spirit of God.

As the story continues, the Holy Spirit plays the essential role of providing for continuity between Jesus and the community that survived him. Jesus, the Son of God empowered by the Holy Spirit, carries out his vocation of kingship through persevering love. The way of Jesus becomes the way of his followers through the empowerment of this same Holy Spirit. After the transition from God as present in the human Jesus to God as present in the Spirit-guided community, the Holy Spirit becomes understood as the "Spirit of Jesus."

Luke tells of the transition in his account that begins the sequel to his Gospel, the Acts of the apostles:

> After his suffering [Jesus] . . . appear[ed] to [his followers] during forty days and speaking about the kingdom of God. . . . They asked him, "Lord, is this the time when you will restore the kingdom to Israel?" He replied, "It is not for you to know the times or periods that the Father has set by how own authority. But you will receive power when the Holy Spirit has come upon you; and you will be my witnesses in Jerusalem, in all Judea and Samaria, and to the ends of the earth." (Acts 1:3-8)

Here Jesus provides the basic focus and outline of what follows in the book of Acts. His ministry will continue due to the presence of his Spirit in a new and powerful way among his followers. The message will be the same, the Jubilee theology of release, new sight, liberation. The Spirit is one with Jesus.

THE FRUITS OF THE SPIRIT

The followers of Jesus self-consciously turned to the Holy Spirit as their guide into the shape of their vocation of continuing Jesus' ministry of making present God's kingdom. The apostle Paul summarized the characteristics of the follower of Jesus when filled with the Spirit of Jesus:

> The fruit of the Spirit is love, joy, peace, patience, kindness, generosity, faithfulness, gentleness, and self-control. There is no law against such things. And those who belong to Christ Jesus have crucified the flesh with its passions and desires. If we live by the Spirit, let us also be guided by the Spirit. Let us not become conceited, competing against one another, envying one another. (Gal. 5:22-26)

We best understand the Holy Spirit as where the holiness of God, the holiness of the created world, the holiness of all living creatures, and the holiness of each and every human being come together. This convergence is all the one Spirit of God.

If we truly seek the fruits of the Spirit, we may first acknowledge what they are *not*. The fruit will not so much be ecstatic experiences. The fruit will not be a strengthening of our sense of our own uniqueness as "Spirit-filled Christians" in a way that justifies our treating creation as a lifeless object to be exploited. The fruit will not lead to justifying our treating other human beings as things, or as enemies and objects of our nation's bombs.

If we seek truly to be filled with the Spirit, we will pray for the courage and wisdom to follow Jesus' path. We will pray for the courage and wisdom to value each and every life—even when doing so may lead to a cross.

Paul, in Romans 5, speaks of the connection between the Holy Spirit and love. "God's love has been poured into our hearts through the Holy Spirit that has been given to us" (5:5). When we receive the Holy Spirit, God's love is poured into our hearts. The fruits of the Spirit all come down to one basic affirmation: "*God loves.*" When we *know* to the bottom of our souls that God loves us the rest follows: joy, peace, patience, kindness, generosity, faithfulness, gentleness, and self-control.

The power of God's love poured into our hearts heals us of hatred and fearfulness. This power helps us move from a world of scarcity to a world characterized by abundant living. The fruits of the Spirit are not about freedom from suffering or knowing all the answers or constant happiness. More so, the fruits of the Spirit have to do with knowing that God loves us, with loving other people, and with living with patience, compassion, and openness to learning and growth.

God offers all of us life, *abundant* life. God offers us the gift of the Holy Spirit to move us to trust in Christ as our savior, to move us to seek to walk in Christ's way, to empower us to live according to the Spirit.

THE WORK OF THE HOLY SPIRIT

God as Holy Spirit provides strength, encouragement, and guidance for people of faith and for faith communities. The Holy Spirit gives gifts of insight, hopefulness, joy, and peace of mind. The Holy Spirit enables us to connect with others, to give and receive love and encouragement. The Spirit is the spirit of reconciliation, empowering those who depend upon it to restore broken relationships, to forgive and to accept forgiveness.

The Holy Spirit is always everywhere. There is no sacred/secular split whatsoever; there is no realm of life that is Spirit-less. Where there is life the Spirit is present. Wherever there is goodness, peace, and justice they are the work of the Holy Spirit.

The Holy Spirit is gently persuasive and enlightening. It clarifies as we go through life and always waits for our openness. It walks the fine line between coercion and passivity, neither forcing a person to trust in God nor simply leaving us to our own devices. As we open to God, the loving persistence of the Spirit moves in our hearts. However, the Spirit is only as powerful in our lives as we let it be. A good analogy for the Spirit's work in the lives of believers, perhaps, is a road map. We need the map to know where to go, but we do the driving.

The Holy Spirit transforms our lives as we let it, moving us toward sanctification and wholeness. The Spirit gives us gradual awareness, flashes of insight, moments of joy, comfort in sorrow, courage to step out, a sense of connection with others, and the ability to love and be loved.

This is God's World: So What?

[The Doctrine of Creation]

I have suggested that Genesis 1 and 2 are crucial texts for our understanding of the Holy Spirit. They make clear that God's Spirit is the Spirit of life—of all life. To see God's Spirit infusing all of creation and to see God's Spirit as the Spirit of Jesus both have enormous significance for our next doctrine, too, the doctrine of creation.

Many years ago, I decided to write a somewhat ambitious masters thesis. I thought that one year of seminary had given me enough expertise to produce something comprehensive about Christian ethics. I would bring together the themes of love, creation, and justice into a grand theory that would vindicate the melding of pacifism and social activism. I am now a bit embarrassed about my audacity in thinking that as young and ignorant as I was then I could write coherently on such big topics. This thesis is definitely *not* something I would want anyone to read now.

My faculty readers were patient with me. However, I did learn later that one of them, my intellectual mentor, John Howard Yoder, had made one suggestion to the M.A. program director. In the future, he proposed, the seminary should work harder to help students reduce the topics of their theses to a more manageable scale.

BRINGING LOVE, JUSTICE, AND CREATION TOGETHER

Nonetheless, now about twenty-five years later, I believe that my instincts concerning my theme (if not the scale of the project) actually were good. I wanted to try to bring together a central Anabaptist theme (the centrality of Jesus' love command) with themes more likely emphasized in Catholic and Reformed contexts (theologies of nature and creation). I still believe that problems we have in developing life-giving understandings and practices related to justice stem from the failure to bring love and creation into direct conversation with justice.

In my thesis defense, John Howard Yoder's only sharp question to me came over my discussion of creation theology. That Yoder brought up this one issue may be telling. In all of his writings (and I have read with great appreciation most of them), he never works very hard at developing a theology of creation. Nor does he seek to elaborate in any detail his claim that the way of Jesus goes with the grain of the cosmos.[1]

Mennonite thinkers and Reformed and Catholic thinkers all generally seem to agree. We go to Jesus to learn about love; we go to the real world, to creation, to learn about "justice." Well, even if I bit off way more than I could chew as a young budding scholar, I still believe I was onto something: Jesus and creation go *together*.

Let me review the basic view of theology I am presenting in this book. Theology, I propose, has to do with our hierarchy of values—the things we actually shape our lives by, the things we *actually* believe as verified by our practices. Theological reflection matters because it is how we gain self-awareness about what our values actually are.

I believe we best understand *Christian* theology as reflecting on how the values embodied by Jesus in his life and teaching might become *our* values. So I am calling what I do "theology as if Jesus matters." Well, I want to pursue this approach as far as I can. So I now turn to this question: when we reflect on the doctrine of creation—including nature, the world around us—might we understand it through an interpretive framework centered on Jesus?

CREATION AS "RED IN TOOTH AND CLAW"?

Some, many, maybe most, Christians—at least modern, Western, educated Christians—have their doubts. Several years ago I presented a conference paper, "A Pacifist Critique of the Modern Worldview."[2] A good friend of mine, an older scholar and in every way an impressive Mennonite Christian, raised some criticisms. My friend suggested I was too quick to see nature as compatible with pacifism. He quoted the famous lines from Alfred Lord Tennyson's poem, "In Memorium" about nature being "red in tooth and claw."

I was not familiar with that poem, so I looked it up. I discovered that the stanza my friend cited raises precisely the question I am asking. Might we understand nature (or, as Christians would say, "creation") as being compatible with Jesus' basic peaceable life and teaching?

"In Memorium" speaks, using Tennyson's word, of "man" as nature's "last work." This "last work" "trusted God was love indeed and love Creation's final law." The poem continues, though, to suggest that there seems to be counter-evidence to the idea that love is creation's "final law": "Nature, red in tooth and claw with ravine, shriek'd against his creed." Nature itself, evinced by its bloodiness, cries directly in contradiction to the belief in love's natural ultimacy.

If we accept that love is creation's "final law," we would seem to be saying that the way of Jesus is built into the way things are. Is this a legitimate position to hold? Does the way of Jesus go with the grain of the universe or not? Is the call to peacemaking that we seek to embrace as followers of Jesus a call to *resist* creation, to go *against* the grain? Or is peacemaking actually a quest to seek harmony with the ultimate character of the universe? Does nature indeed "shriek against" the "creed" that love is "Creation's final law"?

THE BIBLE ON CREATION

I have picked four Scripture texts to look at briefly. These texts are only the tip of the iceberg when it comes to biblical teaching on creation. But they give us a good sense of the terrain. What are some things we can say about creation based on these verses?

Let's begin at the beginning. We read in the first chapter of Genesis that "when God created the heavens and the earth," the first step was the giving of light. "And God saw that the light was good." Then the waters and the land were separated. "And God saw that it was good." What follows is vegetation. "And God saw that it was good."

Likewise with the moon and sun and the stars. And with the living creatures.Then the finale.

> And God said, "Let the earth bring forth living creatures of every kind: cattle and creeping things and wild animals of the earth of every kind." And it was so. . . . And God saw that it was good. . . .
>
> Then God said, "Let us make humankind in our image, according to our image, according to our like-ness. . . . God created humankind . . . ; male and female he created them. . . . God saw everything that he had made, and indeed, it was very good. (Gen. 1:26-31)

Genesis 1 tells us that the universe, the earth, and its hos-pitality to life are from God. The chapter's key refrain is this: "And God saw that it was good." Then, when the sixth day ends: "God saw everything that was made, and indeed, it was *very* good." We get the sense of an artist at work, or a writer, or just about any person creating something meaningful.

I haven't created many things, but I have prepared Mexi-can molé sauce. This preparation is very elaborate, with dozens of ingredients that in the end blend together into something pretty special. It takes five or six hours to make, but when you put in the effort, when you taste your molé (assuming you like that kind of thing) and you say, "Indeed, it is *very* good"—then you are ready for a rest!

For God, it seems, the world, the plants and animals, the creation and sustenance of life—all of this is an act of creative *love*. Genesis one teaches that the world and its teeming life is something beautiful and profoundly meaningful. Creation ex-presses something about God's own self.

Next, let's turn to the Book of Psalms. We read in the thirty-third Psalm about God's creative work.

> The earth is full of the steadfast love of the Lord. By the word of the Lord the heavens were made, and all their

host by the breath of his mouth.

The Lord deserves the utmost reverence for the work of creation. The creator speaks and commands and the world comes into being. In doing so, God is established above the nations.

From where [the Lord] sits enthroned he watches all the inhabitants of the earth—he who fashions the hearts of them all, and observes their deeds. A king is not saved by his great army; a warrior is not delivered by his great strength. The warhorse is a vain hope for victory, and by its great might it cannot save.

Truly the eye of the Lord is on those who . . . hope in his steadfast love, to deliver their soul from death, and to keep them alive in famine. Our soul waits for the Lord; he is our help and shield. . . . (Ps. 33)

Psalm 33 makes a powerful assertion, a foundational definition: *The earth is full of the steadfast love of God*. One way the psalmist portrays God the creator, seen through nature, is God as lover. God is to be trusted because of God's creative love that has made what is and who sustains it.

This psalm is actually a great proof text for what I argued in my MA thesis. We have here all three components I attempted to bring together: creation, love, and justice. God is *creator*. God's creation is full of God's steadfast *love*. And this loving creative work leads to genuine *justice*. God's justice in Psalm 33 *denies* the claims of the warriors and kings to a privileged role in the embodiment of social justice. It is not the rough, coercive, brute-power-enhancing justice of the sword that reflects the grain of the universe seen in God's creation. It is trust in God's steadfast love.

For many years, I have taught a class called "History and Philosophy of Nonviolence." In this class, we look at Mahatma Gandhi's life and philosophy. Every year I am inspired again to see how relevant to the "real world" the practice of steadfast *satyagraha* is—*satyagraha* being the word Gandhi used for loving resistance or nonviolence. Amid all the great movers and shakers of the twentieth century, it's amazing that in the end many "experts" judged Gandhi the person of the century. I'd say it is not so much that he accomplished more than anyone else but that he made imaginable in a century of total war that humanity still might find another way. He helped make W. H. Auden's call at the beginning of World War II seem possible: "We must love one another or die."[3]

Next let's look at some of Jesus' words. In the Sermon on the Mount, he calls upon his listeners to find their way free from worry and anxiety. Life is about much more than food and clothing. God cares for God's creatures. Look at the natural world.

> The birds of the air neither sow not reap nor gather into barns, and yet your heavenly Father feeds them. Are you not of more value than they? And can any of you by worrying add a single hour to your span of life? And why do you worry about your clothing? Consider the lilies of the field, how they grow; they neither toil nor spin, yet I tell you, even Solomon in all his glory was not clothed like one of these. (Matt. 6:25-27)

God cares deeply for the natural world, even in its transience. Much more so will God care for those creatures created in God's image.

> Therefore do not worry, saying, "What will we eat?" or "What will we drink?" or "What will we wear?" For it is the Gentiles who strive for all these things; and indeed your heavenly Father knows that you need all these things. But strive first for the kingdom of God and his justice and all these things will be given to you as well. (Matt. 6:29-33)

Jesus' words in Matthew 6 remind us that God is the sustainer of life for all creation. God sustains life for the birds of the air and the lilies of the field as well as human beings. Jesus then makes his key teaching point: learn from the abundance of life around us that we may trust in God. Learn from the abundance of life around us that we may depend upon God's care for us as we seek the kingdom and its justice.

Again creation, love, and justice are linked. God sustains all kinds of life; creation is abundant in God's love; and Jesus draws this lesson: Because of God's abundant life-giving love, seek justice right now in this world with fearless conviction.

And finally, let's turn to some words attributed to the apostle Paul:

[Jesus Christ] is the image of the invisible God, the firstborn of all creation; for in him all things in heaven and on
earth were created, things visible and invisible, whether
thrones or dominions or rulers or powers—all things have
been created through him and for him. He himself is before all things, and in him all things hold together. He is
the head of the body, the church; he is the beginning, the
firstborn from the dead, so that he might come to have
first place in everything. For in him all the fullness of God
was pleased to dwell, and through him God was pleased
to reconcile to himself all things, whether on earth or in
heaven, by making peace through the blood of his cross.
(Col. 1:15-20)

Colossians 1 presents Jesus himself as being present in all
that is. The Jesus who challenged the powers-that-be in his political and religious world and was executed for doing so embodied the image "of the invisible God." In Jesus, we find
linked inextricably together the presence of the creator God
and the message of genuine restorative justice manifested in
concrete acts of love and resistance. And this Jesus directly participated in the creation of "all things in heaven and on earth."

The work of creation, the reality of our physical world, and
the work of reconciling all things is the *same* work, coming from
the same source, seeking the same end. The Spirit of Jesus infuses all of creation. In Christ, "all things hold together." Fur-
thermore, through Christ, God works God's reconciling, healing wonders for "all things, whether on earth or in heaven."

We can look back to the Genesis creation account—the
Spirit of God moves over the waters at the beginning, the Spirit
of God is breathed into the dust of the earth to enliven the first
human being. Here is where trinitarian ideas make sense to me.
God the creator, the Holy Spirit, Jesus the savior, all join *together*
in the creation and sustenance of life, in the work that brings
healing and reconciliation to all things.

CREATION AND JUSTICE

This healing and reconciliation is what the Bible means by
justice.[4] Not an eye for an eye. Not an impersonal principle of
balancing self-interests. Not holiness and wrath that respond

to human brokenness and sin with punishing anger. No, by "justice" the Bible much more has in mind God's creativity that brought into existence what is—out of love. God's creativity endlessly and steadfastly brings healing when what is is marred by brokenness. Biblical justice restores relationships; it makes whole that which has been damaged.

Justice is for the sake of life. God's justice in the Bible is not primarily retribution but salvation, not primarily punitive but corrective. The justice of God may be seen as God's saving power, God's fidelity to the role as the Lord of the covenant. God created the earth and its inhabitants for harmonious relationships and continually acts, even amid human rebellion, to effect those relationships.

The term *justice* in the Bible tends to merge with concepts like "steadfast love," "compassion," "kindness," and "salvation." Justice has ultimately to do with how a loving creator has made the world. To be just is to live according to the creator's will, to be in harmony with God, with fellow human beings, and with the rest of creation—*and* not to rest until this is the case for everyone else too.

The Bible's connection between justice and life follows from its ideas regarding creation. Biblical writers affirm "creation" as an act of the covenant-making God of Israel. Thus creation's character coheres with the values of the covenant—love, justice, peace, compassion—all the things that sustain and nourish life. We find no disjunction between the creator God and the covenant-making God. In fact creation was God's first covenant-making act. Thus covenant values (justice, love, peace) ultimately are part of the very fabric of creation.

Human life originated as an expression of God's covenant-love. So all human action consistent with that love shares in the basic meaning of creation—and is thereby "just." The creation of humankind in the image of this God means that all people need relationships with each other and with God. The purpose of human activity is to help these relationships. Since all people, simply by virtue of being people, are in the "image of God" and thus have dignity and value, there is no justification for discrimination and disregard of any human life. Injustice is the severing of relationships; justice is their establishment and/or restoration.

The cosmos is created good. Being an aberration, evil can and must be resisted. No evil is such an intrinsic part of the structure of reality that it cannot be conquered by the creator's power. To conquer the power of evil—a power especially manifested in the severing of relationships—is to do justice.

God's will has to do with *all* parts of creation. There is nothing that is autonomous from that will or that is ethically neutral. The Bible challenges people of faith to carry out the creator's will in all spheres of human existence.

Ultimately, the Bible makes no distinction between the order of creation and the order of redemption. The creator-God and the redeemer-God are one and the same. Biblical people would never have recognized the creator-God without their historical experience of the redeemer-God.

The Bible affirms the central theological reality in creation as love. Therefore, faithfulness to the "creation mandate" equals living lives of love. The heart of God's character is steadfast love, which for God means desiring the good of all people. This includes God's enemies and especially social outcasts. God's love provides the model for God's followers.

The Bible presents God's justice as normative for the nations, not just the covenant people. For example, when Amos condemned the nations for their injustices, his readers would not have questioned whether it was legitimate for him to do so. God's will was for *all* people, and all people were to be held accountable to how they responded to that will. This is true because God is seen to be the creator of all that is. Justice is embedded in creation (hence injustice is as unnatural as an ox plowing the sea or a wall being crooked, Amos 6:12; 7:7).[5]

For biblical writers, creation theology came not from reason but from their historical experience of God as redeemer. However, the implications of their creation theology led them to see all people as part of God's creation, all people created in God's image, and all people accountable to God. These beliefs primarily led to negative conclusions (like Amos's) regarding the actual practice of justice on the part of the nations. The accountability generally was used to support the fact that the nations too will be judged by God for being unjust.

However, we do see scattered examples of just people outside Israel (e.g., Rahab the harlot; the repentant people of Nineveh in Jonah; even, to some extent, Cyrus, the Persian leader). These perhaps indicate that God's justice was seen to be knowable and doable by anyone—by virtue of one's humanness. Paul also seems to have this in mind in Romans when he writes about Gentiles who follow the law (2:14-16).

In a nutshell, then, we see in the Bible a doctrine of creation that places the way of Jesus right at the center from start to finish. The Bible teaches that the way of Jesus indeed goes *with* the grain of the universe.

CREATION AND JESUS: WISHFUL THINKING?

But is this belief blind faith? Is it romantic, wishful thinking to believe that creation also witnesses to the way of Jesus? In one discussion, a friend laughed at me as I proposed this way of looking at the world. He invoked Voltaire's *Candide* and called me a Panglossian. Only after a little research did I realize what an insult he gave me; a Panglossis a person who lives by *baseless optimism.*

My friend could be right. However, in thinking of these issues in the context of our discussion of theology as if Jesus matters, I believe we should *start* with the Bible's doctrine of creation. We should recognize that based on our values as followers of Jesus, we see love of God and neighbor as at the heart of reality. So we should begin with the assumption that nature (as God's creation) likely will confirm these values. This is our "hypothesis." Then, we consider the actual evidence. Do we in fact find evidence in nature for a much more optimistic view than reflected in the "red in tooth and claw" assumption?

Well, I will just say that I don't think these friends of mine I have mentioned who see a huge tension between nature and the message of Jesus have proven their case. I recommend the work of Mary Clark, a retired biologist and scholar of peace, who has thought deeply about issues of violence, human nature, and the interrelatedness of living creatures. In her important book, *In Search of Human Nature,*[6] she concludes that *cooperation* may be more fundamental to human nature than selfishness and competition.

She challenges the validity as a descriptor of human nature the metaphor of the "Billiard Ball Gestalt" that "depicts isolated objects moving independently and colliding randomly with each other. It models cause-and-effect, linear events of an atomistic or individualistic worldview. The 'Self' is discrete and separate from the whole."[7]

She proposes as a more accurate metaphor the "Indra's Net Gestalt." Here, the universe is "depicted by a jeweled net where each jewel is connected to and hence reflects upon all the others. No one entity can be its discrete, autonomous 'Self' independent of its connectedness with the whole of reality."[8]

This awareness of our interconnectedness points to cooperation as the basic creative force in human evolution. A key factor that emerged as human beings evolved to greater intelligence was an increase in the need for cooperation.

> Becoming smarter (for whatever purpose) meant birthing ever-more helpless, premature infants, and investing a great deal of extra time and effort in nursing them, teaching them, and protecting them. Females (who incidentally gather well over half the group's calories in extant foraging societies) required increasing assistance from other adults in watching over and protecting their helpless young from predators, and for providing additional food to the group's cohort of mothers, especially during lactation, which eventually came to last four or five years. [These] adaptational requirements ... placed on ... primates were increasingly critical for evolving hominids.[9]

Obviously, given the intense debates swirling around issues of human nature, competition versus cooperation in the evolutionary processes, and the like, we cannot *prove* that cooperation is more central to human nature than competition. We cannot *prove* that service more powerfully furthers human adaptability to life on this earth than domination. That is, we cannot *prove* that the way of Jesus goes *with* the grain of the universe.

However, from the perspective of Christian theology, we should be asking some hard questions of those who *assume* the "red in tooth and claw" hypothesis. Is it merely a coincidence that the emergence of this violent view of the natural world coincided historically with the emergence of what I want to call a profoundly predatory view toward the natural world? What kinds of political and economic practices have tended to be furthered by views that see human life as "nasty, brutish, and short" and characterized by intense competition for life's resources? Human cultures in the "civilized West," those that have been much more receptive to the innate competitiveness view of human nature, have tended to reduce creation to a source for economic goods. Such a reduction has led to the rape and plunder of forests, oceans, waterways, prairie lands, mountains, and so much worse.[10]

I believe projecting *our* violence onto nature has served an analogous function to the way propaganda attributes bloodthirstiness to our "enemies." Since our enemies obviously do not value life, we need not value their lives. That is, our portraying *them* as hopelessly violent serves our desire to rain violence upon them.

Likewise, if we project violence onto nature we more easily treat nature violently. If the universe is "red in tooth and claw," we human beings had better make sure the "red" comes from nature's "blood" and not our own.

I once read a fascinating book, called *The Man Who Listened to Horses*, by Monty Roberts.[11] His father was a well-known trainer of horses, who himself wrote popular books about his techniques. The father firmly believed in overpowering the horse, teaching through pain who is the boss, breaking the horse's rebellious spirit. This is the way of nature, he insisted. Tragically, though not surprisingly, Mr. Roberts treated his family, including his son Monty, the same way—"spare the rod and spoil the child"; nature itself teaches this, the father insisted.

Somehow, Monty intuitively realized that not only should he as a child not be treated with such violence. He strongly suspected that horses be shouldn't either. So he began to develop revolutionary techniques. And they worked. He terms it "gentling" the horse, not "breaking" it. Sadly, Mr. Roberts rejected his son's insights—and rejected his son. He died with the relationship broken.

Monty Roberts bases his understanding of how to gentle horses on his perceptions of how horses relate to each other. He has learned how to make a creature to creature connection with them that fosters a relationship, not a dynamic of brute force and domination. He even tried his techniques out on deer and found them to be responsive, too.

Roberts has gone on to apply what he has learned to human relationships with fruitful results. His basic saying on his website could have come straight from Jesus: "Violence is never the answer." He founded an organization called "Join-Up International" that promotes gentle, more effective alternatives to violence and force in relationships with both horses and human beings.

This is only one story. I find it encouraging, though. I have called this chapter on creation theology, "This is God's World: So What?" As Christians, we do confess that the world we live in is the product of the creative work of God. We also confess that our present lives are the products of the creative work of God. As God's creatures, we are accountable to our creator.

In earlier chapters, we have reflected on Christian theology as reflection on the significance of our confession that Jesus' message is the basis for our hierarchy of values. What matters most to us, as Jesus' followers, is loving God and neighbor. Does this confession about God as creator, God's message of love, and our possibility of living in harmony such a message cohere with our perception of the nature of nature?

This is what I believe follows from our confession that "this is God's world": When we look for evidence of Jesus' way in the world around us, we might well be pleasantly surprised by what we find. We might find that the world around us is home for love, justice, and peace—amid the ambiguities and alienations that remain all too common.

Canadian singer-songwriter Bruce Cockburn, throughout his long career, has produced numerous songs that challenge listeners toward hopefulness in response to well-aimed critiques of current expressions of oppression and injustice. In "Down Where the Death Squad Lives" he tells the all-too-common story of violence in service of power. However, he does not settle for despair but sees evil wrapped in love. It is not only "bombs that fall from above" but also healing responses.[12]

Creation carries in it, reflecting the character of the Creator, the capacity for life's regeneration. To see evil wrapped in love is certainly a statement of faith. However, creation itself does offer some support for such an affirmation.

So, a theology of creation that shares Jesus' hierarchy of values will look for evidence that supports the centrality of love of God and neighbor. It will recognize that all of life is interconnected and that reality itself is eloquently full of creativity; as Gerard Manley Hopkins wrote, "the world is charged with the grandeur of God . . . Nature is never spent. . . . Because the Holy Ghost over the bent world broods with warm breast and with ah! bright wings."[13]

All of life is *interconnected*. Native American philosopher Gabriel Horn writes of the contrast between two ways of knowing. The first coheres with what Horn calls "our Original Intention." "Take only what you need, live in harmony and balance with your environment, love the Earth. Such a thought process does not allow artificial extensions, like the tools we create or even the weapons we make, to become actual extensions of the self." People whose thought processes follow this path do not believe they are superior to other life forms. All things are necessary parts of wholeness.[14]

The other way of knowing "travels on an asphalt road." For this path, people's artificial extensions, on which they increasingly depend, are linked with their very identity. This leads to an ever-widening separation not only from non-Western peoples but also other life forms. The wheel is no longer seen as something sacred but as a tool for moving faster.[15]

Our doctrine of creation should lead to an openness to the richness of life, to what philosopher Albert Borgmann calls "eloquent reality."[16] Many people have characterized recent centuries as ones of deep alienation and brokenness. Such alienation seems to follow from a worldview that has abstracted from the non-human world all conscious intelligence and purpose and meaning and then projected onto the world a soulless machine. Richard Tarnas see that "this is the ultimate anthropomorphic projection: a [human]-made machine, something not in fact ever found in nature. From this perspective, it is the modern world's own impersonal soullessness that has been projected from within onto the world."[17]

However, other perspectives are possible. "Eloquent reality" is that which in this life, this world, is genuinely beautiful, healing, soulful, invigorating. Reality understood thus is not totally orderly, objective, controllable, or quantifiable.

Martin Buber articulated an understanding of the world focused on relationships as the core of what is most real—in contrast to the world of use, control, and exploitation (the "It-world"). Buber argued that the world we live in is where we will encounter our peaceable God:

> I know nothing of a "world" and of "worldly life" that separate us from God. What is designated that way is life with an alienated It-world, the life of experience and use. Whatever goes out in truth to the world, goes forth to God. Only he that believes in the world achieves contact with it; and if he commits himself he cannot remain godless. Let us love that actual world that never wishes to be annulled; . . . in all its terror, [daring] to embrace it with our spirit's arms—and our hands encounter the hands that hold it.[18]

6
....

How Does
God Communicate?

[The Doctrine of Revelation]

*T*HE UNDERSTANDINGS OF JESUS, God, Holy Spirit, and creation that I have developed so far encourage optimism about our possibilities for discerning God's revelation in our lives and in the world around us. We confess that God's Spirit infuses all that is, enlivening the created world.

In this chapter, we will pursue the implications of this confession further in relation to the doctrine of revelation. We will ask more specifically, How does God communicate? How do we work at discerning the message of God amid all the messages with which we are bombarded? What role does the Bible play in this discernment?

AN ALL-AUTHORITATIVE BIBLE?

Back in 1971 when I first began going to church as a teenager, I attended a *Bible* Baptist Church. We were a Bible-centered church. We saw the Bible as the perfect book, the Word of God that provided clear direction for life. We believed that God speaks to us directly through the Bible. When we opened the Bible, we opened ourselves to God.

Most people in that church had beautiful Bibles with supple leather covers. These Bibles looked like no other kind of book. And they were well used. Conversations and prayers were punctuated with Bible verses—in the King James Version. This sense of certainty of our access to clear, authoritative direction straight from God had great appeal for me. The reason I had turned to faith was that I wanted answers; I wanted to know the truth. And it seemed I had found it.

You simply did not question the authority of the Bible. That was one of my first lessons. I realize now that along with this message of the authority of the Bible, I also learned to defer to human authority. My job as a Christian was not to think and ask questions; my job was to listen and obey. Listen to God, for sure, but also recognize that the voice of God comes through the authoritative Bible. And, of more practical importance, listen to God through the authoritative preacher. Our congregation centered around our pastor. He preached every Sunday morning, every Sunday evening, and every Wednesday evening. Straight from the Bible.

So, if I had asked back then how God communicates, I would have had a simple and obvious answer: God communicates through the words of the Bible, each word fully inspired, each word fully authoritative. If I had been honest and at least a bit self aware, I would also have admitted that sometimes it was hard for me to understand each word of the Bible. I was thankful to have an authoritative preacher to help me hear the Bible better and learn how I should obey it.

The question behind the question of how God communicates is the question of *why* God communicates—what is the point of God's self-disclosure? What purposes does God's communication serve?

Now, our preacher was a kind man, not abusive or exploitative. He wasn't on a power trip. Rather, he was a sincere believer following the path that seemed best to him and his congregation. But this is the message I got from him (and others in the church) about why God communicates (which I now believe is pretty much the *opposite* of the Bible's actual message): God communicates to us, I learned, to take us out of the world. The reason God speaks through the Bible is tell us how to have our souls saved and to tell us how Jesus will return and take us away to heaven with him.

I took this message very seriously. When I went to college, I agonized a bit over whether I should stay in college or not, since I expected Jesus to return soon. At one point someone convinced me that the rapture would happen in 1981. Surely my ambivalence about staying in college had nothing to do with the low grades I received my first term!

So I read the Bible as a collection of verses that one way or another all support the same basic idea—get saved and get out of here. One of the study aids I was given was a set of cards with Bible verses about salvation to memorize. These verses were taken out of context and then put together to give the path to salvation.

It is interesting how selective the use of proof texts was, though. We had verses that helped us know that drinking alcohol was a terrible sin—a person really couldn't be a Christian and a drinker. But what about the verse, "a little wine is good for the stomach" or the story of Jesus miraculously providing wine for the wedding at Cana? Well, those verses didn't really say what they seemed to say. When Jesus turned the water into wine, he was actually turning it into unfermented grape juice—which is surely also what Paul had in mind as well when he commended wine as a digestive aid. It was many years before I came to question the authoritative teaching I was given concerning alcohol.

As I look back now, it seems ironic to think of the first step I took toward rethinking my view of the Bible. When I went to college, someone recommended I get this new translation that had just come out, the New International Version. I know now that the NIV was created as a theologically conservative alternative to the Revised Standard Version. But to me then it was radical because the first printings of the New Testament looked just like a regular book. Hard cover, a couple of hundred pages long, just a single column per page with regular-sized print. When I showed it to a friend in my Baptist congregation, he gasped in shock. It looked just like any other book. I still didn't think of the Bible as a human book, but the door had been opened.

All along, though, I struggled with Bible study. I believed with all my heart what I was taught about how important the Bible was. It was God's Word, without error, and the source of the absolutes we need for knowing God's will. But I simply didn't find the Bible interesting. I tried and tried to read it. I kept journals and struggled to memorize the important salvation verses. I attended seminars called "Walk Through the Bible" that helped us learn the names of the books of the Bible and all sorts of interesting tidbits that would help us keep things straight—such as how long it took the hundreds of thousands of Hebrews to walk across the Red Sea at the exodus. But the Bible just didn't catch my imagination.

I realize now that for the Christianity I had joined with, the real issue that mattered is the *idea* of a Holy Book. What was important was our *doctrine* of the Bible (more so, when it came down to it, than its *content*). The issue was authority. Christianity, as I first learned of it, was basically a religion of authority, of security, of certainty.

For my church, what mattered was a sense of having the truth. We needed a point of safety amid a crazy and uncertain world. The Bible helps provide a sense of security. Since the God of all has spoken to us directly and completely reliably in this book, we can simply turn to it and know exactly what's going on. Thus we may have perfect assurance that we are on the winning side.

REIMAGINING BIBLICAL AUTHORITY

The key turning point for my theology came when I became a pacifist. My pacifism did not emerge from my reading of the Bible. I initially became a pacifist more due to a kind of mystical awareness, an inner sense of clarity emerging out of an awareness of the human costs of violence during the Vietnam War era.

However, I certainly still believed in the Bible. I had to make sense of my pacifism biblically. It just so happened that within a few months of my pacifist turn, I discovered the writings of John Howard Yoder and then of other Mennonite thinkers such as Guy Hershberger and Millard Lind.[1] During this exciting time of growth, I would definitely have still advocated for an inerrant Bible. My own inner awareness seemed to match the teaching of the Bible—as made clear by Yoder and the others.

Another issue that I cared about at this time was women in church and society. I became convinced that women should be affirmed in church leadership, and I supported egalitarian relationships. So I now disagreed with my fellow evangelical Christians in being both pacifist and feminist. But I was certain I had the Bible on my side. I taught a class and wrote a 100-page manuscript arguing for biblical feminism.

I did not think I had to change my view of the Bible to hold to my new progressive views. I still believe that, actually, but I have changed my view of the Bible anyhow.

I found a new clarity amid vicious debates that swept the North American evangelical community over the issue of biblical inerrancy in the 1970s. I first encountered these debates as one fully on the side of an error-free Bible. But then I read a book called *The Battle for the Bible*[2] by Harold Lindsell that changed my views.

In fact, Lindsell argued vehemently in favor of inerrancy. However, when I finished his book, I had *abandoned* that view. It was my pacifism that made the difference. I became suspicious of an argument that seemed so hostile, even violent. In my suspicion, I was then opened to see the logical and practical problems with the way I had thought of the Bible. My concerns were deepened when we went through an election in our hometown that ended up denying equal rights to gay people—and our evangelical friends used their inerrant Bible as a basis for a lot of hostility.

So I was ready to go to seminary and learn a new way of thinking of God's communication. Having a chance to study with John Howard Yoder and Millard Lind helped me tremendously. I saw that they were people of profound faith, deeply committed to the Bible and to peacemaking. But compared to what I had been taught in the Bible Baptist Church, Lind and Yoder had a whole different kind of Bible.

Most of all, what mattered about the Bible for my seminary teachers was its witness to Jesus' command to love God and neighbor. The Bible witnesses to this call to love by telling a story—a bunch of stories, of course, but stories that fit together (loosely!) in pointing to one great story. This one great story tells of God's love that created us all with the freedom to resist that love, that remains committed even when we do resist, and that continues to persuade us to trust in that love and find healing.

This was an entirely different perspective than
ful God, fearful humanity, get saved and get out o
lated proof-text, defensive, and obligation-oriented
to the Bible I had learned. The Bible became much i._____
esting to me. It told about the challenges of living life here and
now, in history, with real human sorrows and joys, failures and
successes, struggles and moments of peace. The Bible became
a source of encouragement but also something to be questioned
and argued with. Something truly human in the best sense of
that term. A source for genuine conversation.

I also came to understand that God reveals Godself everywhere. The Bible itself is not this revelation. I can't emphasize
this point strongly enough. *The Bible itself is not this revelation.*
The Bible *witnesses* to revelation, to God's self-disclosure in creation, in the history of God's people, in the human heart, and
in human relationships.

I now believe that, for Christians, the Bible matters because
of how it helps us interpret God's self-disclosures that come to
us in all of life. We understand the big story of the Bible, and
the various little stories, as helping us discern how God communicates, what God communicates, and why God communicates.

HOW DOES GOD COMMUNICATE?

How does God communicate? Through our senses,
through our relationships, through the physical world we live
in. But we have to have eyes to see and ears to hear to recognize the communication as from God—and to respond to it appropriately. Maybe we could think of God's self-disclosure as
being like radio signals that always bombard us but need a re-
ceiver to be heard.

All these signals need to be sorted through. How do we
know *what* precisely God is communicating? This is where the
Bible comes in. We find in the Bible a clear sense of what kind
of things God wants to communicate. When we do theology
as if Jesus matters, we will recognize that Jesus certainly matters for discerning God's self-disclosure. The story of Jesus tells
us that what matters most to God is love, caring for others, challenging injustice, seeking wholeness.

The Bible is not a substitute for our experience, our discernment, and our taking responsibility for learning and acting and listening and thinking. The Bible does not let us off the hook and give us some kind of magical basis to avoid the complexities of life. Not at all. Rather, the Bible is best seen as a stimulus for experiencing and discerning and learning and acting and listening and thinking.

The Bible is meant to help us be more faithfully human, more ourselves, as we become more conformed to the purposes God has for us in life.

WHY DOES GOD COMMUNICATE?

Why does God communicate? Because God wants us to grow in love. God wants us to learn truth. God wants us to find the power and hope we need to help transform the world. God wants us to join in God's work of healing.

For Christians, God is to be seen in all aspects of the created universe—from the immensity of outer space to the mysteries of the atoms. The Psalms teem with allusions to the beauty and majesty of the natural world. They draw from this beauty and majesty a sense of worship and gratitude to Israel's Creator God. We find just one example in Psalm 65:

> By awesome deeds you answer us with deliverance, O God of our salvation; you are the hope of all the ends of the earth and of the farthest seas. By your strength you established the mountains; you are girded with might. You silence the roaring of the seas, the roaring of their waves, the tumult of the peoples. Those who live at earth's farthest bounds are awed by your signs; you make the gateways of the morning and the evening shout for joy.
>
> You visit the earth and water it, you greatly enrich it; the river of God is full of water; you provide the people with grain, for so you have prepared it. You water its furrows abundantly, settling its ridges, softening it with showers, and blessing its growth. You crown the year with your bounty; your wagon tracks overflow with richness. The pastures of the wilderness overflow, the hills gird themselves with joy, the meadows clothe themselves with flocks, the valleys deck themselves with grain, they shout and sing together for joy. (Ps. 65:5-13)

Christians confess that life itself comes from God. Consequently, any birth, the renewal of nature each spring, any thing that enhances life discloses God.

Christians also believe that human rationality, the ability to reason and solve problems, express characteristics of the One in whose image human beings have been created.

In addition, our ability to love others and live in friendship—as well as the devastation of isolation and loneliness—reflect being created in the image of a social, relational God ("male and female we created them," Gen 1:27).

Another way that God is disclosed in human life is in facing consequences when we trust in realities other than God. That is, in biblical language, idolatry carries with it intrinsic consequences that reflect the nature of the created universe. These consequences are best seen not as punishment for its own sake so much as disharmony caused by traveling "off the track" of the universe.

God is also disclosed in acts of liberation and salvation. In the Jewish and Christian traditions, events such as the calling of Abraham and Sarah; the exodus out of slavery in Egypt; the life, death, and resurrection of Jesus have been key examples of God revealed in liberating acts. Since the time of Jesus, God has been revealed when oppressed people gain liberty and when healing communities are formed and sustained. When the way of Jesus is embodied in these ways that are in continuity with the formative acts, they disclose God.

These formative acts, and many other stories of God's healing involvement, were written down along with teachings these communities believed came from God. Such writings, gathered in the Christian "Scriptures," provide the "master stories" that give the Christian community direction for its beliefs and practices.

An early version of reciting the story of God's revelation through liberating acts in the history of God's people—and the use of this story to challenge present-day faithfulness—may be found in the book of Joshua after the people of Israel had entered the Promised Land.

Joshua reminds the people of their heritage. Long ago, their forebears had served other gods "beyond the Euphrates." In mercy, God chose Abraham and gave him many offspring.

Abraham's descendents, however, ended up enslaved in Egypt. God's mercies continued, though.

> Then I sent Moses and Aaron, and I plagued Egypt with what I did in its midst; and afterwards I brought your ancestors out of Egypt, you came to the sea; and the Egyptians pursued your ancestors with chariots and horsemen to the Red Sea. When they cried out to the Lord, he put darkness between you and the Egyptians, and made the sea come upon them and cover them; and your eyes saw what I did to Egypt. (Josh. 24:5-7)

After the exodus, God led the people through the wilderness and eventually to their destination.

> I gave you the land on which you had not labored, and towns that you had not built, and you live in them; you eat the fruit of vineyards and oliveyards that you did not plant. Now therefore revere the Lord and serve him in sincerity and in faithfulness; put away the gods that your ancestors served beyond the River and in Egypt, and serve the Lord. (Josh. 24:13-14)

The Bible, this collection of the master stories, serves as the basis for the community's discernment concerning other apparent disclosures from God. The content of these other forms of revelation is measured against the content of the Bible. So, while Christians understand God to disclose Godself in many ways, they give a privileged status to the Bible. The authenticity of these communications is tested by how well the alleged disclosure coheres with the disclosure of God in Scripture.

A late statement of this conviction may be found in the famous verses from 2 Timothy that also emphasize the point of these stories being the encouragement to faithful living:

> All Scripture is inspired by God and is useful for teaching, for reproof, for correction, and for training in justice, so that everyone who belongs to God may be proficient, equipped for every good work. (2 Tim. 3:16-17)

Other forms of God's self-disclosure to God's people include a variety of personal ways of communication, such as dreams, visions, prayer, meditation, and special insights. Christians see these all as subservient to God's self-disclosure in Scripture and evaluate them in relation to Scripture. They also understand the ongoing discernment of the community of faith ("tradition") to be a form of revelation, likewise subject to Scripture.

Echoing the language of 2 Timothy 3, Christians confess that the Bible is "inspired" by the Holy Spirit—meaning essentially that God participated in the writing, preservation, and interpretation of the books of the Bible. The God who created the universe and who has acted in history in ways that have fostered healing the brokenness of relationships between human beings and God, also guided the writings that were ultimately collected into the book Christians confess to be their Scripture.

THE BIBLE AND JESUS

The Bible's meaning for Christians rests most of all on its being our source for information about Jesus. From the Bible we learn of God's entry into human history in a particular human being whose life and teaching reveal the character of God, the will of God for human beings, and the approach God takes in providing salvation for all who trust in God. The rest of the Bible, Old Testament and New Testament, provides the context we need properly to understand God's revelation in Jesus.

The Bible gives us the story of Jesus and the broader setting in which the Jesus story makes sense. Thus, it provides us with the "master story" we need for an orienting framework to understand human existence. As the master story, the Bible provides direction, clarity, norms, and standards for what is true and for what is God's will for human life.

The nature of the Bible as the meaning-full Scripture of the faith community follows from the *confession* that Christians make concerning its status. The meaningful element of the content of the Bible most of all takes the form of an ongoing story that is persuasive, relational, and evocative of faith for those who confess it to be revelation from God. The meaning of the Bible, then, is not so much coercive and "outside-of-us" as it is trust-based, the consequence of a freely made choice to accept its normativity.

The core meaning of the Bible takes the form of a story that we are invited (not forced) to join, to identify as our own story. As such a story (Christians confess, *the* foundational story), the Bible is *not* seen as a blueprint believers follow out of fear and in a spirit of legalism. Rather, it is a friend and guide whose power stems from its trustworthiness as a basis for healthy living and belief.

We fully grasp the Bible's truthfulness only as we live with it, following its directives. It is not so much objective, obvious to all eyes, outside-of-us, scientifically verifiable "truth" as it is "personal truth." The Bible's truth becomes operative as we assent to it, trust in it, and live in relationship with it.

The story of Jesus provides the "angle" for interpreting the broad variety of materials included in the Bible. As believers accept Jesus' authority as their savior, teacher, and guide, we will recognize the authority of the source of our understanding of Jesus—and understand the materials in that source in light of the message of Jesus.

CHALLENGES IN UNDERSTANDING THE BIBLE

One of the major challenges in understanding the Bible correctly is that it comes to us from a great distance. It was written thousands of years ago, in languages very different from our own, and in cultures very different from ours.

Nonetheless, we are able to assume significant common ground between ourselves and the biblical people. We are all human beings with similar questions and more commonalities than differences. The kinds of issues that were alive for the biblical writers remain alive in our world.

We have biblical translators who build on a remarkable history of careful scholarship. Yes, we must recognize the lack of perfect understanding of the languages of the original writings of the Bible (not to mention that we do not have the original writings but only copies dating from much later times than their original composition). Nevertheless, we may trust that we are able to approach with a pretty high level of accuracy the intentions of the biblical writers.

However, these various distances do remind us that the truths of the Bible are most reliable in their broad articulation.

The most meaningful content of the Bible begins with its general themes of God's love and the people's response to that love over time. Many of the more specific statements in the Bible are difficult to apply directly—such as the commands for parents to execute rebellious children (Deut. 21:18-21) and the commands for women to be silent in the church (1 Cor. 14:34-35)—because we cannot be certain of their precise context and their specific intent. However, we may with great confidence apply the more general thematic truths that tell us of God's character and human struggles. What matters most as a source for our beliefs and practices is the story of the Bible as a whole that witnesses to the reality of Jesus Christ.

Another problem for many people in relation to the Bible is the existence of what seem to be many internal inconsistencies and historical inaccuracies.

A key element to dealing with this problem is to recognize the nature of the biblical materials. The Bible is not a history book in the modern, scientific sense. It is a collection of premodern stories and exhortations that were written according to the standards of ancient expressions of faith, not the standards of modern historical research. Readers of the Bible should not read it expecting perfection of facts and details.

The Bible itself emphasizes that heroes of faith are very human—but still serve as channels of God's truth. "We have this treasure in earthen vessels," Paul wrote of his own ministry's frailty (2 Cor. 4:7). The principle here applies to the Bible itself as well. The value of the "treasure" is measured by its capability to connect people with God and to provide clear direction for faithful living.

In the overall scheme of things, the historical accuracy of the Bible is quite remarkable. The biblical stories, as near as we can ascertain, are believable on historical grounds to a surprising degree. Yet we must also remember that the biblical writers intended to tell stories that would buttress faith and challenge life practices. The writers are preachers, proclaiming the "good news" of God's saving love. The Bible succeeds in its intent as a confession of faith, not a "proof" based on irrefutable facts.

Another type of problem with the Bible is that it seems to contain numerous ethically problematic emphases. Three prime examples are positive portrayals of sexism, military violence, and slavery.[3]

The presence of these emphases must be acknowledged; they are too prominent to be denied. For Christians, though, the Bible is to be read directionally. Jesus provides the center to the Bible. The rest of the Bible outside of the immediate stories related to Jesus are to be read as in some sense pointing toward the core message of Jesus.

For example, let's consider the sexism of the Bible. Reading the Bible as being centered on the message of Jesus (and remembering the deep sexism of Jesus' culture) helps us to see the remarkable ways that Jesus overturned the sexism of his day. Jesus' message clearly points toward the equality of the sexes in God's eyes. With Jesus' message in mind, we then look at the Old Testament in a way that especially notices hints that point ahead to Jesus. We should assume, I believe, that in relation to sexuality as with other issues, Jesus understood himself as being compatible with the basic thrust of the Old Testament.

We will see such hints—for example, we will notice that the creation story in Genesis 1 emphasizes that both male and female constitute the image of God. We will notice that at times women play a surprisingly important part in the story—prophets and judges such as Sarah, Miriam (Exod. 15:20-21), and Deborah (Judg. 4–5). There are stories such as Judah and Tamar (Gen. 38), the Levite and his concubine (Judg. 19), and David and Bathsheba (2 Sam. 11–12) that point toward implicit critiques of sexual violence and exploitation. The special emphasis of prophets on the responsibility of Israel to care for widows (for example, Exod. 22:22-24 and Deut. 24:17-22) also reflects an implicit critique of oppressive patriarchy that left these women in particularly vulnerable positions.

When read as a whole and in light of Jesus, the Bible ultimately points to the affirmation of the equality of women with men. The Bible provides bases for *refuting* sexism.

The Bible is a document written by human beings, written in specific times and places, written about human experiences and human perceptions of God. Ultimately, it is only as a *human* document that the Bible mediates the divine.

The reality of what the Bible is reflects the reality of what human life is. Human life is tentative, ambiguous, mixed, and fragile. We find greatness, beauty, wisdom, and joy in human experience. We also find violence, selfishness, ugliness, bitterness, and anger. To see truth, to grow in wholeness, to experience love—these all take perspective, insight, faith, and trust. That's how we benefit from the Bible. The Bible is not something from the outside of human experience. Rather, it is a record of human experience. With insight, we find in this record stories, images, pictures that can engender our growth. These help us to understand truth now, here in our world of human ambiguity.

In many ways, the trust we develop in the Bible is similar to trust we develop in a friend. It grows gradually as we experience the friend to be trustworthy. Sometimes the friend isn't always trustworthy; then we have to let the trust gradually grow back. This is all part of human relationships. Ultimately, though, the growth of this trust is also a matter of a series of choices. We decide that yes we will trust at least a bit more, believing that this trust is worth some work. Our approach to the Bible is similar. So, too, is our approach to God and to life itself. We trust a little, we find the trust rewarded—but we also must choose to risk, to test. To fall back a little and then build back up.

Gabriel Josipovici points out that we say our yes to the Bible "as we do to people, to the degree that we grow to feel we can trust" Scriptures. He suggests that "moments of ordinariness" and of "vulnerability," when we're hungry, when we're in tears, are what allow us to experience both person and Bible "*as* our own."[4] At these moments, we find that the Bible is authentic to life. We find we can trust that, yes, here is something that offers insight and empathy—and spiritual nourishment and encouragement.

The Bible meets us in our ambiguity with its own ambiguities. We gain the most from the Bible not by looking to it expecting perfection. Doing that leads us either to bow down before it with a closed mind or to reject it when we realize that it doesn't meet our ideal of perfection. Either case cuts off the conversation before it gets started. Rather, we gain the most by accepting the Bible as it comes to us.

The Bible reflects the nitty-gritty realism of everyday life. It contains contradictory voices. It blesses kingship and power politics *and* it condemns them. It pictures Jesus as a super-human, faultless stranger from heaven *and* as a flesh-and-blood Jewish carpenter sweating and crying and doubting God. It promises wealth and happiness to the faithful *and* it promises a cross to the faithful. We can't read the Bible with an attitude that now we can turn off our critical faculties and just be told what is true. We have to keep thinking. We still have to make choices and interpret and weigh. Just like we do in life.

Most of all, though, the Bible gives us stories of human beings. Finite, at times broken human beings, almost always with very realistic strengths and weaknesses. These are human beings who fail, who grow, who make poor decisions, who are weak and yet capable at times of great deeds.

We read of scoffing Sarah giving birth at an old age. We read of stuttering Moses resisting the great Pharaoh God-king. We read of arrogant David, given power and wealth due to his wisdom and courage and trust in God, and wasting it all by acting on his lust toward another man's wife. We read of shattered Jeremiah, speaking profound words of grief and insight and hope, during Israel's darkest days. We read of trembling Mary, accepting her fate despite great cost, to mother the greatest prophet of all. We read of self-righteous Paul, brought to the end of his pious rope with his shattering encounter with God on the road to Damascus. He is then restored to proclaim the most radical kind of mercy.

These people meet God and gain a measure of healing. However, the healing is always partial. Moses doesn't make it to the Promised Land. Jeremiah dies in exile. Paul never escapes the struggle with his thorn in the flesh. Nonetheless, this partialness indicates the measure of healing we may hope for—incomplete at best, but still genuine.

To listen to the Bible is to be better able to listen to life. The Bible speaks out of the heartbeat of actual life—everyday people wrestling with God, wrestling with disappointment, wrestling with brokenness. Out of this ongoing process of wrestling, some healing, they do know some growth, they do know some joy—with hope for more.

To know there will be some healing is part of what we have to gain from assenting to the world of the Bible. The Bible witnesses to healing power. This power works tocreate goodness out of chaos. This power works to liberate slaves from Egypt. This power works to sustain faith amid the rubble of the shattered ancient Jerusalem temple. This power keeps life and love going even after the crucifixion. The Bible witnesses to this healing power. That witness seeks to find listeners, even today.

Humanness: A Blessing or a Curse?

[The Doctrine of Humanity]

QUITE A FEW THEOLOGIES TAKE HUMANITY as their starting point. I can understand why, since theology is human work—our reflections as human beings on the big issues of life. However, I have chosen to pick up the doctrine of humanity ("theological anthropology") only in this seventh chapter. I believe our reflections up to now have given us a better perspective for a *theological* affirmation of our humanity.

One of my favorites theologians is Abraham Joshua Heschel, the great Jewish thinker who died in 1972. A little over forty years ago, he wrote a profound little book called *Who is Man?* Heschel laments the negative view of humanness in our modern world. The human being, he writes, "is being excessively denounced and condemned by artists, philosophers, and theologians."

Heschel asks, What does the modern worldview say about us? That we're "beasts" except with the great difference that we know we'll die. So "You must cling to life as you can and use it for the pursuit of pleasure and of power." Heschel concludes that humans have "few friends in the world, certainly very few in the contemporary literature about them. The Lord in heaven may prove to be humanity's last friend on earth."[1]

While some Christian thinkers would tend to agree with Heschel's perspective, a great deal of Christian theology—academic and popular—more likely reinforces the problems Heschel laments. In the actual view of humankind, Christian theology often has differed little from secular philosophy.

HOSTILITY TOWARD HUMANNESS

The roots of this hostility toward humanness go back a long way. In the Christian tradition, I'd say, they go back at least to the fourth century, to the theology of Augustine, to the powerful doctrine of original sin. This doctrine evolved into John Calvin's doctrine of total depravity. Human life, in the immortal words of a later Augustinian named Thomas Hobbes, is inevitably "nasty, brutish, and short." We are born sinful, rebellious, and basically despicable.

It is highly ironic though, that these views led to strong support for violent governmental control over the general population. I have never understood the logic. Why does belief in human depravity lead to trust in people with power? Why do we think rulers will transcend their own depravity and use their monopoly on violence in *undepraved* ways?

Tying together negative views of humanness with support for domination systems has a long and still vital history. Read the newspaper editorials—we're all pretty bad, we're told. That's why we need so much military and police violence, to keep our human proclivity toward evil in check. But what about the human proclivity toward evil of those building, buying, and wielding the guns?

It's not just theology that is hostile toward human nature. A lot of modern science is, too. Read popular writers such as Edward O. Wilson, Richard Dawkins, and Steven Pinker. These avowed atheists talk about total depravity in ways that would make a Calvinist nod in vigorous agreement. Our behavior stems from our selfish genes. We males *naturally* fight and struggle for dominance. It's a dog-eat-dog world. (I have to say that after years of living intimately with our dogs Sophie and Trika, I believe this slander against dogs *does* reflect a kind of human depravity!)

The air we breathe in our culture, the images with which we are bombarded, and the lifeblood of our economic life all tell us that the natural human condition is based on our innate selfishness. And our received theology does little to challenge this. Indeed, we are told humans are born sinful, rebellious, and alienated. We are born in sin.

Most Christians, in face of their belief in humanity's profound depravity, have focused their energies on *escaping* this world of sorrows. Going back to Augustine, we are taught of the "city of man," the city of brokenness and inevitable sorrow, pain, and conflict. This is the fate of all human historical existence. Then we have the city of God, the hope for after we die. Only *after* we die will the way of love be the norm. Only then will we be transformed, cleansed of our original sin, and finally empowered to be good. The best we can do *now* are small, almost symbolic, nods toward peace and love—mostly experienced as peace as order and love as kindly feelings.

JESUS: LOVE DEFINES HUMANNESS

However, if we seek to do our theology as if *Jesus* matters, we will shape our values by Jesus' own hierarchy of values. We will take seriously what Jesus himself taught about our humanity and his expectations for how human beings might live in this life. As we do so, we will be in *tension* with these negative notions of humanness that see humanness much more as a curse than a blessing.

My conviction, in light of Jesus' message, is that love defines humanness. And the humanness love defines is not only "pre-fall," Adam and Eve before they ate the forbidden fruit and changed forever our possibilities as human beings in this world. The humanness that love defines is not only an ideal for the heavenly city of God beyond history and death.

The humanness that love defines is the humanness of the woman who bathed Jesus' feet in her tears and "costly ointment" because of her love (Luke 7:36-50). The humanness that love defines is the humanness of the father who greeted his wayward, prodigal son with unconditional welcome when he returned from the dead (Luke 15:11-32). The humanness that love defines is the costly and risky generosity of the Samaritan merchant who stopped along the Jericho road to save the life of a person he had been socialized to hate as an ethnic and religious "other" (Luke 10:25-37).

Human love, according to theology done as if Jesus matters, is a description of our basic nature. It is a realistic expectation. It is why we are here. When we love we are most ourselves. It is the most natural thing we can do.

However, and this is a huge "however," the "however" that explains the entire biblical story following Genesis 3, we are damaged. We are not fully in touch with and do not act fully in harmony with our basic human nature. Each of us is damaged, our human societies are damaged, our world as a whole is damaged. So it is not enough to define humanness in terms of our basic nature as loving beings. We are also damaged.

And the terrible irony is that our damage *exploits* our basic nature as compassionate, loving beings born to affiliate with others. Our damage exploits our loving nature and turns it against us. We need others as a fundamental part of who we are. We are made to connect with, to join with others. Because of this basic need, we are vulnerable and fragile. We are, that is, *easily* damaged.

A terrible example of our fragility, of how our human loving nature is easily exploited, may be seen in the sophistication of our present-day American military. Journalists interviewing American soldiers have been surprised to learn of the educated antiwar sentiments expressed by many soldiers. How can these young people, at least some of whom know what's going on and do not support it, nonetheless keep fighting? One major reason is the military's technique of creating cohorts of soldiers. They go through basic training together, bond closely with each other, and then go to war together. Thus, many will say, sure this war sucks, it's a fraud, but I'm still going to go fight because my buddies depend upon me.

This human need for connection, even for friendship—one of our strongest drives—carries much more weight than the drive to violence, or the drive to support one's home country. And this need can be exploited to create fighters.

So, even in the heart of the beast we see evidence of a very different take on human nature than we get in the theological tradition, in the modern worldview, and in popular culture. We are not isolated billiard balls, inherently selfish and competitive. We are part of a web of life.[2] We seek affiliation. We need love, and we are naturally capable of sharing love.

BIBLICAL SUPPORT FOR JESUS' PERSPECTIVE

Jesus' affirmation of humanness as a blessing fits with other parts of the Bible. From start to finish the Bible portrays human beings addressed by God as responsible beings, capable of understanding and responding to God's call—in *this* life.

Let's look briefly at just a few biblical texts that support this assertion, beginning with Genesis one, where we read of our being created in God's image.

> God said, "Let us make humankind in our image, according to our likeness; and let them have dominion over . . . all the wild animals of the earth. . . ." So God created humankind in his image . . . ; male and female he created them. God blessed them, and God said to them, "Be fruitful and multiply, and fill the earth and subdue it; and have dominion over . . . every living thing that moves upon the earth." God said, "See I have given you every plant yielding seed that is upon the face of all the earth, and every tree with seed in its fruit; you shall have them for food. And to every beast of the earth, and to every bird of the air, and to everything that has the breath of life, I have given every green plant for food." And it was so. God saw everything that he had made, and indeed, it was very good. (Gen. 1:26-31)

This final act in the creation story stands as the culmination of creative work that is good, very good, so good that when it was done God could take a rest, a time of contentment. The image of God, male *and* female, provides human beings with a vocation—be fruitful, multiply, cultivate life and abundance in this good creation God has placed human beings in. It is *natural* for human beings to do this work of creativity and bringing forth fruit in community, to all the ends of the earth.

Although Christian theology in the Augustinian tradition has placed a huge break between human beings before the fall of Adam and Eve and after, Psalm 8 actually pretty much repeats Genesis one in speaking of *post*-fall humanity.

> O Lord, . . . when I look at your heavens, the work of your fingers, the moon and the stars that you have established; what are human beings that you are mindful of them, mortals that you care for them? Yet you have made them a

little lower than God, and crowned them with glory and honor. You have given them dominion over the works of your hands; you have put all things under their feet, all sheep and oxen, and also the beasts of the field, the birds of the air, and the fish of the sea, whatever passes along the paths of the seas. (Ps. 8)

God has made human beings just a little lower than God, crowned with glory and honor, and given us dominion over the works of God's hand—a call to be stewards, to work fruitfully, to glorify the maker of heaven and earth.

Genesis 1 and Psalm 8 anchor the celebration of humanness in God's creative work and in God's love for us. We also find texts in the New Testament that convey a sense of God's love for human beings as the foundational reality concerning our worth. Here are words from Jesus:

Do not worry about your life.... Is not life more than food, and the body more than clothing? Look at the birds of the air; they neither sow nor reap nor gather into barns, and yet your heavenly Father feeds them. Are you not of more value than they? ... Consider the lilies of the field, how they grow; they neither toil nor spin, yet I tell you, even Solomon in all his glory was not clothed like one of these. But if God so clothes the grass of the field, which is alive today and tomorrow is thrown into the oven, will he not much more clothe you—you of little faith? ... Strive first for the kingdom of God and God's justice, and all these things will be given to you as well. (Matt. 6:25-33)

Jesus anchors the high value that human beings have in the care and respect God has for us. He also emphasizes that because we are loved by God (and therefore are good), we may devote ourselves to seeking to further God's justice in the world. Jesus actually presents quite an optimistic view of human possibilities—along with his sober realism about the powers of injustice that oppose the kingdom of God in the world.

Paul reiterates Jesus' affirmation of God's love that gives worth to humankind.

While we were still weak, at the right time Christ died for the ungodly.... God proves his love for us in that while we were still sinners Christ died for us. . . . If while we were enemies, we were reconciled to God through the death of his Son, much more surely, having been reconciled, will we be saved by his life. But more than that, we even boast in God through our Lord Jesus Christ, through whom we have now received reconciliation. (Rom. 5:6-11)

Paul clearly understands that humanity lives in an alienated condition, separated from God's love by our bondage to the power of sin. However, he emphasizes powerfully that God responds to this alienation with transforming love. God proves the worth of human beings by reaching out to us in the most profound way possible, bringing reconciliation through Jesus' self-sacrifice.

Our passages from Matthew and Romans reemphasize God's love and care as the basis for our value. As Abraham Heschel wrote, the Lord of heaven and earth *is* our best friend. Jesus states in Matthew 6 that we get clues of just how much God cares for us as human beings when we see God's care for the birds of the air and the lilies of the field. God cares for us even more.

Paul states in Romans 5 that even when our damage leads us to live in rebellion, God values us so much that Jesus brings us salvation. God loves us even when we make God our enemy. Paul goes on in Romans to summarize the most fundamental law that we are called to follow as saved people. "'Love your neighbor as yourself.' Love does no wrong to a neighbor; therefore, love is the fulfilling of the law" (13:9-10).

THEOLOGICAL ANTHROPOLOGY IN LIGHT OF JESUS

Paul, of course, only repeats Jesus' core statement of faith: "You shall love the Lord your God with all your heart and all your soul, and you shall love your neighbor as yourself" (Matt. 22:37-40). Jesus' words here provide a good jumping off point to summarize a theological anthropology in light of Jesus.

This statement by Jesus tells us several important things: (1) The core meaning of life is love, trust, and mutuality. We are valued. It is appropriate for each of us to take up space in the world. (2) We find ourselves insofar as we are oriented toward God, the God of love. That is, we find ourselves insofar as we may say yes to God, and to life. Life is characterized by abundance and not scarcity. (3) We find ourselves insofar as we are oriented toward other people. We are social creatures with a need and an ability for friendship—and we wither without friendship.

As human beings we are worshiping creatures. We orient ourselves toward that in which we place ultimate value. As the psalmist wrote (115:3-8), we become like that which we worship. When we genuinely worship the true God, we become like God—loving, merciful, just, peaceable, kind. When we are unloving, judgmental, unjust, violent, and unkind, we make clear that we are worshiping something other than the true God.

Human beings contain a mixture of attributes that foster a sense of tension. On the one hand, we are limited, finite, and dependent on God and other human beings. On the other hand, we are imaginative, spiritual, and creative. We are limited by our earthiness yet also able to imagine not being limited. We are material creatures with a sense of life beyond the material.

As well, we are language users. We communicate with one another through our use of language. We communicate across time through the language people in other times and places have used. Being language users means that we are linked with traditions, uses from the past.

We are communal, communicating with others through language. We are rational, using language to reason and solve problems. We are symbolic—our language tells about reality but is also removed from the reality it describes. Hence, our words are perspectival, limited, capturing only incompletely that of which they speak.

The Christian view recognizes that we gain our essential humanness in relation to God, even while it also recognizes that as language users we are not capable of fully describing God or our experiences.

Scripture presents human beings as having been created *good*. This "goodness" is not the same as perfection. Goodness is an attribute assigned by God, meaning that we are created as God wants us to be. We remain good in this sense—loved by God. As God's good creatures, we are of intrinsic value. We are created good also in the sense that this means that we are able to be responsive to God, able to live in relationship with God.

Let's return to Genesis 1. In considering the story of humanity's creation in Genesis, we encounter a powerful metaphor that Christian theology has been highly interested in. Genesis tells us that we are created in "the image of God" (1:27).

Based on this text, we should begin our reflections about the "image" with the exercise of creative power. Human beings, echoing characteristics of God, are given the ability to shape our environment. In Genesis 1, God's "kingly" power creates what is. Human beings, then, are created to share this power. Thus we are given the vocation of exercising responsible stewardship in relation to God's creation.

Genesis 1 also tells us that as beings created in God's image, we have been created male and female. Inferred here, human beings created in God's image are relational creatures. We are created to relate with God and with one another.

The New Testament speaks of Jesus as being the "image" of God (2 Cor. 4:4; Col. 1:15). This identification implies that Jesus' way of being human provides the norm for all of us. God created us in God's image, and Jesus reveals the core characteristics of that image. Jesus' way of being human meant being loving, just, willing to suffer, intimate with God, in partnership with others, inclusive of outcasts, in general revealing a kingdom "upside-down"[3] in relation to the sense of "kingship" of his day and age.

Jesus as King (Messiah, Christ) in the New Testament shares central characteristics with God as King in Genesis 1. These include using creative, non-coercive power and giving to human beings the vocation to "be fruitful and multiply" (Gen. 1:28), with the New Testament version being to "go into all the world and make disciples" (Matt. 28:19).

HUMANITY IN THE IMAGE OF GOD

Genesis 1 refers to humans being in the "image of God," and the New Testament refers to Jesus as being in the "image of God" (Col. 1:15). Hence, affirming that humans exist in God's image means that we are, in our essence, relational, creative, powerful, rational, communicative, aware, and gifted with free will.

Linking the two references to the image of God, we may conclude that Jesus indeed is the model human being, our guide for our theological anthropology. In Jesus we see two key aspects of the calling of human beings. First God calls us to live responsibly. We are to take responsibility to follow God's will, to live with trust in God, to care for other people and creation, to be creative, and to respect others. Second, God calls us to love. Jesus showed this love in his "Abba relationship" with God and with his openness to all sorts of people.

In the Christian confession that in Jesus God was incarnated in human flesh, we also confess that God endorses and is committed to humanness. Jesus shows what *all* human beings might become. We tend toward God. We also tend toward nature. We are spiritual *and* material. Human beings are "bio-historical creatures."[4] That is, our physical life begins and ends. We have instincts. We exist in time. We share many essential characteristics with other animals. We are "flesh and blood."

From within a Christian framework, we confess that as finite, fragile, limited creatures we depend upon God for life. We confess that our origins rest in God's creative intent. We also confess that our ongoing sustenance depends upon God "providing rain and sunshine in due season." Our hope for life beyond death rests on God's resurrecting power, not on something inherent in our physical or spiritual makeup.

While recognizing our bio-historical nature, we also confess that we are *not* reducible to physical and instinctual elements (in contrast, say, to the thought of evolutionary psychologists such as E. O. Wilson and Steven Pinker). We are not simply quantifiable machine-like entities—though we also believe (in contrast to some forms of modern scientism) that nature itself is also not simply a quantifiable machine-like entity.[5]

We understand life to be the breath of God, not mere random chance. Each human being has inestimable value. Each has non-quantifiable and non-reducible elements. Each of us has a spiritual aspect that touches on all aspects of our being with creativity and love.

Human beings are unique in the animal realm in having consciousness ahead of time of our inevitable deaths. This knowledge shapes our lives.[6] We also have consciousness of our spiritual natures and an ability (and longing) to relate to God, to the infinite, to the eternal and transcendent, a sense of mystery. Human beings combine in volatile ways, flesh and spirit, an anchoring in earthly existence combined with imagination, a longing for the stars.

When we look at the development of newborn human beings, we also find evidence that love is of the essence of our humanness. Humans are born utterly dependent on others. Requiring nurture to live, we enter the world powerless to care for ourselves. Our first and most primal experience is of needing nurturing love simply to exist. And this dependence continues for much, much longer than it does for any other animal. Without love, human beings would be extinct.[7]

Think about our ongoing lives and these two questions: What are our most fundamental survival needs as human beings? And what elements of our lives give us the most pleasure? Notice that several of the exact same things are high on both lists. Our survival needs and our pleasures often go together.

We need to eat. Our lives, like other animals', are to a large extent organized around our meals. We think in terms of working so we may "put food on the table." At the same time, we *love* to eat. Most us, when we think back to the times in our lives when we have had the most fun, find that these have often involved food. Our taste buds generally give us pleasure—as does the feeling of have a satisfied stomach after we have been hungry.

We need to drink. We love to drink. Few pleasures are as intense as a glass of cold water when thirst is strong. We also enjoy many other beverages beyond simply satisfying our thirst.

Sex is very pleasurable, and we don't continue as a species without it. When we talk about our "sex drive" we do not simply have in mind some kind of need we feel to have children. We also know that the sex drive is linked with a "pleasure drive." As social creatures we need friendship to survive. Friendship brings us great joy.

The overlapping of our survival needs and our deepest pleasures tells us something profound about the nature of life.

)eings are not simply automatons with strong sur-
:ts that govern our behavior. Much more so, we are
ho *love* the activities that keep us alive. Life is meant
Our humanness is meant to be a source of joy.
ɘ is the basic picture: Our humanness is a blessing,
ɘ. We are created by a loving God to love and to be
ɪd we can do just that, we *must* do just that. Maybe
)f the fittest is the law of life—but what makes us fit?
ɘst for domination. Not selfishness. But love and shar-
nutuality.

HUMANITY AS DAMAGED (SINFUL)

As I said before, we cannot avoid the reality, however, that
we humans are damaged. We live in a damaged world. Our
lovingness is turned against us. Look at the basic survival
needs I mentioned—food, drink, sex, friendship. Each is a
source of profound pleasure, but each can become an obsession, an occasion for disease, even a source of bondage.

For many of us in North American society, our wealth has
lifted us above the need to devote all our energies simply to
survival. Yet we are plagued with inability to limit our use of
the goods that allow us to survive. So the pleasure we derive
from food and drink, when overly indulged in, leads to obe-
sity, alcoholism, heart disease, and various other health problems.

An obsession with sex simply as individual pleasure leads
to myriad problems of broken relationships, sexually transmit-
ted diseases, and emotional trauma. As I mentioned, the need
for friendship lends itself to exploitation by forces that use the
close ties we develop with friends as a strategy for wreaking
violence on designated "enemies" outside the circle of our
friends.

We may be good; we certainly are loved by the Lord of
heaven and earth. But we are also in desperate need of salvation. Sin is a *relational* (more than legal) concept. It involves
alienation in the relationships of human beings with God first
of all. Sin also involves alienation in the relationships with
other human beings, with one's self, and with the natural
world.

Sin finds expression in *harmful* activities and in the lack of good activities. It leads to brokenness among human beings, characterized by violence, exploitation, objectification, exclusion, and avoidance. Humanity in the image of God is humanity with power, creativity, the ability to shape our surroundings. Under sin's influence, this power remains—but it becomes destructive rather than life enhancing.

Human beings are uniquely creative in our ability to destroy. This destructive ability is the flip side of our unique ability to create as stewards of God's creation. Human beings, distinct from other animals in the main, act violently toward other members of our species for purposes that do not serve our own survival needs.

Sin is connected with lack of trust in God, with false worship (given that we are "worshiping creatures"), with building walls of separation, and with fearfulness. The story of Adam and Eve in Genesis 2 and 3 captures this connection between sin and fearfulness in a powerful way. After they disobey God, God approaches them as before for fellowship, but this time the human beings hide from God, fearfully. In so doing, they set in motion a terrible spiral of fearfulness leading to violence leading to alienation.

Human false-worship interrelates with the structures of human social life (the "principalities and powers" referred to in the New Testament). When created things (including institutions and ideologies) are "worshiped" they take on a power *outside* of individual consciousness. This power fosters idolatry, sin, and evil. We trust in things other than God leading to a spiral of death.

These empowered "idols" may be seen to epitomize the demonic realm. They take on a will of their own aprt from God's will and, as Paul writes in Romans 8, seek to separate human beings from God.

Sin corrupts our humanness. Human beings under the power of sin fail to achieve our potential as God's creatures. However, even as "fallen," even as living under the power of sin, humans remain "good" ("good" here being defined as loved by God). As "good" creatures, all human beings retain value in God's eyes and ability to respond in faith toward God. The "fall" does not change human nature from good to evil.

Human beings remain good—loved by God, creative, power-ful, and capable of loving God and other human beings.

Sin is best thought of in "public health" terms.[8] We need to consider sin not to condemn and punish and eradicate and avoid. Rather, we seek healing. Just as public health officials focus on understanding the causes of the disorder and finding ways to treat the problem, thus also should Christians think of sin. We should hope to foster honesty about the sins, objectiv-ity about their causes and consequences, and seek to undo the harm caused by the sins and find healing and restoration for all involved.

How is sin overcome? This question brings us to the theme of salvation. In chapter two above on Christology, we learned of two core christological concerns: (1) Jesus' person and (2) Jesus' work. We reflected on Jesus' person in that chapter—his identity as God's Son. And we postponed considering Jesus' work until we learned more about our broader theological framework—and the human predicament. Now we are ready to look more closely at the theme of "salvation."

Salvation:
Healing Our Damage

[The Doctrine of the Work of Christ]

WHEN I FIRST BECAME A CHRISTIAN, now over thirty-five years ago, I was taught a certain view of salvation. Confess to God that you are a sinner. Acknowledge that as a sinner, you are bound for eternity in hell. Recognize that belief in Jesus as your savior is the only way to go to heaven instead of hell. Pray the sinner's prayer, confessing that you trust in Jesus. And be saved—once and for all.

Now, I have to say that this schema actually worked pretty well for me. I admit that by personality I'm not prone to doubt and anxiety, so perhaps I shouldn't draw too many *theological* conclusions from my experience. But from that night in late June 1971, when I accepted Jesus as my savior, I have never once wondered whether I was a Christian or not.

However, my understanding of what salvation is has changed tremendously from those early days. And I now wonder: Is it God we are saved *from* or God we are saved *by*? If not God, what *are* we saved from? And, what are we saved for?

BEING SAVED *FROM* GOD?

The theology I was first taught as a Christian implicitly told me that it was God from whom I needed to be saved. In a college freshman lit class, I read Jonathan Edwards' famous sermon, "Sinners in the Hands of an Angry God." The professor kind of mocked Edwards, but I took him seriously. This is what I had been taught.

God is furious at each of us because of our sin. So we are doomed—and we fully deserve our doom. Our only way out is through Jesus' sacrificial death on the cross. God visits on Jesus the violence we deserve because God must punish sin. Jesus is our substitute who saves us by paying the price required to satisfy God's righteous anger.

Why did I come to question this theology? Well, I saw too many people who were afraid of God. In one church I worked with two older people who were close to death—in both cases, they had made clear professions of faith but still felt great fearfulness. What did God *really* think of them? They knew they were unworthy of God's love—and deserved God's anger. The gospel songs only helped them so much.

Plus, this picture of an angry God simply did not jibe with my own experience. As is true for most of us, my deep-down experience of God has been closely related to my experience of my parents. I never doubted my parents' love. I think of an image. My wife Kathleen and I reach out toward our grandson, baby Elias, and he reaches back, meeting our reach with his. I likewise see my father moving toward baby Teddy, hands outstretched. Would I flinch, fearing his anger? Or would I move toward him, expecting his embrace? It would always be the embrace.

So it has been with God. At the times of my greatest vulnerability, of coming face to face with my failure or loss, there has been no question that God has been present with me, the source of comfort not condemnation.

So how could it be believable to me that God's disposition toward me was one of anger, that God would be the one I needed to be saved *from*?

I also came to see that the Bible does *not* support that view of a fundamentally angry God. The God of the Bible gets ticked off with humans—sometimes *deeply* ticked off. However, I believe it is a mistake to see these instances as definitive of God. Let me quote two representative passages, one from the Old Testament, one from the New, that make it clear that *God is savior.* God is not the one to be saved from, but the one who saves.

First, the prophet Hosea. In God's voice, Hosea 11 recounts the history of Israel. God loved Israel, calling "my son" out of slavery in Egypt. Yet the people keep turning from God and "sacrificing to the Baals," despite God's ongoing care for them. Naturally there will be consequences. A return to slavery in Egypt. Swords devouring cities: "My people are bent on turning away from me. To the Most High they call, but he does not raise them up at all" (Hos. 11:7).

Amazingly, however, God cannot accept this eye-for-an-eye kind of response. God is *God*. That means God will respond differently. Mercy will win out over vengeance.

> How can I give you up, Ephraim? How can I hand you over, O Israel? How can I make you like Admah? How can I treat you like Zeboiim? My heart recoils within me; my compassion grows warm and tender. I will not execute my fierce anger; I will not again destroy Ephraim; for I am God and no mortal, the Holy One in your midst, and I will not come in wrath. (Hos. 11:8-9)

This passage has interest for us partly because God here seems to acknowledge the temptation to act in such a way as to evoke terror in God's people. But ultimately this kind of punitive response is a *human* response, not the response of a holy God. The Holy One in Israel's midst is free. God may choose simply to forgive and to heal. Because of holiness, Yahweh "will not come in wrath."

Jesus taught equally poignantly about God's initiative in salvation.

> All the tax collectors and sinners were coming near to listen to [Jesus]. And the Pharisees and the scribes were grumbling and saying, "This fellow welcomes sinners and eats with them."
>
> So [Jesus] told them this parable: "Which one of you, having a hundred sheep and losing one of them, does not leave the ninety-nine in the wilderness and go after the one that is lost until he finds it? When he has found it, he lays it on his shoulders and rejoices. And when he comes home, he calls together his friends and neighbors, saying to them, 'Rejoice with me, for I have found my sheep that was lost.' Just so, I tell you, there will be more joy in heaven over one sinner who repents than over ninety-

nine righteous persons who need no repentance." (Luke 15:1-7)

Jesus goes on in this same encounter to tell two more parables illuminating God's initiative and unilateral mercy. He tells of a woman who looks hard for a lost coin and rejoices when she finds it (15:8-10). Then he tells a longer story, the powerful account we call "The Parable of the Prodigal Son" (15:11-32), a parable many justifiably have called "the gospel in miniature."[1]

This is the crucial point in both the Hosea and Luke passages: God does not need sacrifice. There are no complicated cosmic transactions necessary. In fact, as Hosea tells us, because God is *holy*, God simply forgives. *Because* God is holy, God seeks healing, not punishment.

Hosea 11 tells the Bible's salvation story. The Egyptian empire enslaves the children of Israel. The Israelites cry out in their pain. God hears—and acts to liberate them from their oppression. At its heart, this is simple mercy. God does not need to be appeased, or manipulated by sacrifices, or convinced by good deeds, to bring salvation. God simply does it because that is the kind of God that God is.

We need to notice the picture of God's "holiness" in Hosea. When Jesus tells his remarkable parable of the Prodigal Son, he simply lifts up what the prophets had already taught about God. God desires mercy, not sacrifice (Hos. 6:6; Matt. 9:13; 12:7). God responds to brokenness with justice that brings healing. God wills for God's people to bless all the families of the earth with peace and kindness, providing a place for the nations to beat their swords into plowshares.

God seeks out broken, damaged people to *heal*. That's the core reality of God's character. So we get to Luke 15 and hear Jesus telling us several stories to illustrate what God is like. Jesus, God's very son, "welcomes sinners and eats with them" (15:2). In doing so he sets to grumbling those who speak of God's righteous anger, those who want a God who cares only for those "worthy" of God's care. Jesus doesn't back down a bit. This is what God is like: the shepherd who, after desperate searching, celebrates finding his lost sheep. God is also like the woman who rejoices finding her one lost coin (15:10).

And, most powerfully, God is like the father who welcomes back his wayward son with a big party. First the son actively hurts his father, taking his inheritance and deserting the family. But then he hits bottom and has no place left to turn. He "comes to himself" (the key moment) and heads home. On the way, he plans his speech—"Father, I have sinned against heaven and before you; I am no longer worthy to be called your son" (15:18).

Now we come to the truly powerful part: The father does not need this speech: While the son "was still far off [before he could say a word], his father saw him and, filled with compassion; ran and put his arms around him and kissed him." Only then does the son give the speech—and the father brushes it off. "Quick, bring out a robe." Let's celebrate; "this son of mine [that's right, this son of mine] was dead and is alive again."

I think the son's speech was important for his own healing; it showed that he truly had come to himself. But it seems not to have mattered one whit to the father. This is what God is like (just as Hosea had said, just as was seen in the exodus): God saves because God wants wholeness. God saves because God wants damage to be healed. God saves because God wants all the families of the earth to be blessed.

So I have an answer to my first question. Are we saved *from* God or *by* God? The prophets and Jesus make it clear: God *saves*; we don't need to be saved from God.

SALVATION FROM OUR DAMAGE

So, what then do we need to be saved *from*? In a word: our damage. We *are* damaged. Human beings, when we fail to trust in God, trust in idols. Doing so diminishes our humanness and damages us.

From the beginning of Genesis, we learn that a consequence of the damage that human beings suffer is violence. Cain murders Abel, the first outworking of damaged social life. The ancient Israelites in Egypt needed to be saved from the damaging violence of the empire. If we add a thought from Luke 15, we could also say we need to be saved from the damage caused by views of God that portray God as unmerciful and retributive.

Violence tends to follow a fairly self-conscious logic. At the core of this "logic" rests a commitment to the necessity of retribution; using violence is justified as the appropriate response to violence. When the moral order is violated by wrongdoing, "justice" requires punitive retribution (defined as repayment of violence with violence, or pain with pain).

The legitimacy of retribution seems almost a cultural universal in Western culture—as it has been in many other cultures. Where does this commitment to retribution come from? In the West, affirmation of retribution links directly with mainstream Christian theology. We find deeply ingrained in our religious consciousness the belief that retribution is God's will.[2]

That the nature of the universe (as created and sustained by a holy God) requires retribution is a part of what most Western Christians, especially those in the United States, appear to believe. A theological framework we could call "the logic of retribution" underlies many rationales for the use of violence. The logic of retribution understands God most fundamentally in terms of impersonal, inflexible holiness. Here God's law is seen as the unchanging standard by which to measure wrongdoing.

This framework understands human beings to be inherently sinful. God responds to sin with punishment. Jesus *necessarily* died on the cross as a sacrifice to provide the only basis for sinful human beings to escape deserved punishment. We Americans justify violence as an expression of this deserved punishment ("punishment" defined as inflicting pain in response to wrongdoing). The logic of retribution requires violence in response to violence.

According to the logic of retribution, then, inflexible holiness in effect governs God's behavior. Because of the fundamental nature of this holiness, God may not freely act with unconditional mercy and compassion toward rebellious human beings. Simply to forgive would violate God's holiness. Compassion without satisfaction is not possible for God.

The doctrine of the atonement enters here. Due to the extremity of the offenses of human beings versus God's law, God can relate to us only if there is death on the human side to restore the balance. This can happen only through the enormity of the death of God's own son, Jesus, whose own holiness is so powerful that it can balance out the unholiness of all of humanity.

Human beings, when we confess our own helpless sinfulness, may claim Jesus as our savior from God's righteous anger. Jesus satisfies God's retributive justice (pain for pain) on our behalf. Within the logic of retribution, salvation (defined as the restoration of harmony with God), achieved as the result of violence, is consistent with the basic nature of the universe as founded on impersonal holiness. Salvation happens only because the ultimate act of *violence*—the sacrificial death of Jesus Christ—satisfies God's holiness. In this view, God is no pacifist. In fact, it is part of God's plan that God's own son be violently put to death.

In light of this understanding of the nature of God and of the fundamental nature of the universe, the logic of retribution indeed tends to lead to acceptance of "justifiable violence." Violence may be the best response to violence.

Let's reflect on one expression of this viewpoint.[3] In the criminal justice tradition of the Western world, the overriding justifications given for harsh punishments, even to the point of death, are tied to a belief that requires retributive justice when fundamental natural or divine laws are violated. Such "justice" restores the moral balance. In religious terms, retribution is needed to "satisfy" the need God has that violations be paid for with pain.

By making the "satisfaction" of impersonal justice (or of God's impersonal holiness) the focus of our response to criminal activity, the personal human beings involved—victims, offenders, and community members—rarely find wholeness. In fact, the larger community's suffering often only increases. Instead of the healing of the brokenness caused by the offense, we usually find ourselves with a rising spiral of brokenness. Many victims of violence speak of being victimized again by the impersonal criminal justice system. Offenders, often alienated people already, become more deeply alienated by the punitive practices and person-destroying experiences of prisons.

Prison psychiatrist James Gilligan asserts that "a society's prisons serve as a key for understanding the larger society as a whole."[4] When we look through the "magnifying glass" of the United States prison system, we see a society focused on trying to control violence through violence, a society that willingly inflicts incredible suffering on an ever-increasing number of desperate people.

Gilligan writes that United States prisons have become "cruel, inhumane, and degrading, with severe overcrowding, frequent rapes and beatings, prolonged and arbitrary use of solitary confinement, grossly unsanitary, disease-inducing living conditions, and deprivation of elementary medical care."[5] Ironically, it would appear that the effect of treating prisoners with brutality and other dehumanizing tactics actually puts the broader society more at risk.

Gilligan argues that "if the purpose of imprisonment were to socialize men to become as violent as possible—both while they are there and after they return to the community—we could hardly find a more effective way to accomplish it than what we do."[6] Treating people violently makes them *more* violent. A large amount of the violence that is part of our criminal justice practices, of course, is segregated behind prison walls and invisible to the outside world. However, since nine out of every ten prisoners eventually return to society, we cannot escape the truth that treating prisoners violently and thereby making them more violent endangers all of us.

Gilligan states that the strongest predictor he has found for men being violent is that they have been treated violently themselves, especially as children.[7] He asserts that "violence does not occur spontaneously or without a cause, it only occurs when somebody does something that causes it. Therefore, all we need to do to prevent violence is to stop doing what we have been doing to cause it."[8] In other words, the logic of retribution is not an answer to the problem of violence; it is one of the central causes.

A GOD WHO HEALS OUR DAMAGE

In contrast to the assumptions of the logic of retribution, the Bible from the start presents us with a God who shows us (and tells us) that life lived in trust in God heals the damage that has so diminished our humanity.

In the Bible, salvation has to do with wholeness. To have salvation implemented leads to harmony with God, harmony with other human beings, and harmony with the rest of creation. We *need* salvation when we experience brokenness instead of wholeness. After the very beginning of the book of Genesis, the Bible presupposes the realities of disharmony and brokenness—and focuses on the struggle for salvation amid these realities. Salvation results in healed brokenness, restored health, and wholeness.

The Old Testament presents salvation through concrete events communicated in stories told and retold. Such an approach locates this salvation in history and not in a cosmic, transcendent context. Salvation, in the Old Testament, is not about some transaction in the heart of God or some sort of weighing of the cosmic scale of justice. Rather, salvation has to do with flesh-and-blood actions.

The core of the basic story line of the Old Testament may be seen as three moments of salvation: the calling of Abraham and Sarah (Gen. 12), the liberation of the Hebrews from slavery in Egypt (Exod. 1–15), and the proclamation of mercy to the Hebrew exiles (Isa. 40–55). Salvation in each of these three key moments is given clearly to *unworthy* recipients. Abraham and Sarah are portrayed as having no particular virtues; they are simply "wanderers." The Hebrews in Egypt were lowly, demoralized slaves who showed no evidence of worshiping the God of their ancestors. And, the exiles of Isaiah 40–45 had lost all their pillars of identity as a consequence of their unfaithfulness to Torah.

The explicitness of the unworthiness of those being saved by God makes clear that they had done nothing to earn God's intervention. The logic of retribution tells us that God must act to destroy the unclean and unworthy, not to save them unless somehow the "balance of the scales of justice" might be restored through punitive acts. The biblical story tells us something quite different.

God the savior acts in such moments purely with good will. In each case the action is clearly mostly God's, due to God's free choice simply to intervene. The recipients did nothing to "buy" God's favor, nothing to force a legalistic God to act. God required no human acts to balance the scales of justice.

God's desire for relationships with God's people fuels the saving acts of God. God's intervention is *personal*, born out of compassion and love, leading to liberating acts that effect and sustain the human/divine relationship. At its core, according to the Old Testament story, salvation has to do with a loving, passionate God desiring a personal connection with human beings. The work of God to establish and sustain these relationships emerges from this personal, passionate, and loving disposition.

For salvation to enter the Hebrews' world, *nothing* is needed that would change God's disposition. The Hebrews are *not* called to find ways to appease God's anger, satisfy the demands of God's balance-the-scales justice, or find ways to avoid impurities that violate God's absolute holiness. Instead, God calls for human beings who receive God's mercy to act mercifully toward others. God calls them to follow Torah regulations that provide guidance for such merciful actions. In doing so, they form Israel into a merciful society (see Exod. 20, the first account of the Ten Commandments, where the first word is God's gift of salvation and the second word is the appropriate human response).

Contrary to many Christian doctrines of salvation, for *Jesus* the salvation story of the Old Testament remains fully valid. He does not seek to tell a different story but to proclaim the truthfulness of the old story.

Luke's birth story sets the stage for a proper understanding of Jesus' life and the meaning of his role as savior. In the birth story we learn that indeed something new is at hand—but that this "new thing" is in full harmony with the Old Testament portrayal of salvation. Israel's God has "remembered" the promise to Abraham (Luke 1:54-55), the covenant with Abraham's descendents. This remembrance leads to new acts of profound *mercy*. Nothing here hints that something has to happen to *God* to make restoration possible. God *initiates* the reconciliation. God unilaterally declares that salvation has come and is especially available to the vulnerable and marginalized people—those with ears to hear the good news.

Throughout the Gospels, Jesus never hints at seeing his teaching as anything but in full continuity with Israel's Scriptures. Matthew presents Jesus making this point explicitly:

"Do not think that I have come to abolish the law or the prophets; I have come not to abolish but to fulfill. For truly I tell you, until heaven and earth pass away, not one letter, not one stroke of a letter, will pass from the law until all is accomplished" (Matt. 5:17-18).

Jesus' God does not demand repayment of every ounce of indebtedness. Rather, Jesus taught that debts would be released without any kind of payment (Luke 4:19). The nature of the salvation Jesus proclaims turns the debt motif on its head. His Jubilee theology does not accept the logic of retribution that portrays human beings having an overwhelming debt to God. That logic sees this debt leading God to demand perfect obedience or a violent sacrifice as a necessary basis for paying the debt and thereby earning God's favor. Instead, Jesus began his ministry by proclaiming a word of pure acceptance—the poor, the captives, and the oppressed are given a simple word of unilateral acceptance by God. God simply forgives the debts.

Jesus indeed liberates ("saves"), but he does so simply by announcing that it is so (see Mark 1:15 and Luke 4:16-21). In this way, he stands in full continuity with the core salvation story of the Old Testament. Nothing has changed in the content of that story. The close parallels with the Old Testament story reinforce our sense that Jesus totally fits within the gift/response dynamics of God's saving efforts there. Jesus presents the kingdom of God as *already* present for his listeners. Because it is present, listeners are to "repent" and "believe." That is to say, there is no sense here that the repentance and belief in any way are conditions God requires before making the kingdom present.

Jesus' gospel message does lead directly to his death. This death, though, is not required to bring about the salvation Jesus the Savior offers the world. Rather, the death stems from the response of the Powers to the salvation *already* given by God. Jesus' straight-out mercy reveals to the world God's saving will with unprecedented clarity.

Jesus' death adds nothing to the means of salvation—God's mercy saves, from the calling of Abraham on. Rather, Jesus' death reveals the depth of the rebellion of the Powers, especially the political and religious human institutions that line up to execute Jesus.[9] Even more so, Jesus' death reveals the power of God's love. Jesus' death does indeed profoundly heighten our understanding of salvation. It reveals that the logic of retribution is an instrument of evil and that God's love prevails even over the most extreme expression of (demonic) retribution.

We learn more about salvation from Jesus' own teaching. The synoptic Gospels include two stories where Jesus is asked directly about eternal life. Both stories illumine Jesus' understanding of salvation—in what they say *and* in what they do not say. One story, that includes the parable of the Good Samaritan, occurs only in Luke's Gospel (10:25-37). All three synoptic Gospels contain the other story, Jesus' encounter with the "rich young ruler" (Matt. 19:16-26; Mark 10:17-22; Luke 18:18-25).

An "expert in the law" (Luke 10:25 NIV) asks Jesus about inheriting eternal life. This question arises after Jesus blesses seventy of his followers who returned to him after sharing his message. The "expert" asks, in effect, what about those of us who are not privileged to be part of this group: How do we enter into God's blessing of salvation?

Jesus asks the lawyer to say what he thinks. The lawyer answers with his summary of the Tradition. He quotes Deuteronomy 6:5 ("You shall love the Lord your God with all your heart, and with all your soul, and with all your strength") and Leviticus 19:18 ("You shall love your neighbor as yourself"). When Jesus affirms this response—"you have given the right answer; do this, and you will live" (10:28)—we see one more explicit statement of Jesus' continuity with the Old Testament understanding of salvation. The lawyer's answer reflects accurately the biblical teaching on salvation, and Jesus fully affirms this teaching.

Granting that the way to salvation includes loving *both* God and neighbor, an inseparable combination, the lawyer asks for clarity concerning who the neighbor is. Jesus' powerful story underscores that "neighbor" is an all-encompassing category. "Neighbor" includes even one's national enemies—the "Samaritan" being a neighbor to the Jew even while representing Jews' longtime enemies.

In portraying neighborliness in this way, Jesus characterizes eternal life in terms of mercy toward the one in need. Jesus unites his own way of life as God's Messiah (seen in his healing ministry) with the way of life characteristic of those who gain salvation. As the Hebrews learned with God's two central gifts (liberation from slavery in Egypt and Torah to guide their lives of grateful response to that liberation), so Jesus' listeners now hear reiterated: Love of God results in love of neighbor.

In Luke's version, Jesus' encounter with the rich ruler follows immediately after he asserts that little children, with their open hearts and trusting spirit, show what is needed for entry into God's kingdom. The ruler, perhaps wondering if Jesus' statement about children leaves him out, asks about how he might inherit eternal life. As with the earlier encounter with the lawyer who asked the same question, the basic answer here is quite similar. "You know the commandments: 'You shall not commit adultery, you shall not murder, you shall not steal, you shall not bear false witness, honor your father and mother'" (Luke 18:20).

Again, Jesus understands himself fully in harmony with the biblical tradition. This time, he links salvation with the Commandments that introduce Torah. Surely the love command from the earlier story and this summary of the Commandments should be seen as equivalent. Implied in any summary of the Commandments are the prelude to the Commandments (*because* "the Lord your God brought you out of the house of slavery," Exod. 20:2) and the first Commandment ("you shall have no other gods before me," Exod. 20:3; that is, love God *fully*).

The rich ruler, like the lawyer, agrees with Jesus concerning this understanding of salvation. Again, Jesus goes on to add depth to the basics. Here, too, Jesus surely understood his clarifications to be totally in line with biblical teaching. Jesus makes clear that two elements lie at the heart of the Commandments: (1) do not idolize wealth; and (2) commitment to God leads to caring for vulnerable folks in one's community. Both elements clearly were central in Torah and were reflected in prophetic reiterations of the expectations of Torah.

When we consider Jesus' two responses to questions about how salvation is attained, we see something utterly unremarkable if we understand Jesus to be in continuity with the Old Testament. Jesus actually adds nothing to the Old Testament portrayal of salvation. What must one do to be saved? Love God wholeheartedly (Deut. 6:5). Love one's neighbor as oneself (Lev. 19:18). Follow the Commandments (Exod. 20:1-17).

Jesus follows the prophets and Torah: God initiates salvation, always. God does this out of love and with the intent—reflecting God's total commitment to human beings—to bring healing to the alienated human race. Nothing needs to happen to change God's disposition toward human beings or to enable God to overcome limitations imposed on God's mercy by "holiness." God does not need some sort of sacrificial violence to satisfy God's honor or appease God's wrath so that God might provide salvation for alienated human beings.

Jesus' saving message was simple. Turn to God and trust in the good news of God's love. That is all there is to it. To make this message perfectly clear, Jesus expressed the good news of God's love in concrete ways. Jesus healed physical damage. Jesus overpowered demonic oppression. Jesus reached out especially to the vulnerable ones, the ones labeled "sinners" and outcasts who were excluded and oppressed due to the *sin* of the powers-that-be in Israel. There is little hint of salvation according to the logic of retribution in Jesus.

Trusting in God as peaceable frees us from the damage of trusting in "the myth of redemptive violence" (the belief that violence solves problems[10]) and damaging our souls by acting violently toward others. Trust in the ultimacy of this peaceable God frees us from the damage of trusting in *things* as ultimate, such as possessions, nation-states, religious structures, or social status that when idolized deprive us of our humanity.

Trust in God as merciful frees us from the damage of fearfulness. It is telling that in Genesis 3, after Adam and Eve eat the fruit, God still reaches out to them, walking as always in the garden to be with them. But Adam and Eve hide from God; the alienation comes from their fear, not from God's anger.

I think of an old friend of mine from my hometown in Oregon. After finishing school, my friend moved to California, got married, and had a couple of kids. When his son was two or so, they visited the grandparents back in rural Oregon. My hometown was the kind of place that when my family went on a six-week trip, we didn't even bother locking our house while we were gone. So, Grandpa asked the child if he wanted to go outside to play.

The boy was reluctant. Why? Grandpa wondered. The little boy pointed outside and said, "Strangers."

Now I am sure it was wise to teach the boy caution, especially for life in the big city. But this also strikes me as an example of what we could call "surplus fearfulness." The world can be scary, but it is God's world—and God's presence with us is one of empowerment and generosity, not fearfulness and retribution.

So, we are saved from our damage. We are saved from fear. We are saved from idols and powers that dehumanize us.

WHAT ARE WE SAVED FOR?

What are we saved *for*? As the prodigal son's father insisted, we are saved for celebrating. When damage is healed, and it will be when we turn to our merciful God, God is like the shepherd finding the lost sheep and the woman finding the lost coin—and God invites us to join this joyful celebration (Luke 15).

What are we saved for? Romans 12:1-2 puts it like this:

> I appeal to you, brothers and sisters, by the mercies of God, to present your bodies as a living sacrifice, holy and acceptable to God, which is your spiritual worship. Do not be conformed to this world, but be transformed by the renewing of your minds, so that you may discern what is the will of God—what is good and acceptable and perfect.

Because of God's transforming mercy, we may devote ourselves to being agents of that mercy, blessing all the families of the earth. We may live a life of creative and healing nonconformity to the ways of empire, creative and healing nonconformity to the dehumanizing ways of the Powers, creative and healing nonconformity to the violence caused by our projecting anger and retribution onto God.

God's mercy does indeed transform. I'm sure we all know salvation stories we could tell—stories from our own lives, from our friends and loved ones. I have a short one to end with.

When I was in high school, I became close friends with a guy who was several years older. He had been a star basketball player and liked to give pointers to us younger guys. He was kind of drifting in his life, living at home and working in a plywood mill. Then he got saved—and in fact he was the biggest influence on my own conversion not long afterwards.

My friend left Oregon and went to Bible college. He bought into the theology I began this chapter describing. He went on for a graduate degree in counseling, got married, and had a child. We stayed in touch even as my theology evolved—he respected my changes but remained true to his adopted theology. But over time, things didn't work out for my friend and his family. He ended up divorced and his daughter left home in her mid-teens.

We visited my friend not long after these events, and his life seemed at a low ebb. He had basically lost his faith. He had left his counseling profession and seemed completely at loose ends. Several years later, we were back home and met my friend for dinner. He was being resurrected. His theology was being reconstructed. He had embraced Eastern Orthodoxy. As I talked about the new thinking I was doing on understandings of salvation, he nodded enthusiastically. Yes, the God he now worshiped was a God of love, not a God of judgment and fear. And this God was helping him put his life back together.

The Church: Why Bother?

[The Doctrine of the Christian Community]

*I*N THE BIBLE, HUMAN BEINGS ARE GIVEN salvation so that they may embody God's will in this life. From the calling of Abraham and Sarah to the final revelation of the New Jerusalem, the Bible portrays lived salvation as community centered. Faith communities provide the context for human flourishing. However, in our fallen world faith communities also in practice have not always fulfilled their calling. So their legacy is ambiguous. This ambiguity also characterizes the post-biblical churches.

Thus when I think about the doctrine of the church ("ecclesiology"), the questions come pretty quickly—especially one set of questions. The church: comforter or afflicter? The church: a place that heals or a place that hurts? The church: oppressor or liberator? The church: blessing or curse?

I have an answer to these questions: "Yes!" What I mean is, in my experience, the church has been *both* a blessing and a curse. We invest ourselves in this community, we make ourselves vulnerable to each other, we care deeply. The rewards can be great—but so too can be the disappointment and hurt.

WHEN THE CHURCH IS A CURSE

I co-pastored a large rural congregation in the Midwest with my wife Kathleen back in the mid-1990s. This congregation had an enormous impact on many peoples lives, mostly for the good. However, some people were hurt by the church.

So we joked ruefully of our congregation having "road kill" spread around the countryside.

When is the church a curse? Sometimes a relatively powerless individual or group becomes the focus of "church discipline." This scapegoat gets the boot, and the larger group finds momentary peace. This is how I understand what happened in a regional conference I was part of once. During a time of great anxiety, a small, counter-cultural congregation became the focus of concern. This congregation was quiet and unobtrusive. However, the conference challenged its participants' beliefs, and they were unwilling to toe the party line. Soon this congregation was expelled from the conference (for the sake of the "unity of the whole"—to appease various people who threatened to leave the conference).

The church tends to be a curse when it places a priority on perceived purity over compassion and understanding. I mentioned our congregation in the Midwest. Kathleen learned to know an elderly man, a former member, who lived near our church. He had experienced great pain back in the 1950s when he married a woman who had been divorced. This young couple was made to feel unwelcome and removed themselves from the congregation. But our neighbor's family had been deeply invested in the congregation, and he never felt at home in a different church. So forty years later he remained mostly alone, his pain still very present.

Desmond Tutu, the great South African peacemaker, has lamented over the church. He points out that in just about every movement for justice and liberation over the past few centuries, the strongest opposition to change has come from the church. I have read of many Christians who argued strenuously *in favor* of slavery right up until the Civil War.[1] Even today, it is said that Sunday morning is the most segregated time of the week in our society.

The general message the churches have given is one of support for the status quo. In Britain, a long effort lasting much of the nineteenth century to end the death penalty came to the brink of success early in the twentieth century—but was held up for one more generation. The bishops of the Church of England continued to insist that the death penalty reflected God's will. Abolition only came when the bishops relented.[2] Is it a coincidence that as the church has lost power in Western Europe, rejection of the death penalty has spread?

WHEN THE CHURCH IS A BLESSING

Of course, this is only one side. The church indeed has been and continues to be a *blessing* as well as a curse. Many of us have found love and care in the church. I have. I can think back now more than thirty-five years when I first chose to attend church. I was stunned when I learned that people in that church had cared enough about me to be praying for my well-being, even when they barely knew me. The experience of genuinely being loved remains the legacy of that experience—an experience that decisively shaped the rest of my life.

My most meaningful moments as a pastor came in being community with people I likely would not have ever had occasion to learn to know otherwise. Being invited into others' lives as they face death, bury loved ones, and struggle with loneliness and illness—and sharing with others the joys of new life (babies, weddings, the coming to faith), indeed constitute a blessing.

The church is also a blessing when it provides enough clarity and faith to be a counterweight to our wider society's violence and imperialism. In every college class I teach, I feel a sense of gratitude to our congregations. Some, at least, do shape their young people to question materialistic and militaristic values in American culture as they seek to follow the way of Jesus.

The church is a blessing when it provides an anchor for our workaday lives, a place where we come to sing and pray together, where we come to be around people whose lives inspire us to try just a bit harder to love and care for others.

Many years ago, my best friend in graduate school, who himself had a very ambiguous relationship with faith, said, "Well, the church has a lot of problems, but it is the one place in our society where people gather to confess together that they do not want to be jerks. And that's worth something."

THE PRACTICAL VALUE OF THE CHURCH

How do we negotiate this blessing/curse tension? I believe a key step would be to *desacralize* the church. Maybe we should not think of the church as something unique and special in God's eyes, a "sacred place" akin to the temple in the Bible. Maybe we should not think of the church as a place that exists over against the secular world. Maybe we should think of the church simply as one possible human community.

The church is a human structure. As such it is one of the Powers; as such it is one of the fallen Powers—capable of good, certainly. But the church, like all human structures, like all fallen Powers, can easily become an idol. The church can seek to take God's place in our lives. The church, like many other human structures, can become an absolute that demands to be defended—even with violence if necessary (witness various inquisitions and crusades).

If we no longer look at the church as sacred and recognize our tendency to make it an idol, will there be any reason to want to "redeem" it nonetheless? Is there any reason to bother with the church if it is simply a human structure?

Well, yes. . . . One reason for bothering with the church is a "mundane" or everyday reason. Even if the church is not sacred, it still serves the life-enhancing role that any authentic human community does. A second kind of reason is a "Christian" one. If we do theology as if Jesus matters—if we do ecclesiology (the doctrine of the church) as if Jesus matters, we will have reasons to bother with the church.

What about the mundane rationale? Human beings are, by nature, social creatures. We need other human beings to be human. We may see this need clearly in a negative sense when we look at how it is exploited by oppressors.

The most powerful weapon prisons have to control prisoners is solitary confinement. Hundreds of years ago, in their desire to make prisons more humane, Quaker reformers argued for solitary confinement to take the place of beatings. If prisoners are isolated, the argument went, they will search their souls and seek to change. Well, what happened instead is that solitary confinement drove prisoners *insane*. And, bingo, tragically, pacifist Quakers gave prisons a powerful weapon for violence.

We are learning of the careful research into torture methods that our government has sponsored. These methods include intense efforts to disorient and isolate detainees. Such trauma triggers detainees' need for human contact. When the need is strong enough, detainees reach out to their torturers since they are so desperate to connect with humans. Then the torturers have them where they want them.[3]

Of course this story is terribly upsetting—but we may learn from it. These occasions of the cost of isolation underscore just how important human community is. The *positive* side, the joy we receive from friendship, underscores just how central community is to being whole human beings. And the church is one place where we can find such community. Probably all of us, if we were to list the moments in our lives when we have experienced genuine joy, would include times with friends, likely friends in church.

Just recently, Kathleen and I discovered an old cassette tape from our wedding in the late 1970s. Talk about bringing back old memories. We were quite impressed at the simplicity of the service. From welcoming guests to the recessional took all of seventeen minutes! Neither of us wanted to bore anyone, I guess. The big memories, though, are of our friends, our congregation. The music, the sermon, the reception, the sense of joy and encouragement the two of us felt all arose out of our faith community.

Church communities also at times have been crucial to wider social movements—think of the role of the Catholic Church in Poland in resisting Communism and the role of black churches in the American South during the civil rights movement. So, one set of reasons to bother with church might well be simply our human need for community.

Still, I also want to insist on a set of reasons that are Christian. Remember, I define theology as reflection on our hierarchy of values. I propose that our "God" is seen in what we value the most. *Christian* theology emerges when we see Jesus' own values as the basis for ours. When we do theology as if Jesus matters, we will seek to have our hierarchy of values to fit with Jesus' values.

To think of the church as if Jesus matters is to say that the church is faithful when it self-consciously furthers Jesus' way—

through its teaching and preaching, through its worship and communal prayer, through its practices and projects.

We should bother with the church as Christians because it can be, it should be, it *must* be (if it is to be faithful), a place where people work together to embody, to make real and concrete, the basic message of Jesus: Love God and neighbor. And as social creatures, we need other people to help us do this.

FAITH COMMUNITY IN THE BIBLE

Let's look at four Bible texts that can help us think about why to bother—or, maybe I should say, *how* to bother with the church.

I will begin with Psalm 15:

O Lord, who may abide in your tent? Who may dwell on your holy hill? Those who walk blamelessly, and do what is right, and speak the truth from their heart; who do not slander with their tongue, and do no evil to their friends, nor take up a reproach against their neighbors; in whose eyes the wicked are despised, but who honor those who fear the Lord; who stand by their oath even to their hurt; who do not lend money at interest, and do not take a bribe against the innocent. (Ps. 15:1-5)

Psalm 15 emphasizes that living justly and compassionately is the prerequisite for abiding in God's presence and among God's people. The identity of the community imagined by the Psalms centers on people in this community living here and now in ways that foster life and resist evil.

For a second Old Testament text, let's look at Jeremiah 7. Jeremiah receives the calling from God to challenge the people of his day as they enter the gates of the temple to worship God. He is to tell them,

Do not trust in these deceptive words: "This is the temple of the Lord, the temple of the Lord, the temple of the Lord." For if you truly amend your ways and your doings, if you truly act justly one with another, if you do not oppress the alien, the orphan, and the widow, or shed innocent blood in this place, and if you do not go after other gods to your own hurt, then I will dwell with you in this place, in the land that I gave of old to your ancestors for-

> ever and ever. . . . Will you steal, murder, commit adultery, swear falsely, make offerings to Baal, and go after other gods that you have not known, and then come and stand before me in this house, which is called by my name, and say—"We are safe!"—only to go on doing all these abominations? (Jer. 7:3-10)

Jeremiah 7 denies that ritual acts and public worship are in and of themselves of value to God. When they coexist with easily accepted injustice, ritual acts and worship are acts of *rebellion* against God. When the church places a higher priority on status and comfort than on caring for vulnerable people, than on rejecting violence, than on serving as a house of prayer for all nations—it is tending toward idolatry.

Now let's look at a text from the Gospels.

> A dispute arose among [Jesus' disciples] as to which one of them was to be regarded as the greatest. But [Jesus] said to them, "The kings of the Gentiles lord it over them; and those in authority over them are called benefactors. But not so with you; rather the greatest among you must become like the youngest, and the leader like one who serves. For who is greater, the one who is at the table or the one who serves? Is it not the one at the table? But I am among you as one who serves." (Luke 22:24-27)

Luke 22 establishes the political style that must characterize Jesus' followers—not power-over, not claiming to be a benefactor while actually practicing domination, not to seek status and to be served. The political style of Jesus is a politics of service, a politics of simplicity, a politics of authentic humility and equality of status.

Finally, consider Paul's thoughts from Romans 12. He begins with a call to intellectual transformation, commitment to God in response to God's mercy. This transformation turns the believer from cultural conformity with the wider world and enables one to discern God's will. Such discernment will lead to mutual up building in the faith community.

> We, who are many, are one body in Christ. . . . We have gifts that differ according to the grace given to us: prophecy, in proportion to faith; ministry, in ministering; the teacher, in teaching; the exhorter, in exhortation; the

giver, in generosity; the leader, in diligence; the compassionate, in cheerfulness.Let love be genuine; hate what is evil, hold fast to what is good; love one another with mutual affection; outdo one another in showing honor. (Rom. 12:4-10)

Romans 12 points to the faith community as a counterculture that *thinks* differently. This counter-culture makes Jesus' priorities its priorities in contrast to the priorities of the "domination system,"[4] that is, in contrast to the ethics of power-over all too common in the world.

The church is worth bothering with *insofar* as it understands its existence as a way to help its people to embody these attributes. The church is not an end in itself. It serves the true ends: love of God and neighbor. To such service is where ecclesiology in light of Jesus leads us.

THREE SENSES OF "THE CHURCH"

In working at a theology of the church in light of these reflections, I start by suggesting that we may think about the church in three senses: the structural, the visible, and the invisible church.

In thinking about the *structural church*, we may understand one aspect of the church's existence to be an organized group of Christians with a recognized (usually ordained) formal leadership, with membership, regular rituals (most commonly baptism and communion), a regular meeting place and meeting times.

The church in this sense serves as the location for weddings and funerals with designated officiants. It is as the structural church that we talk about official beliefs (such as confessions and creeds), legal status as incorporated entities, regional conferences, and denominations.

To speak of the *visible church* is to refer to the church as the concrete fellowship of followers of Jesus Christ who form a community, meet regularly; worship together (usually with singing, prayer, and preaching); study Scripture together; offer one another encouragement; organize for service, social action, and witness; and share in rituals such as baptism and communion.

There is overlap between the structural and visible aspects of the church. The distinction may be seen in terms of an analogy with language. Vocabulary and rule of grammar provide the structure of language, but the actual face-to-face interaction of human beings using the words is what makes the language alive.

To talk about the *invisible church* is to speak metaphorically of the mystical "communion of the saints" made up of all those who trust in Jesus Christ. The church in this sense exists throughout time and all over the world.

The second sense, the visible one, takes precedence over the first and the third senses. The structural church and the invisible church only have meaning in relation to the visible church. There is no invisible church apart from many visible congregations. Without authentic, face-to-face discipleship, the structural church is only a calcified human institution.

The church gains its direction from the life and teaching of Jesus. Jesus provides criteria for the church's authenticity: love, openness, peaceableness, opposition to the powers of death, willingness to suffer for the sake of the truth, suspicion of institutions and human self-aggrandizement, and adherence to the prophetic faith of the ancient Hebrews.

The church's mission includes at its heart witness to God's love to all the ends of the earth—as Jesus challenged his followers just before he left them in Acts 1:8. The church so witnesses (1) by embodying in the present, in its common life, the reality of God's promised kingdom; (2) by finding ways to communicate this reality to the wider world as invitation; and (3) by confronting the powers of death through exorcism and *disillusionment*.

The church, by definition, is "political" (with "politics" defined as how human beings order their common life). However, the church lives in the tension of ambivalence toward the "world" (defined both as that which God created and loved and as that which opposes God). There is no part of the world to which Christians should not bear witness. At the same time, *all* parts of the world (including churches) may manifest opposition to God and hence may seduce Christians. The key criterion for avoiding such seduction is adherence to the peaceable way of Jesus.

The focus of the church should be *positive*. It seeks to understand and live out its mission of witnessing to God's love. Christian existence is based on God's mercy, not human strictness and purity. The key metaphor for the aspiration of the church is "health." Health is found through self-awareness and identity security.

We may actually think of such a positive focus as a form of "church discipline." Church discipline should primarily be a matter of people in the church living with openness and integrity. That is, the church best sustains its health by being a community from which those who do not want to live with openness and integrity will choose to excuse themselves.

The center of the church is faithfulness to Jesus' way, not doctrinal formulations or legalistic purity. The focus is on the center, sustaining the community's core identity—not on the boundaries, striving to divide between insiders and outsiders.

The church may need (on *rare* occasions) to withhold fellowship from troublesome members ("troublesome" defined primarily as those who harm others). This withholding must always be done with a spirit of love and concern, in hopes of effecting restoration of fellowship and healing for all involved. The withholding should never be done with a punitive intent or for the sake of the church's "purity" or "reputation."[5]

Since the church is the "church of Jesus Christ," membership is tied to a public expression of one's willingness to follow Jesus and his way. Typically this expression happens with the rite of baptism. The baptized person confesses Jesus as God's Son (that is, as the definitive revelation of God) and Jesus' way as God's will for all human beings.

As an *inviting* fellowship (more than a fellowship focused on purity), the church is open to a variety of expressions of faith under the rubric of following Jesus. As a *voluntary* fellowship, the church does not coerce or claim to hold the "keys of salvation." As an *active* fellowship, the church expects its members to join in the task of witness. As a *discerning* fellowship, the church expects all its members to be part of the church's work of perceiving the "signs of the times" and to share and receive counsel for personal life and social discernment.

As a human organization, the church requires some sort of formal leadership. Leaders are "ordained" (called out) in recognition both of the practical need for recognized leaders and of the gifts and motivations of the person being called out. However, the basic standards for ordination are essentially the same as they are for membership. Leaders are not above the congregation. Their leadership is primarily practical.

We need to recognize (and confess with regret) the scandal of intra-Christian enmity. Probably nothing has (or continues to) undercut the message of the gospel as much as Christians doing violence toward other Christians. Some historians argue that the "Christian wars" in Europe during the sixteenth and seventeenth centuries fostered the emergence of atheism more than any other factor.[6] However, the diversity of Christian traditions has also led to a richness of expression and understanding that has enhanced the witness to God's love in Christ.

Structural unity of all Christians is a dangerous ideal. In part, this is so because top-down conformity quenches the creativity of the Spirit. In part, this is so because such "unity" tends to exclude and coerce dissenters. For life-enhancing Christian unity, what is required is openness, respect, corporate cooperation, and sharing across the differences while each particular tradition also maintains its own unique expression of faith.

Within the diverse umbrella of my own Mennonite tradition, for example, the service organization Mennonite Disaster Service models the exercise of common Christian witness amid respect for diverse institutional structures. Various Mennonite denominations work together to help people in need following natural disasters while retaining their distinct identities.

THE CHURCH AND WORSHIP

A final area of reflection in relation to our theology of the church is worship, the communal times when people of faith gather to share with one another in hymns, public prayer, and the ministry of the word.

The Sunday morning worship service plays a key role for group spirituality. In many North American congregations, we tend toward busy lives, with many interests, activities, and other circles of friends. Church is not the all-week cultural and religious center that it used to be. So worship time is precious.

Something should happen during those one to three hours Sunday morning that plays a major role in helping us to make sense out of our lives. This time should help us to find strength and encouragement and hopefulness.

A pastor friend of mine once told me about a woman who regularly attended his worship services and became involved in his congregation. She was from a Catholic background. She had told him that she was going to the Mennonite church for the social contacts. She liked being with the people, sharing many interests and concerns, and working with them on social issues. However, when she wanted to *worship*, she went back to the Catholic mass. She told my friend that Mennonites do not really know how to worship.

In thinking about what my friend said, I had to question the woman's apparent division between worship and fellowship. At least, I thought about why that distinction did not fit with my experience and understanding. That helped me to think about what I find to be important elements of my worship experience and why I find them a source of encouragement.

When I was a pastor, my Sunday mornings meant more than simply carrying out pastoral responsibilities. My encouragement did not stem only from successful completion of my tasks. It also had to do with what had gone on in the worship experience in general. I felt that *something* had happened to lift my spirits and touch me with a reality outside of myself. In authentic worship, in being pointed toward God, we are simultaneously being pointed toward the kind of people we want to be, the kind of world of which we want to be part.

This "something" is what I want to reflect on. I will do so not so much by trying to define what this "something" is. Rather, I will structure my comments on various elements that make up the worship service and how I think they combine to provide encouragement. These elements I am calling emotional, intellectual, social, and meditative parts of worship.

These different elements all overlap. We sing—engaging in what I am calling an emotional element. However, the singing includes our minds, so it is also intellectual, and we do it together, so it is certainly social. As well, it often includes a prayerful, meditative element.

When I use the term *emotional*, I am not meaning that worship makes us intensely emotional. I do not mean emotional in the sense as when we say that someone who is fighting back tears is "emotional." Certainly intense emotions may occur. What I have in mind, though, is simply that part of us that we might call the emotional part of our being. The part that maybe transcends words or is at least something we can't describe in strictly a linear way. You could call this the inarticulate speech of our hearts.

The part of our worship that I have especially in mind as "emotional," in this sense, is our music. There is something about singing, hearing others sing, and hearing instrumental music that often touches our hearts in significant ways. As well, music evokes something from our hearts, something that touches the emotional part of our being.

Singing especially, in ways beyond the actual word content of the hymns, can act as a kind of salve on the hurting soul. It's not magical; the hurt typically remains. However a kind of soul soothing may be felt. It is partly the act of singing, of expressing something with at least a bit of abandonment. It is also partly the act of hearing—the instruments, the other voices. As well, I have also experienced in times when I feel joyful that hymn singing may be an opportunity to voice that joy.

The *intellectual* element comes more to the fore in other aspects of worship. When we actually do talk, what we say is crucial. I am thinking especially of sermons here, though also our children's stories, Scripture readings, and other times when just one person speaks. My Mennonite tradition has placed a high priority on hymn singing. This has always been a central part of Mennonite worship. So, too, have sermons.

Sermons can be a significant source of spiritual encouragement. In Romans 12 we hear Paul calling for "spiritual worship." This has to do with the "renewing of our minds." He calls for us to think—and in new ways. He wants us grow in understanding God's ways of peace and justice and of our world and our place in it. He urges us to find words to express our soul's longings and hurts and joys.

Sermons can be opportunities for encouragement to think. The intellectual part of us needs the nourishment of deeper perspectives. It needs the challenges of ways of seeing that are different from ours and the support that maybe some of our ideas are worth staying with after all. The best sermons I have heard provided this nourishment through various means—stories, images, evoking memories, touching emotions, as well as analysis, definition, explanation. I came away thinking about new ways to see. At times I've felt encouraged that some of the old ways are still okay. My mind as well as heart have found spiritual nourishment.

So our worship includes hymns and sermons, both of which in different degrees and different ways touch our hearts and our heads. A third element that also does both is what I am calling the *social* or *interactive* element. Here I am thinking of when we talk with each other. We talk both in formal settings such as Sunday school and worship service discussions and in informal settings when we visit before and after our service.

When Kathleen and I began attending the Eugene (Ore.) Mennonite congregation in the 1970s, we came from a pretty intense, zealous church. We had wanted to change the world—through evangelism, through activism, through the intensity of our common life. Our first sense of the Mennonites was certainly positive, which is why we kept going back. However, we also thought that the group was not that far from being, as we said, "just a social club." We did not see that the congregation was doing that much—certainly not compared to what we thought a church *should* do. So we felt a little disdainful.

However, my thinking has changed since then. I do think that congregation is and always has been more than just a social club. I also am not nearly so critical of the idea of being a social club. At least, I think being the kind of social club we are is not *just* a social club. Maybe no social clubs are. I see the social-ness of our being together as part of our worship of God. It is a powerful force in encouraging us to be spiritually alive and fruitful in our lives in the world.

We need to have a sense that we are part of something bigger than just our individual selves. We need other people whom we like, who like us—more than that, whom we trust and respect and who trust and respect us. We need to have a sense that we matter. We need to have people with whom we can talk, people who affirm us as significant beings. We do not get this in that many places—certainly not in our consumer culture. Our church community and our socializing especially offer to meet these needs, at least in part. As I stated, this socializing includes our formal discussions. Here we have opportunity to make ourselves heard to other people who actually listen and act as if what we say is worth listening too. We have the chance to think together on big issues (and little issues) that interest us and affect our lives. We also find enjoyment in the human contact, our senses of humor, and the give and take and stimulation of thought processes.

This socializing also includes our informal conversations, where we touch base, make new acquaintances, share news and hopes and fears. None of this probably happens enough to make us fully content. However, it does happen and we do well not to take this rareness of human fellowship for granted.

The element of our worship having to do with talking with each other is a crucial part of the whole. In this area, I am pretty Quaker in my theology. Some people accuse Quakers of being non-sacramental because they do not observe the Lord's Supper. However, they believe they are sacramental, in that they experience communion in their fellowship with one another. I think there is something to that. We can understand our time together as the "sacrament" of communion occurring through talking and listening, enjoying each other, learning of the God that is part of each of us. This is a central part of worship. I reflect more fully on the "sacrament" of the Lord's Supper in the next chapter.

I believe that our worship is encouraging to me because with our worship we join in constructing an alternative world to the rat race around us. Our singing, our thinking, and our talking and listening all help shape that world. We connect with values, with hopes, and with a spirituality. These all point toward a new world. This is where people, where relationships, where love, respect, and compassion—all enlivened by a caring God—are affirmed. We confess these as true, as genuine, as at the center of what we want to be as human beings.

We call forth this alternative world tentatively and imperfectly. However, we do make contact with it. In doing so, we find some hope, some encouragement, and some reason for continuing on. That is what church is about and why it is worth bothering with.

Evoking the Presence of God

[A Theology of the Sacraments]

*T*HE ALERT READER MAY HAVE NOTICED something missing from the previous chapter. In our discussion of worship as part of our theology of the church, we did not consider sacraments such as communion except for my brief comments at the end. The main reason for this omission no doubt stems from my experience as a Christian. I have mainly participated in "low-church" congregations that do not emphasize communion as a regular part of worship.

Since I have generally found worship to be meaningful in my various congregations, I drew on the elements of worship that have made it meaningful in my experience. I left out practices that have not been central to this experience.

I could also argue that if we are thinking of the church in light of Jesus' life and teaching, we would not expect communion to be a major element of our theology of the church. Of course, communion is not absent from the story of Jesus. We have the "Last Supper." But in Jesus' ministry and teaching, this "sacramental" event plays a peripheral role in the overall story.

Nevertheless, even among Mennonites and other low-church traditions, an appreciation for the sacramental practices of the broader Christian tradition has been growing. Plus, many from Christian streams that have seen the sacraments as more central to church life have become attracted to the Jesus-centered, ethically oriented focus of "baptist"[1] churches. So, the theme of the sacraments, in particular, the Lord's Supper or communion, requires our attention. I do feel reluctant to take up the issue of communion. It's not so much that I have personally had negative experiences with communion—actually my experiences have trended positive.

But I do know people who have had hard experiences: the denial of participation in the Lord's Supper for my friend's father back in the 1930s for owning life insurance, a trauma that still hurts her; the gay man who was refused communion when he returned to his home congregation hoping to rebuild a sense of connection; the teenager who was told she was too young to take communion, making her feel like a second-class Christian even though she deeply desired to follow Jesus. . . . These exclusions bother me.

COMMUNION'S SYMBOLISM

As I reflect on communion, I find it helpful (though also troubling and confusing) to think about what this ritual *symbolizes*. It seems to me that the meaning of communion varies according to what we think lies behind the service. What do these acts symbolize for us? Well, lots of different things at different times. For example:

Back in the late 1970s, my wife Kathleen and I were part of a non-denominational church made up of people in their twenties, many of whom were new Christians. We took communion every week—in wildly varying ways. Whoever wanted to could lead the service. One Sunday we might have saltine crackers and Kool-Aid. The next would be grape juice and bread. And every once in a while this one guy would try to get us to use regular wine—even though about half the people in the church were teetotalers! Communion often symbolized people's joy and enthusiasm in knowing Jesus and in being with others who shared those feelings. Everyone was welcome; I don't think any of us had a very sophisticated theology of the sacraments—to say the least.

Most of us in the congregation were from Baptist and other believers church backgrounds; many others were new Christians who hadn't been in church much at all before. So we didn't have a particular formula we felt we needed to follow. We had no desire to make communion a sacrament that required a priest to legitimate it. Rarely, if ever, did we talk about anything happening to the elements—they were bread (or crackers) and juice, that was all. What mattered was that they provided an occasion for us to thank Jesus for saving us through his sacrificial death—and usually, in some sense, to express our commitment to follow him.

A second example would be from about the same time. Kathleen and I often visited her family in Arizona, and when we could we would go to Mass with her widowed Roman Catholic grandmother. Gramma loved for us to accompany her. And she loved for us to take communion with her, even though she knew we weren't Catholics. She said she was sure the priests wouldn't mind, though she never asked any of them about it. To her, our sharing in the Mass with her was a familial affirmation of her faith. (The rest of the family was not Catholic, and for many years Gramma felt somewhat ostracized due to her faith.)

For Kathleen and me, the Mass was meaningful partly because of the connection with Gramma, partly because we liked the content of the liturgy, partly because we were pretty ecumenical in spirit and liked sharing this ritual with fellow Christians from a tradition different than ours. However, I started learning more about Catholic theology and realized that according to the teaching of the Catholic Church we were not legitimate participants. I found this offensive and eventually began to decline to go forward to take the elements.

A little later, while I was in graduate school, a close friend took her final vows as a Catholic nun. The service to celebrate her taking this step was quite meaningful. But when it came time to take communion, I did not feel that I could go forward. The sisters and the priest who was officiating (one of my professors and also a good friend) all urged me to go ahead even though they knew I was a Mennonite, but I could not bring myself to do so.

Another example would be when my parents retired and moved to a new community. My father had grown up the son of a Lutheran pastor, but in the small town in Oregon where I grew up, we had no Lutheran church. So I had never attended a Lutheran service.

In their new town, my parents now had a Lutheran church to attend. So Kathleen and I went along the first Sunday they were there. This was the first time in forty years my dad had a chance to be part of the kind of church he grew up in. When it came time for communion, Kathleen and I hopped up and partook, even though the pastor said it was only for people who believed in the "real presence." But my parents stayed seated.

I found out later that in the church where my dad grew up, communion was open only to church members. So he didn't think he should take communion in this church until he joined. As I thought about it later, I felt that part of what was symbolized both by the pastor's statement about the need to believe in the "real presence" and, even more, by my dad's views, was that communion could represent the church as a kind of closed club—if you believe in the right thing, or if you have a certain kind of congregational membership, you can take part. It could be kind of like a lodge; the value of my membership is heightened by the fact that some *aren't* members.

As a final example, I noticed a letter in a church periodical from a seminary professor arguing against an essay that had advocated opening communion to anyone who is thirsting for God. To open communion in this way, so that we "open the breaking of bread to people who have not made the covenant with Jesus," is to jeopardize our understanding of the church according to this professor. Church, it would appear, is a place where it is important to make clear distinctions between who belongs or not. The symbolism here seems to be, in part, that communion is one place where we must clearly draw lines between in and out.

From these examples, I mostly perceive a sense of communion as a boundary marker, a way to make distinctions between worthy participants and those who, due to theology, congregational membership, or some other factor, are not worthy to partake. The one counter-example would be the chaotic practices of my old house church. That congregation took communion very seriously, practicing it every week, but strictly as an activity symbolizing the wonders of the merciful salvation God makes available to everyone.

However, another element of communion symbolism comes to mind when I think of a good friend of mine who models faithfulness to Jesus' gospel of peace. This friend works hard for justice and reconciliation both inside and outside the church. He puts his very life on the line—in fact, he was nearly killed while witnessing for peace in Iraq in 2003. He also puts his reputation and ministerial status on the line by welcoming sexual minorities to his congregation.

For my friend, sharing in communion is extraordinarily important as a source of spiritual sustenance. While not formally a Roman Catholic, he feels strongly drawn to Catholic sacramental theology. For him, communion symbolizes solidarity with other peacemaking Christians, an identification with the long Christian tradition, and his receptivity to the Spirit's nourishment through the bread and wine.

I know many other Christians who share my friend's convictions about peacemaking *and* his experience of the depth of meaning in the communion service. So I would not want to try to drive a wedge between sacramental practices and costly discipleship—even though I am suspicious that the sacramental tradition tends to emphasize external churchly ritual over actual deeds of justice and compassion.

These issues keep getting more complicated for me, though, as I reflect more on the symbolism of communion.

THE PROPHETIC CONCERN

Let me turn to a biblical passage that touches on my concerns as I reflect theologically on communion. One starting point for such reflection could be the writings of some of Israel's prophets, beginning with these sharp words from the prophet Amos.

> I hate, I despise your festivals, and I take no delight in your solemn assemblies. Even though you offer me your burnt offerings and grain offerings, I will not accept them; and the offerings of well-being of your fatted animals I will not look upon. Take away from me the noise of your songs; I will not listen to the melody of your harps. But let justice roll down like waters, and righteousness like an ever-flowing stream. (Amos 5:21-24)

The book of Amos as a whole focuses on the spiritual state of the nation of Israel. This people had been formed by God for the purposes of living faithfully to the message of Torah. Amos understood that at the heart of Torah lay God's concern for justice and equity among all the people of the community. Community rituals were meant to encourage this justice and equity.

Instead, according to Amos, Israel had departed from God's intentions for its common life. An expression of this departure was the *delinking* of rituals from the ethical core of Torah. Shockingly, in Amos's view, the rituals themselves became an occasion for sin. They were not an expression of faithfulness to God but actually expressed the opposite—utter disregard for the core message of God's will found in Torah.

Here we have the image of people who share in religious rituals as a means of demonstrating their piety to onlookers while being blind to profound social injustice. The rituals had become ends in themselves: go to services, get blessed, and you are set. God is in the holy sanctuary; God's presence is mediated through the religious leader—the only demand on the believer is to show up, go through the ceremonies, and go on with life as if God's commands for social justice are optional.

Virtually any ritual runs the risk of evolving into the kind of approach that Amos spoke so harshly against. When faithfulness can be equated with simply sharing in an external ritual, the ethical practices of the participant easily become marginalized, secondary, and optional. Only in this way could we have the endless repetition of the practices Amos condemns—people of faith actively attending services while also actively participating in unjust social practices.

COMMUNION AS WELCOME

Let me mention yet another symbolic expression of communion. I learned of this story from reading an encouraging book—*Take This Bread*, by Sara Miles.[2] Miles grew up an atheist. She cared deeply for justice in the world, devoting years of her life to working in Central America. She eventually ended up in San Francisco, a bit burnt out from her work.

One Sunday she found herself attending an Episcopalian worship service. Miles went simply to watch, not even sure what had drawn her to attend. Then in the middle of the service, when the priest announced, "Jesus invites everyone to his table," she found herself caught up in the movement forward and took the bread and wine.

Miles was suffering in many ways at this time. Her father had just died unexpectedly. The father of her daughter had separated from her. She carried the pain of her experience in Central America. Taking the bread and wine seemed to speak to her need, though she didn't know how that could be. She remained skeptical but couldn't stop going back to church and accepting the invitation to Jesus' table.

About the time she accepted that she had become a Christian, an opportunity arose for her to begin a food pantry at this church. So, as she grew in her faith and her understanding of what it meant to share at Jesus' table, she found herself sharing food with others who also were hungry, as she had been, though in more literal sense.

Ultimately, Miles links these two experiences *inextricably* together. Jesus' table symbolized by the communion service at Sunday worship complements Jesus' table symbolized by sharing with hungry people at Friday food pantry. Both expressed God's welcome: to all who hunger for spiritual wholeness and to all who simply hunger for food.

She found inspiration in stories such as Jesus feeding the five thousand, breaking bread and sharing it indiscriminately with all who were hungry for physical food. Typically, Christians oriented more in a sacramental direction do not view this story as a precursor to the communion service. After all, Jesus shared indiscriminately here. He did not limit the "elements" to believers. However, for Miles, the key points of continuity between Jesus' sharing food in this Gospel story and her own experience of coming to his table at communion could be seen in Jesus' compassionate response in providing nourishment in face of people's hunger and his blessing of the "elements" before sharing them with those in need.

> Jesus . . . saw a great crowd; and he had compassion for them and cured their sick. When it was evening, the disciples came to him and said, "This is a deserted place, and the hour is now late; send the crowds away so that they may go into the villages and buy food for themselves."

> Jesus said to them, "They need not go away; you give them something to eat." They replied, "We have nothing here but five loaves and two fish." And [Jesus] said, "Bring them here to me." Then he ordered the crowds to sit down on the grass. Taking the five loaves and the two fish, he looked up to heaven, and blessed and broke the loaves, and gave them to the crowds. And all ate and were filled; and they took up what was left over of the broken pieces, twelve baskets full. And those who ate were about five thousand men, besides women and children. (Matt. 14:13-21)

Miles also drew inspiration from this text from Luke's Gospel where Jesus sits down for table fellowship with tax collectors and sinners, announcing that his message of healing was for all who needed their brokenness bound up.

> Jesus went out and saw a tax collector named Levi, sitting at the tax booth; and [Jesus] said to him, "Follow me." And [Levi] got up, left everything, and followed [Jesus].
>
> Then Levi gave a great banquet for [Jesus] in his house; and there was a large crowd of tax collectors and others sitting at the table with them. The Pharisees and their scribes were complaining to [Jesus'] disciples, saying, "Why do you eat and drink with tax collectors and sinners?" Jesus answered, "Those who are well have no need of a physician, but those who are sick. I have come to call not the righteous but sinners to repentance." (Luke 5:27-32)

Amos, representing many of Israel's prophets, warns of the dangers of ritual separated from ethics. Religious people attend services; they share a ritualistic "meal" that invokes God's presence within the sanctuary. But in their lives they accept (or actively participate in) social injustice that leaves the poor and needy oppressed and disenfranchised. In doing so, according to Amos, these religious people are partaking in hateful "festivals" and "solemn assemblies" that God actually promises to ignore. "I will not listen" (Amos 5:23). Earlier, Amos even asserts that the people have a choice—*either* seek life (and establish justice for the needy) *or* attend religious services (5:4-5).

Let us note that Jesus provides a model for a different kind of celebration, one that includes at its heart sharing with people in need and welcoming "sinners" (rather than excluding them). The food blessed and shared meets people's physical needs while also symbolizing God's welcome and promise to heal their souls.

IS GOD NEEDY?

I have to mention one last kind of symbolism. This is the symbol pointed to by Psalm 50.

> Our God . . . calls to the heavens above and to the earth, that he may judge his people: "Gather to me my faithful ones, who made a covenant with me by sacrifice! . . . Hear, O my people, and I will speak, O Israel, I will testify against you. I am God, your God. . . . I will not accept a bull from your house, or goats from your folds. For every wild animal of the forest is mine, the cattle on a thousand hills. I know all the birds of the air, and all that moves in the field is mine. If I were hungry, I would not tell you, for the world and all that is in it is mine. Do I eat the flesh of bulls, or drink the blood of goats? Offer to God a sacrifice of thanksgiving, and pay your vows to the Most High. Call on me in the day of trouble; I will deliver you and you shall glorify me." (Ps. 50:3-15)

Some Christians may have a tendency to think of communion similarly to the ancient Israelites in the psalm. Thinking that it is an offering to God of something God needs to be favorably disposed to them.

We can see two expressions of giving God something God needs. Maybe God needs our *obedience*, so taking communion regularly pays God to accept us. Instead of the communion symbolizing and celebrating God's mercy already shown to us, it symbolizes payment God needs *to* accept us. This sense of communion as obligation probably reflects a kind of popular spirituality more than an explicitly articulated theological affirmation, but it is a widespread part of the meaning of communion for many.

A second, more theologically developed, understanding would see that communion either symbolizes or in some sense manifests how Jesus, through his death, offered a sacrifice to a needy God. This sacrifice satisfies God's holiness and allows

God to offer forgiveness. Communion may be seen as necessary for the Christian so the sacramental act covers us with the needed sacrifice and thus protects us from God's condemnation.

The psalmist, though, makes it clear in Psalm 50 that God is not needy. Simply offer God a sacrifice of *thanksgiving*. What God wants is gratitude for God's bounteous mercy. If we apply this message to our understanding of communion, we could say that communion is not something we do to gain God's favor. Rather, communion is an expression of gratitude for the favor God has *already*, *unconditionally*, granted us. The ritual is purely a ritual of thanksgiving. Of course, the thankful believer recognizes that if we truly know God's mercy and if we truly have the Spirit of God active in our hearts, we will share this mercy with others simply as part of our existence as healthy, God-oriented human beings.

Such thanksgiving *is* a transformative act with powerful ethical elements. The ritual serves as a reminder and a reinforcement. It is a public statement of our humanness as creatures in God's image who thrive best in loving relationships with God and our fellow human beings. The ritual also serves as a reminder that to be human before God is to resist and seek to overcome all the forces in the world that break relationships and oppress our fellow humans.

SORTING THROUGH THE SYMBOLS

So where does this cacophony of symbols (note, s-y-m-b-o-l-s!) leave us? Communion can symbolize God's mercy, God's empowerment for peacemaking, communities of generosity and support. Communion can also symbolize boundary lines between insiders and outsiders; communion can symbolize human efforts to find assurance that God is on *our* side.

Let me suggest this: No human ritual is in and of itself sacred. God is not to be evoked mechanistically, through the performance of some specific ritual that guarantees God's presence when the correct words are recited and the appropriately credentialed leaders officiate.

We could say, instead, that rituals *may* provide a context to be encouraged to love. We should see our practice of communion as continuing in the line of the biblical practices of keeping Torah, especially keeping the Sabbath. Jesus gave us definitive guidance when he asserted that human beings are not made for the Sabbath, but the Sabbath for human beings.

The purpose of the Sabbath from the start was to serve human well-being, not to be ritual that works as an end in itself. Sabbath observance began, according to the story, as a political statement: The Hebrews were free from slavery. After their liberation, they were to live as free people. To symbolize this freedom, they were to keep the Sabbath—a time for rest, communal fellowship, and worship of God. The ongoing practice of Sabbath observance meant to remind the people of God's mercy *and* of God's radical transformation of their social lives.

We may say the same thing about communion. Certainly for Christians, as well as for Jews, the radical memory of God's liberation in the exodus and creating the community of God's people as a light to the nations remains central. Complementing the memory of the exodus, Christians also point to the liberation effected by Jesus' life, death, and resurrection—liberation memorialized in the communion service.

So, I do not believe we should focus on communion as the ritualistic re-enactment of Jesus' death as a necessary sacrifice that brings about salvation by enabling God to offer forgiveness in a way God could not before. Rather, the Lord's Supper may better be linked with the liberation Jesus himself evoked when he talked about his impending death as a "ransom for many" (Mark 10:45). "Ransom" was used in the Old Testament as a metaphor for the liberation of God's people (see Exod. 6:6; 15:13; Isa. 43:1-7; 44:21-23).

Communion, as with Sabbath observance and Torah in general, best serves its purpose when understood as a human response to God's mercy. This response, like all life-fostering ritual, helps make concrete the experience of healing that God offers. This evocation of God's healing mercy is why we do well to hold the stories of Jesus feeding the multitudes and sharing meals with tax collectors and sinners together with the story of his sharing his "last supper" with his disciples.

The stories of these meals all add important dimensions to the meaning of our communion service. The feeding of the multitudes reminds us that Jesus indeed cares about actual food and actual hunger. And this care reflects his inviting disposition that compassionately welcomes all to hear his word and be nourished both spiritually and physically. By sharing meals with sinners, Jesus reminds us that he means to reach out to and welcome people on the margins. The "last supper" underscores the cost of following Jesus' way of mercy and justice. It is a reminder of his call to his followers to take up our crosses, sharing his life of resistance to tyrannies. It also points to the importance of a coherent community as the host for the ongoing remembrance of Jesus' message.

Ultimately, Jesus' message underscored the heart of the message of Torah. We have been noticing throughout this book the centrality of his great commandments to love God and neighbor. Let us remember Jesus' affirmation that these commandments summarize the core message of the law and prophets. This love is what Torah (and our rituals) should foster. As the Jewish theologian Abraham Heschel wrote, "Above all, the Torah asks for love—love of God and love of neighbor—and all observance is training in the art of love."[3] I believe that our task is to work at making the rituals work in this way.

EVOKING GOD'S PRESENCE IN SERVICE OF LOVE

How do we evoke God's presence in ways that serve the call to love? I don't think there is a set formula. But, as 1 John 4 helps remind us, we can count on God's presence as we do love.

> Beloved, let us love one another, because love is from God; everyone who loves is born of God and knows God. Whoever does not love does not know God, for God is love. God's love was revealed among us in this way: God sent his only Son into the world so that we might live through him. In this is love, not that we loved God but that he loved us and sent his Son to be the atoning sacrifice for our sins. Beloved, since God loved us so much, we also ought to love one another. No one has ever seen God; if we love one another, God lives in us, and God's love is perfected in us. (1 John 4:7-12)

Rituals serve the call to love when they make us aware of God's presence. With our doctrine of the Holy Spirit, we affirm that God is always everywhere present. But we don't always realize that. Rituals can *remind* us, open us up, and heighten our awareness.

This is basically what I understand "sacrament" to mean, some act that makes us aware of God's presence in ways that serve our call to love. Some have said that singing together is a quintessential Mennonite sacrament. Maybe potlucks are too. Certainly sharing generously with a person in need or finding reconciliation in the face of damaged relationships—these fit the definition of "sacrament."

Maybe then we could say that to live "sacramentally" is not so much about constantly sharing in official church rituals. Surely such rituals do have the potential to heighten our awareness of God's presence when practiced with care. More so, though, living sacramentally has a lot to do with openness to perceiving God in all our social interactions.

Sara Miles' book is full of examples of such sacramental living. She tells of one Friday at the food pantry. As is usually the case, she feels a bit overwhelmed at the needs represented by the several hundred hungry people and the stress of making sure everyone gets food in an orderly manner. She steps outside to catch a breath of air. Her coworker Paul spots her and sympathizes with her weariness.

Then two regular pantry clients spot Sara and Paul and come to say hello. "The two old women started over to us," Miles writes.

Miss Lewis came to the pantry weekly, took her food back to her room, and prepared it to share with homeless people. She shared greetings. Paul asked how everyone was. Miss Pollen replied that though she had a little flu, she was "blessed."

> Miss Lewis smiled at us all. "Are you thirsty?" she asked her friend. "You need to drink plenty of liquids. Wait a minute." She rummaged in her shopping cart and pulled out a bottle of cranberry-grape juice and a Dixie cup. "Here you go," she said, filling the cup for Miss Pollen.

Miles thinks to herself, *this* is the sacrament.[4]

Indeed. So if we use as our criterion for evaluating the validity of any particular sacrament the evoking of God's presence, we will embrace all acts that bring healing, reconciliation, renewed awareness of God, and love of neighbor as, in a meaningful sense, "sacramental." Religious rituals can and do evoke God's presence in these ways—and at times they do not.

When we think about sacraments as if Jesus matters, we will not privilege any particular rituals as "objectively" evoking God's presence simply because they are authorized by church hierarchies or because they follow certain prescribed formulas. All rituals and all other attempts to evoke God's presence face the same test. Do they help us love God and neighbor? Do they foster healing and reconciliation? Do they empower us to see Jesus and to follow in his way?

Sometimes formal Christian rituals (the traditional "sacraments") do pass this test—and sometimes they do not. Our challenge is always to hold together the life-giving elements with the ritualistic practices.

We should be thankful for those formal occasions that do indeed evoke God's presence, such as a "high church" communion service officiated by a duly authorized priest. Likewise, we should be thankful for those informal occasions that also evoke God's presence, such as when Sara Miles' friend Miss Lewis shares a cold drink with her other friend Miss Pollen.

When Jesus is our model and our central source, we will refuse to make a sharp distinction between these formal and informal occasions. They all face the same question (echoing Jesus' implied question of sabbath observance): Do they serve human beings or not?

Sacramental theology as if Jesus matters will refuse to assume that God's "real presence" always happens in the formal communion service. It will remember the prophetic critique of Amos and others that reminds us that formal religiosity without justice is an affront to God. Likewise, sacramental theology as if Jesus matters will refuse to delegate informal sharing of cups of cold water to less than sacramental status. If acts evoke God's presence, they are sacramental.

As we saw in our previous chapter, we do nonetheless recognize the importance of the church's ongoing existence. The organized church provides for the Christian faith's continuity, solidity, and practice of mutual accountability.

We should bother with the church as Christians because it can be, it should be, it *must* be (if it is to be faithful), a place where people work together to embody, to make real and concrete, the basic message of Jesus: Love God and neighbor. And as social creatures, we need other people to help us do this.

And as *ritualistic* creatures, we gain encouragement and a sense of coherence in our lives when we do have practices that concretely remind us of our convictions, our values, our sense of solidarity with one another, and our continuity with those who have gone before us. One such practice is our communion service. We do well to attend to this service, to be self-conscious about its meaning and its importance—and about its dangers.

We too easily let our core ritual become a "solemn assembly" in the sense that Amos (5:21) critiqued. Rather than evoking God's presence, such an "assembly" may actually obscure the reality of our *distance* from God stemming from our failure to embody Torah in our social lives. We too easily let our core ritual become a boundary marker that provides insiders with a sense of validation and exclusivity that undermines the welcoming message of Jesus.

However, when we do let the ritual serve human well-being, when we remember that God has placed us here—and sustains us here—so that we know and share God's love to the ends of the earth, then indeed we remember Jesus aright.

Bless All the Families of the Earth

[Theology of the Religions]

As we christians affirm the centrality of the church in spreading healing to the entire world, we still face many questions concerning our understanding of other religions. How do we think of Christian faith in relation to the world's other faith traditions?

A number of years ago, my wife Kathleen and I visited a Sunday school class in a large Mennonite congregation. The speaker was a member of the congregation who had just returned from a year in the Far East, and he was reporting on the experience. He talked about how he found the religious beliefs and practices that he had seen so interesting. He then told how he tried to encourage his new friends to be the best Buddhists (or it could have been Hindus) they could be.

I learned later that this comment caused a bit of a furor. People who believed that faith in Jesus as Savior is the *only* way to find salvation were distressed. The speaker's embrace of religious pluralism, his implied belief that any number of religions can lead a person to God, raised concerns.

RELIGIOUS PLURALISM AS A FACT OF LIFE

This issue of Christian faith in relation to other religions grows ever more challenging for Christians in our globalized world. Here in the United States, we can no longer avoid asking about different religions. Many of us travel around the world, doing business with people from many cultures and religious traditions, and, if nothing else, rub shoulders in grocery stores and ethnic restaurants with other-than-Christian religious folks.

I teach at a tiny Christian college in small, pretty isolated town in Virginia's Shenandoah valley. I have had students who are Muslim, Jewish, and Buddhist. Our favorite places to eat include restaurants operated by recent immigrants from Nepal, Vietnam, China, Thailand, India, El Salvador, Mexico, and Ethiopia. Our local public high school in 2006 had students from sixty-four different countries who spoke forty-four different languages—and represented many different faiths. Religious pluralism has become part of our everyday life, like it or not.

So, what do we think of the various religions of the world? How do we relate our own Christian faith to Buddhism, Islam, Hinduism, Judaism, and so on? How does our understanding of the religions fit with our broader theological convictions?

In my Introduction to Theology course, we spend several class periods discussing questions such as these. I ask the students to imagine a hypothetical person from Mongolia. This person is exemplary in every way, loving, kind, morally upright, active and faithful within her religious community. Then I ask them to imagine a similar American (perhaps someone they know) who is also exemplary in every way *and* an active and faithful Christian. The Mongolian has not heard of Jesus or Christianity—any more than many Americans have heard of the key faith commitments of more than a few of the world's many faith traditions. We assume the American is right with God—what about the Mongolian? . . . Often we then have a pretty lively discussion.

This discussion of the Mongolian, part of a bigger discussion of religious pluralism, comes near the end of the semester, after we have sketched out our understanding of basic Christian convictions. The idea is to apply our Christian convictions to the issue of religious pluralism. The Mongolian scenario is hypothetical, but the need to think about Christian faith in relation to other religions most definitely is not.

JESUS AND RELIGION

In reflecting on all these issues here, I want to return to the way I have addressed all of our theological topics in this book. Does it matter if, as we have done throughout this book, we think self-consciously of our theme here, the religions, as if Jesus matters? If we keep Jesus' hierarchy of values central, will doing so influence our approach to the issue of religious pluralism?

I suggest that, following Jesus, we should place at the center of this discussion the call to *love* God and to love our neighbors. We should focus our reflections more on serving Jesus' love command than on devoting our best energy to dividing lines between different religions.

In this light, one of my first thoughts is that we should recognize that the category *religion* is a *human* category. We seem to think that religions exist as fundamentally real things, rather than as labels we have created to try to place some kind of ordering framework on to our experiences. We do need such labels, but they are artificial, they exist only in our minds.

The universe does not explode when my friend Sallie identifies herself simultaneously as a Quaker and a Buddhist. The universe does not explode when my friend Dan has membership in a Jewish synagogue and in a Mennonite church—both at the same time.

John's Jesus did say, so famously, "I am the way, the truth, and the life, no one comes to the Father except through me" (John 14:6). But I don't think he meant to say that *Christianity* is the one true religion. I don't think he meant to say that a person must pass some kind of doctrinal test that clearly identifies one as a Christian and gives one a token to use for exclusive access to heaven after one dies. I don't think these words from Jesus were ever meant to negate his call to love our neighbors.

In fact, right after his statement about being "the way . . . to the Father," Jesus goes on to respond to Philip's request that Jesus would "show us the Father" by asserting that when the disciples saw Jesus they indeed saw the Father. Jesus' way of life is how he revealed to the world the character of God—in his works of love. He encourages his followers; they will do the same works (John 14:8-12).

I am not certain what precisely Jesus did mean by being "the way," but these words were spoken before Christianity even existed. So he couldn't have been talking about the religion Christianity. Perhaps a key point is to reflect on what it means to think of Jesus as "the way." What is the "way" Jesus tells us about?

He gives us a crucial criterion for discernment in a story from Mark's Gospel in which the Pharisees are angry because, they believe, Jesus' disciples are violating the Sabbath by plucking grain. But Jesus responds,

> "Have you never read what David did when he and his companions were hungry and need of food? He entered the house of God, when Abiathar was high priest, and ate the bread of the Presence, which is not lawful for any but the priests to eat, and he gave some to his companions." Then [Jesus] said to them, "The sabbath was made for humankind, and not humankind for the Sabbath; so the Son of man is lord even of the Sabbath." (Mark 2:23-28)

Jesus states that the Sabbath (a religious practice *par excellence*) is meant for human beings, not human beings for the Sabbath. Let me apply this thought to our thinking about religions. Viewed in light of Jesus' words, we could say that religious identity, religious practice, and religious faith are meant to serve human well-being. The "way" of Jesus as a religious leader, as the object of religious devotion, focuses on the question: Does our religiosity serve human well-being or not?

I suggest that our "God" is what we value most in life, what we orient our lives around, what rests at the top of our hierarchy of values. Theology reflects on and articulates the values and convictions that matter the most to us in life. "Christian" theology emerges when such reflection takes as its central set of criteria for evaluating our values the life and teaching of Jesus.

When I say "Christian theology" here, I have in mind what it *should* be, not simply what it is in practice. By "Christian" I mean something like Christ-follower, something that befits a follower of Jesus.

What about "religion," then? I would say that our religion has to do with the practices, rituals, and such that reflect and sustain our theology. I want to use Jesus' life and teaching as our criterion for discerning how Christian (or how befitting of Christ-followers) our religious practices are.

In my previous chapter, I wrote about sacraments as practices that make us aware of God's presence. Sacraments, in their best sense, help concretize God's fundamental disposition of mercy toward us. We shouldn't observe sacraments *to* gain God's favor. We observe sacraments *in response to* God's favor that has been given as a gift.

What are core Christian sacraments? If we link them with Jesus, we would say sacraments are practices that empower us to love God and neighbor. Sacraments remind us of God's love in ways that help us to love others. In his book *Body Politics*, John Howard Yoder discusses sharing food and possessions as being sacramental. Also, the practice of open conversation in the community that leads to decisions and policies that serve the community's well-being. Other "sacraments" for Yoder, in this sense, are the practices of forgiveness and reconciliation in the face of conflict.[1]

Hence, Christian theology is *not* an exercise in buttressing the human religion we call Christianity. Theology with Jesus as its center does not focus on religious structures, institutions, doctrines, and ideologies of exclusion. Rather, Christian theology has to do with reflection that empowers us to follow Jesus and his way of love of God and neighbor. Good theology empowers us by clarifying God's mercy for us and guiding our response embodied in our faith faithful living.

THE BIBLE AND JESUS' HIERARCHY OF VALUES

The Bible gives us a wide-angle look at Jesus' hierarchy of values. His core message was not esoteric, it was not out of the blue, and it was not an absolute departure from what went before. Jesus anchored his message directly in the broad message of the Bible, the message God had given to Israel through God's prophets. The Bible teaches that God desires peace (health and wholeness) for the whole world, that God has formed a people to know this peace and to share it with the rest of the world. The religion that God endorses embodies this teaching.

We see this basic message at the beginning of the story in Genesis 12. Just before these verses, we are introduced to

Abram and Sarah and told that Sarah was *barren*. God would change that condition.

> The Lord said to Abram, "Go from your country and your kindred and your father's house to the land that I will show you. I will make of you a great nation, and I will bless you, and make your name great, so that you will be a blessing. I will bless those who bless you, and the one who curses you I will curse; and in you all the families of the earth shall be blessed." (Gen. 12:1-3)

God shows mercy to the barren couple, gifting them with offspring. In doing so, God calls Abraham and Sarah to establish a community. Their descendants will carry the promise of God. God will, through these people who know God, bless all the families of the earth. We could understand this calling of Abraham as the beginning of a religion. However, these verses make clear that the purpose of this religious vocation had to do with "blessing all the families of the earth," not simply the edification of the chosen people. The religion here is centered on service toward others regardless of their religious affiliation.

The story continues with another founding moment. Following the journey of Abraham's descendents into slavery in Egypt, God liberates the people under the leadership of Moses. God then gives Moses an extended set of commands (Torah) to guide the people in their common life and to order their religious practices. These practices in some sense did have exclusive elements—setting the Hebrews over against the surrounding nations. However, at the beginning of the revelation of the commands, God reiterates the calling to Abraham and his descendents that includes the task of mediating God's love to the rest of the world.

> If you obey my voice and keep my covenant, you shall be my treasured possession out of all the peoples. Indeed, the whole earth is mine, but you shall be for me a priestly kingdom and a holy nation. (Exod. 19:5-6)

The priest's task includes serving as a channel of God's message to the wider world. God calls this "holy nation" to know God and to share that knowledge with, and thereby bless, all the families of the earth. The exclusiveness serves to protect the Hebrews from reverting to the unjust ways of the Egyptian empire. And, this distinctiveness should enable God's people to witness to God's way of peace in order ultimately to *bless* the nations.

Abraham's descendants do form a people who hear again, from the prophet Isaiah, about their vocation, in an echo of God's words to Abraham and Sarah.

> In the days to come the mountain of the Lord's house shall be established as the highest of the mountains. . . ; all the nations shall stream to it. Many . . . will say, "Come, let us go up . . . to the house of the God of Jacob; that he may teach us his ways and that we may walk in his paths." For out of Zion shall go forth instruction, and the word of the Lord from Jerusalem. He shall judge between the nations . . . ; they shall beat their swords into plowshares, and their spears into pruning hooks; nation shall not lift up sword against nation, neither shall they learn war any more. (Isa. 2:2-4)

The faithful religious practices of God's people will bring people from all the nations of the earth to learn the ways of peace. God's will for God's people is that they will lead the way in the conversion of swords into plowshares, of spears into pruning hooks. God's people are to help all the families of the earth break their addiction to violence and to study war no more.

This vision in Isaiah, which the prophet Micah also repeats word for word (4:1-4), does not speak of the "many peoples" converting to a different religion. The emphasis is on the ways of peace, the transformation of weapons of war into tools for peace.

Isaiah's "the word of the Lord," as mediated to the nations through Israel, has potency. This potency may be seen in the word's ability to bring social and political healing in a world all too often at war. The locus of the prophet's concern lay not with religion as an exclusive, closed community, but with changes in how people live—people from all over the world.

Jesus gives a similar message. Near the end of his ministry, he addresses themes of salvation and condemnation. Like with Isaiah, he focuses not on religious beliefs and membership but on practical living. He says that "When the Son of man comes in his glory" all the nations will gather before his throne and the king will invite those on his right to "Come, you that are blessed by my Father, inherit the kingdom prepared for you" because when he was hungry, thirsty, naked, a stranger, they gave him food, drink, clothing, and welcome.

> "Then the righteous will answer him, "Lord, when was it that we saw you hungry and gave you food, or thirsty and gave you something to drink? And when was it that we saw you a stranger and welcomed you, or naked and gave you clothing? And when was it that we saw you sick in prison and visited you?" And the king will answer them, "Truly I tell you, just as you did it to one of the least of these who are members of my family, you did it to me." (Matt. 25:31-40)

Jesus presents his message here in almost shocking terms (at least to those with doctrine-based, exclusivist theology who think what matters most is religious membership). Those who practice the kind of religion that unites them with God, those who inherit the kingdom, are the ones who give food, drink, welcome, clothing, caring to the sick and imprisoned.

The kicker here is that the faithful people don't even recognize the significance of their actions. It's not the overt acts of religiosity that matters here; it's the simple acts of caring. "Just as you did it to one of the least of these, you did it to me" (Matt. 25:40). In this parable, Jesus clearly subordinates explicit confessional religious practices to concrete ministry. Jesus does not picture an ethics-less religious universalism in which everyone finds God no matter what. However, he likewise does not picture an ethics-less religious exclusivism in which only those with the correct doctrine find God.

The distinction that matters for Jesus is not a distinction that separates religious traditions from each other. The separation Jesus speaks of follows from faithfulness in how we live. Ones who bless others with water and food when needed go with God. And those who do not. . . .

At the very end of the Bible, Revelation provides a concluding vision of the New Jerusalem, the fulfillment of God's healing promise, and finds the nations being healed—also clearly an echo of the original calling given Abraham and Sarah.

> Then I saw a new heaven and a new earth; for the first
> heaven and the first earth had passed away, and the sea
> was no more. . . . Then the angel showed me the river of
> the water of life, bright as crystal, flowing from the throne
> of God and of the Lamb through the middle of the street of
> the city. On either side of the river is the tree of life with its
> twelve kinds of fruit . . . and the leaves of the tree are for
> the healing of the nations. (Rev. 21:1; 22:1-2)

The kings of the earth, who are God's enemies throughout
the Bible, find *healing*. These former enemies bring their "glory"
into the circle of God's community. The witness made by those
who followed the Lamb's path of persevering love contributes
mightily to this final healing.

In these various passages, representative of numerous others that could also be cited, we have a clear message that the
religiosity that matters to the God of the Bible finds expression
in works of service and social transformation. This religiosity,
we could say in our context today, has little to do with formal
membership in any particular religious institution. Such membership has authenticity before God only insofar as it serves
the practices that truly matter: beating swords into plowshares,
giving water to the thirsty, offering food to the hungry.

Going back to Jesus' great commandment, such love of
neighbor is anchored in love of God. The call to mercy and compassion throughout the Bible clearly is anchored in knowing
that we are loved *by* God. We are not presented with a calling
to be "do-gooders" by force of our wills. We are called to trust
in our loving God and, as an outworking of this trust, to share
love with others in concrete, transformative ways in *this* life.

From these passages (representing the core message of the
Bible when read in light of Jesus) we see bases for understanding biblical faith to center more on acts of love and healing justice than on formal institutional confession and membership.
So, we may say that what matters most, biblically, about religion is that it serve human well-being. *This* service is our core
criterion—and provides the positive calling of all people of
faith. Understanding religion in this way does provide great
potential for mutuality among different organized religions.

Once consequence of this understanding of the Bible for
Christians is to perceive a *challenge* toward faithfulness—that

our religious practices conform to God's will. We run a high
risk of violating God's intentions for our faith communities
when we *center* on excluding access to God. Our task, instead,
is to center on the love and healing justice that our religious
practices should serve. When we do so, we will thereby bless
all the families of the earth.

RELIGIOSITY AND INJUSTICE

We may also see a shadow side to the Bible's call for our
religiosity to serve love and healing justice. This shadow side
is that all too often God's people have *failed* to let their religion
serve. To the contrary, all too often God's people have allowed
their religion to co-exist with, even, reinforce, *injustice*. We see
this concern clearly in the prophets.

The book of Isaiah begins with sharp words from the
prophet summarizing the core concerns not only of this
prophet but many others. This is the problem in a nutshell from
God's point of view: "I reared children and brought them up,
but they have rebelled against me." The "children" here, of
course are the children of Israel."The ox knows its owner, and
the donkey its master's crib; but Israel does not know, my people do not understand" (Isa. 1:2-3). These children "have for-
saken the Lord [and] despised the Holy One of Israel" (1:4).

> Why do you continue to rebel? The whole herd is sick, and
> the whole heart faint. From the sole of the foot even to the
> head, there is no soundness in it, but bruises and sores and
> bleeding wounds; they have not been drained, or bound
> up, or softened with oil. (1:6)

Isaiah then speaks of the destruction of the northern kingdom, Israel, at the hands of the Assyrian empire. "If the Lord
of hosts had not left us a few survivors, we would have been
like Sodom, and become like Gomorrah" (1:9).

The Lord emphasizes that the practice of sacrifices does
not outweigh the injustices.

> What to me is the multitude of your sacrifices? says the
> Lord; I have had enough of burnt offerings of rams and
> the fat of fed beasts; I do not delight in the blood of bulls,
> or of lambs, or of goats. . . . Trample my courts no more;

bringing offerings is futile; incense is an abomination to me. New moon and sabbath and calling of convocation—I cannot endure solemn assemblies with iniquity. (1:11-13)

When the unjust people offer their prayers and sacrifices, they will be of no value. God will not honor them. "When you stretch out your hands, I will hide my eyes from you; even though you make many prayers, I will not listen; your hands are full of blood."

The answer to move toward healing is not more religiosity, ritual observance, public worship. The way back in changing the way the people live. Put Torah into practice.

Wash yourselves; make yourselves clean; remove the evil of your doings from before my eyes; cease to do evil, learn to do good; seek justice, rescue the oppressed, defend the orphan, plead for the widow. (1:16-17)

Similar passages in Amos, Micah, Hosea, and Jeremiah, among others, also emphasize the blasphemy of religiosity that disregards practical love and justice. Perhaps the most famous example comes in the book of Amos. Amos sharply criticizes Israel for its blasphemous *combination* of social injustice and active religiosity. Because of the injustices, when Israel goes to worship, they actually reinforce their alienation from God.

Amos provides sarcastic directives to the people. Go to the religious services at Bethel and Gilgal—and *sin*, and *multiply* your sins (4:4). Simply the act of public worship is itself blasphemous and sinful when injustice prevails so blatantly in the wider society. Because of their injustices, God says, "I hate, I despise your festivals, and I take no delight in your solemn assemblies" (5:21).According to the prophets, the kind of religious practices that matter to God are caring for the needy and resisting injustice.

Jesus reiterates this message, criticizing exclusivist religiosity:

Woe to you, scribes and Pharisees, hypocrites! For you tithe mint, dill, and cumin, and have neglected the weightier matters of the law: justice and mercy and faith. It is these you ought to have practiced without neglecting the others. You blind guides! You strain out a gnat but swallow a camel! (Matt. 23:23-24)

These critiques demand that we recognize how dangerous religion can be. Religion may actually push us to rebel *against* God. So we should be very careful about setting our religion over against others as the "only true faith." Religion, to be acceptable to God, must *serve* mercy (not seek to monopolize it).

THE HEART OF TORAH (AND THE GOSPEL)

The heart of Torah, according to the prophets and Jesus, may be found in the concern for serving others and opposing oppression and injustice. These are the commitments that religious faith and religious practices are to serve. Consequently, Jesus and the prophets surely provide a basis for Christians making common cause with people of other faiths who also are committed to caring for others and opposing oppression and injustice.

The Bible places the highest priority on such commitments more so than on fostering religiously sanctioned boundary lines that imply that formal religious affiliation matters more to God than works of love. The prophets at times do emphasize the need for boundary lines—but for the sake of protecting faithfulness to Torah's message of justice, mercy, and shalom over against the injustices of surrounding empires.

We see the emphasis on works of love when we return to that well-known passage from Luke central to theology done as if Jesus matters. This story of the "Good Samaritan" captures the general message of all these other texts.

> A lawyer stood up to test Jesus. "Teacher," he said, "what must I do to inherit eternal life?" [Jesus] said to him, "What is written in the law? What do you read there?" [The lawyer] answered, "You shall love the Lord your God with all your heart, and with all your soul, and with all your strength, and with all your mind; and your neighbor as yourself." And [Jesus] said to him, "You have given the right answer; do this, and you will live." (Luke 10:25-28)

Jesus was asked about eternal life. How is this found? The gospels tell of only one other occasion of Jesus being asked this same question. That time Jesus' answer first summarized the commandments then zeroed in on an ethical demand: "Sell all that you own and distribute the money to the poor" (Luke 18:18-25). Here in Luke 10, Jesus' answer also summarizes the law and the prophets. Love the Lord your God and love your neighbor. That's it, in a nutshell. "Eternal life" is not about membership in an exclusive religion nor about correct creeds. It's about being loved and loving others in return.

The story does not end there. Jesus needs to spell out in a more pointed way what he means by love of God and neighbor. Jesus' questioner presses him. So *who* is my neighbor? That is, "Isn't this what we all do, love our neighbors who share our same religious practices and practice formal worship of God?" Jesus' answer could not be more radical. He tells the story of the Jewish man traveling to Jericho who is mugged, robbed, and left for dead. Several people pass him by, including leaders of his own religion. It seems quite likely that these religious leaders placed a higher priority on the avoidance of impurity than on compassion.

Then, unexpectedly, the beaten man is helped and his life saved by the extraordinary generosity of a traveling merchant. Jesus' story makes it clear: The neighbor is the person who especially needs your help.

There's more to it, though. The exemplary neighbor who shows what Jesus has in mind (the one who finds salvation!) is not even a Jew. He's not a part of the religion of Jesus and his listeners. Jesus makes clear that saving faith that finds expression in works of mercy is available to all people of good will. It does not follow from formal membership in any particular religion. In fact, the people who are "members" of the correct religion in this story fail to help the person in need. That is, they are not neighbors; they disobey Torah's most important commandment.

Jesus takes it even farther. The person who models neighborliness in this story not only is not a member of the correct religion; he is a member of the most incorrect religion imaginable to Jesus' listeners. He's a Samaritan, their sworn enemy. The saved person in Jesus' story is the one who does genuine justice, the one who loves his neighbor—not the card-carrying member of the correct religion.

Now, let's think back to the core text for those arguing for Christianity's exclusive truthfulness, John 14:6. In light of this story of the Good Samaritan, would we be willing to go so far as to see this story as an explanation of Jesus' famous saying about being the way, truth, and life? Is the "one way" to God that he proclaims in fact the way of the Samaritan in this story?[2]

When Jesus asserts that he is the way, the *only* way to God, could he be actually asserting that this "way" is precisely the way followed by the "good Samaritan"? Is the Samaritan giving evidence of his own love of God by his actions? Are any who practice that kind of costly, risky love for others in need in fact following this one way to God? I don't think we can answer these questions "yes" with absolute certainty. However, such a possibility certainly seems consistent with Jesus' own life. Jesus' words in John 14 make this clear when he follows up his statement about being the "one way" with asserting that the "works" he did will be the same as his followers will be empowered to do—in this way revealed the Father.

Not only is the possibility that the "one way" Jesus revealed had to do with his kind of costly, risky love for other consistent with Jesus' own life; the one way is also consistent with important teachings in the rest of the Bible (including Old Testament).

Jesus' attitude toward religion seems to center on its danger. Religious practices can (and *should*) serve human well-being. However, often they do not. Too often and too easily, religious people (including Christians) imitate the Levite in the Good Samaritan story and simply pass by people in need. Jesus, in the context of the entire message of the Bible, challenges his followers to find inspiration in texts such as Isaiah 2:2-4; Matthew 25:31-40; and Revelation 22:1-2. Our task is not to focus on boundary lines that separate us from other religions. Rather, our task is to witness to the ways of peace to bring healing to the nations.

One of the big tragedies of Christian exclusivism and its focus on formal religion over Jesus' values is how blatant so much Christian history and so many present Christian practices are in contradicting the message of these Bible passages.

Christians, especially American Christians, are all too often a *curse* to the families of the earth, not a blessing. Christians all too often *fuel* warfare rather than teaching against it. Christians all too often *benefit from* the building of swords and spears rather than transforming them into plowshares and pruning hooks. Christians all too often *reject* strangers rather then welcome them, all too often *isolate and punish* prisoners rather than befriend them, all too often *privatize* water supplies rather than give water to the thirsty.

These kinds of things are possible when we do theology as if Jesus does not matter, as if love of neighbor is something optional, something peripheral in our theology, at most an add-on after we get our basic doctrine right.

Ultimately, I believe we need to confess uncertainty about the fate of people such as my hypothetical Mongolian. Those of us who have decided to follow Jesus and his way do so because we are convinced that his way is *true*—not that it's only one valid option among many. Our uncertainty, though, arises because the way of Jesus is an approach to life—Jesus values love of neighbor much more highly than formal religious affiliation. The Bible makes it clear that "correct" religious affiliation is no guarantee of faithfulness.

How do we understand this inextricable link between "loving God" and "loving neighbor"? Let me suggest, on the basis of the biblical emphases I've summarized in this chapter, that we should see in people loving their neighbors evidence that they are also genuinely loving God. Such love, when unaccompanied by overt trust in Jesus, does not make a person a Christian. We have good reasons to believe, though, that such love does reflect harmony with God. We may wonder whether this harmony might not ultimately be more important than formal religious affiliation.

A couple of years ago, I had the privilege of speaking at a conference on religion and peace. I was profoundly affected by what happened there. I have not had a lot of experience seriously interacting with people of faith from other religious traditions. The content of the papers both inspired and challenged me.

We each prepared our papers independently of each other. But what happened is that three of us, the Buddhist, the Muslim, and I (the Christian) all gave pretty much the same paper! We followed similar outlines, talking about the core peace convictions present at the founding of our traditions and how those have been marginalized in later developments. The Jewish speaker did not follow this same outline, but his presentation reflected a similar understanding. And numerous speakers drew directly on the Hindu convictions of Mahatma Gandhi.

I have to conclude from this experience—and from the Bible's message—that Jesus' values, the core stuff of Christian theology, provide a clear call for us to join hands with peaceable people from all faiths. We all share a calling to transform swords into plowshares.

If we understand ourselves as having a core calling as followers of Jesus to love our neighbors, shouldn't we rejoice whenever anyone practices such love—and join hands with them?

The End Times Are Now

[The Doctrine of Eschatology]

*I*N MOST SURVEYS OF CHRISTIAN THEOLOGY, the concluding topic
is "eschatology," often called the doctrine of the "end times."
This book will be only somewhat different in that it will close
with some ethical reflections. Our final doctrine, though, will
be eschatology.

Every two years, I am allowed to teach a class called "Topics in Christian Theology." This is a genuine privilege that not
all faculty at our school receive. It is a chance to teach on whatever subject I want without having to go through a process of
gaining approval for a new course. In the past I have taught
classes of great interest to me, such as "Violence and Human
Nature" and "Vengeance and God."

As a consequence of writing this book, I decided that the
next time I teach my topics course, I want to do a class I will
call "The End Times." Now, I have to confess that I may be a
little devious in using this title. I expect to attract some students who want a class that will discuss the *Left Behind* scenar-
ios—when's the Rapture going to be? When exactly is Christ
coming back? When and how is all that biblical prophecy going
to be fulfilled?

Such students, when they take the End Times bait, might
be disappointed when I do a kind of switch and propose a different view of eschatology. The class will indeed be on "eschatology," the doctrine of the end times. But it will be eschatology in light of Jesus, not eschatology in light of our fortune-

telling curiosity. I will present a different take on eschatology than the future-prophetic views so popular with TV preachers and best-selling "contemporary Christian" books.

WHAT IS OUR PURPOSE?

I approach eschatology in the same way I have the other core convictions in the rest of this book on "theology as if Jesus matters." I believe that authentic Christian theology is about gaining clarity on our values. What matters the *most* for us who seek to follow Jesus? The values that shape our actual lives reveal more than anything else what our "God" is like.

If we look at Jesus' own life and teaching, we won't find a clearer statement of his hierarchy of values than his concise summary of the law and prophets: You shall love the Lord your God with all your heart, mind, and soul—and, likewise, you shall love your neighbor as you love your own self. This love of God and neighbor (and we must keep in mind how broadly Jesus defined "neighbor": our neighbors include our enemies) is why we are alive. It is what matters the most. That is to say, the "end" that matters is our *purpose* for being here, not any knowledge we might think we have about future events. Our *purpose* is to love—that purpose is the eschatological theme that is central if we do eschatology as if Jesus matters.

In the Bible (and, I want to propose, for us today) the best reason for talking about the "end of the world" and the "end times" is *not* to focus on what is going to happen to the world in the future. Rather, to talk about the "end of the world" biblically points us to the *purpose* of the world. Or, more directly, our purpose for living in the world.

The word *end*, of course, can have two different meanings. (1) "End" means the conclusion, the finish, the last part, and the final outcome. In this sense, "the end of the world" is something future and has to do with the world ceasing to exist. (2) "End" also, though, means the purpose, what is desired, and the intention. "End of the world," in this sense, is, we could say, what God *intends* the world to be for. Why is the world here and why are we here and what are we to be about? In this sense of "end," the end times have to do with *why* we live *in* time, here and now.

PROBLEMS WITH FOCUSING ON THE FUTURE

In the years right after I became a Christian as a teenager, I thought of the end times strictly in terms of the future and how things will conclude. I looked for the return of Christ soon—and would have been shocked to know I'd still be living in the twenty-first century.

When I was in college in the mid-1970s, I seriously contemplated dropping out. Why should I work at preparing for the future when the future wasn't going to come? In those days, I welcomed the development of nuclear weapons, the conflicts in the Middle East, and the likelihood of war with the Soviet Union and possibly also China. I welcomed wars and rumors of wars. These problems all meant that the second coming was at hand. The "end of the world" was coming soon, and in that I rejoiced.

At some point, though, I realized that what I would be welcoming, actually, was incredible human suffering and the destruction of created life, unprecedented death and bloodshed. I welcomed, in a word, extreme *evil*. And, I understood God to be the agent of this evil. In this view, God's purposes could only be worked out if God killed human beings and other living creatures on an unimaginable level.

When my eyes were opened, I recoiled at my old worldview. But it has taken many years since then to further think through these issues and decide that I don't need to reject the Bible's understanding of the end of the world. Rather, I need to reject the Bible-reading lenses I was given as a young Christian.

I do not fully understand how this view of the end of the world as its *destruction* came to dominate Christian thinking. However, as with many problems in the "Christian" worldview (such as seeing God as punitive, supporting so-called just wars, and viewing human beings as corrupted by original sin), I suspect that the "Doctor of the Church," Augustine of Hippo, had something to do with it.

Augustine's great fifth-century book was *The City of God*. He links Greek philosophy with biblical theology and comes up with a notion of heaven (the "city of God") as something *outside* of time and history, future, otherworldly. This city, "heaven," is sharply distinguished from the world we live in, from historical life in the here and now (the "city of man"). For

Augustine, life in history is characterized by brutality, sinfulness, and the struggle for power.

We have thus a disjunction between heaven and life in the here and now. This split between heaven and history led to a notion of Christian hope that focused, in effect, on the destruction of this world. Genuine salvation requires an escape from this life to heaven and eternity and something totally different and separate.

As Augustine's follower Thomas Hobbes wrote during the seventeenth century, life on earth is "nasty, brutish, and short." The end of the world is coming (thank God), and the sooner the better. It is tragically ironic that the worldview that looks to the future for salvation and achievement of heaven tends in the present to justify violence and punishment and domination—and to use the Bible to support all of this.

Such a worldview fosters a self-fulfilling prophecy. Since we believe that life in the here and now is nasty, brutish, short, violent, we act to make it so—as Augustine and so many other Christians since have in supporting death-dealing violence toward heretics, pagans, and criminals.

CHANGING OUR LENSES

Well, what if we change our lenses? What if we look at the Bible and at the world differently? What if we could realize that our key question is not about the future destruction of the world but about our purpose here and now? What if we looked at the Bible with new eyes, watching for what it tells us about the purpose of the world rather than how the world will end at any moment?

Let's look at some biblical texts that provide a glimpse. Psalm 46 was Martin Luther King Jr.'s favorite passage in the Bible. We can see why.

> God is our refuge and strength, a very present help in trouble. Therefore, we will not fear, though the earth should change, though the mountains shake in the heart of the sea; though its waters roar and foam, though the mountains tremble....
> There is a river whose streams make glad the city of God, the holy habitation of the Most High.... The nations

are in an uproar, the kingdoms totter; God utters his voice, the earth melts. The Lord of hosts is with us; the God of Jacob is our refuge.

Come, behold the works of the Lord; see what desolation he has brought on the earth. God makes wars cease to the end of the earth; he breaks the bow, and shatters the spear; he burns the shields with fire. "Be, still and know that I am God! I am exalted among the nations, I am exalted in the earth." The Lord of hosts is with us; the God of Jacob is our refuge.

God is our strength—and we need not fear even though "the mountains shake in the heart of the sea." God is present; God's city is in history. For the people of God, wars cease. God destroys the weapons of war. The "end times" are the times for God's city, the people of God, to embrace the ways of peace—right now, in this life.

Isaiah 2 also presents a picture of the purpose (or "end") of history.

In days to come the mountain of the Lord's house shall be established as the highest of the mountains, and shall be raised above the hills; all the nations shall stream to it. Many peoples shall come and say, "Come, let us go up to the mountain of the Lord, to the house of the God of Jacob; that he may teach us his ways and that we may walk in his paths." For out of Zion shall go forth instruction, and the word of the Lord from Jerusalem. He shall judge between the nations, and shall arbitrate for many peoples; they shall beat their swords into plowshares, and their spears into pruning hooks; nation shall not lift up sword against nation, neither shall they learn war any more. (Isa. 2:2-4)

God calls together a people to form communities in history, in this world. This people witnesses to all the nations of the world. God's people must teach genuine peace, genuine justice, genuine mercy. Isaiah's vision promises that when God's people truly teach peace to the nations, swords will be transformed into plowshares and nations will learn war no more.

This same vision is repeated in Revelation when John of Patmos sees a vision of heaven and earth transformed.

I saw no temple in the city, for its temple is the Lord God the Almighty and the Lamb. And the city has no need of sun or moon to shine on it, for the glory of God is its light, and its lamp is the Lamb. The nations will walk by its light, and the kings of the earth will bring their glory into it. Its gates will never be shut by day—and there will be no night there. People will bring into it the glory and the honor of the nations. (Rev. 21:22-26)

The city of human self-will and domination, called "Babylon," is transformed. It becomes a new city where God truly is worshiped. And the nations and the kings of the earth join in this worship. Those who had rebelled against God are healed—through the witness of the Lamb and people of faith who follow the Lamb wherever he goes.

These three passages unite in insisting that the "end times" of healing are for now. People of faith are called to make the "end times" present in this world, in this history. People of faith are called to serve the God who makes wars cease and who purposes to heal (not destroy) the rebellious nations.

A STRATEGY FOR READING THE BOOK OF REVELATION

Looking through lenses that help us see the end times of healing being present may especially transform the way we perceive the book of Revelation, which is usually seen as the book of the Bible most concerned with end times. It has the reputation of being about whistles and bells, great drama, the shattering of the old and forceful entry of the new.

Many people welcome these visions, reading Revelation to predict a bloody future period of Tribulation that could begin at any time. This tribulation is to be welcomed as part of God's work to bring ultimate salvation (for some) and condemnation (for others). Wars and rumors of wars, the likelihood of a nuclear holocaust, these were all foretold in Revelation; let's praise God when they happen. This is the message of Hal Lindsey's *The Late, Great Planet Earth* (the best selling of all books published in the U.S. during the 1970s).[1] This is the message of Tim LaHaye's phenomenally popular *Left Behind* books.

Other people also read Revelation as being about violence, catastrophe, and the shattering end of life as we know it—but they are appalled by these visions. Jonathan Kirsch, a writer for the *Los Angeles Times*, wrote a bestselling "exposé" of Revelation called *A History of the End of the World*. He characterizes the core message of Revelation in this way:

> The moral calculus of Revelation—the demonization of one's enemies, the sanctification of revenge taking, and the notion that history must end in catastrophe—can be detected in some of the worst atrocities and excesses of every age, including our own. For all of these reasons, the rest of us ignore the book Revelation only at our impoverishment and, more to the point, at our own peril.[2]

Both Lindsey and Kirsch read Revelation looking for it to contain a message of violence, severe judgment, and condemnation for God's human enemies. I want to suggest a reading of Revelation that follows from looking for something else. [3]

We *are* well-advised, I think, to read Revelation looking for guidance as we live amid wars and rumors of war, imperial violence, and threats to creation itself. However, we need to take with utmost seriousness Revelation's place in the New Testament, and in the Bible as a whole. The message of the Bible finds its sharpest and clearest expression in these brief words of Jesus: "Love the Lord your God with all your heart and love your neighbor as yourself."

I believe we best read Revelation looking for confirmation of Jesus' words. We should look for inspiration to make those words the center of our response to the world around us. We seek a sense of hope that as we follow Jesus' command and (like he did) face strong resistance from the powers that be in our societies God will not abandon us. When we read Revelation thus, we will be able to make sense, the best sense, of the "words of this prophecy" (1:3).

What we find in Revelation truly does depend on *how* we see. I think of the little Christmas story attributed to Leo Tolstoy about a character called Papa Panov. Panov had a dream the night before Christmas that on the next day he would see the Christ child. He expected to encounter the mighty and wonderful Baby Jesus of his pious imagination.

Throughout the day as he awaits the Christ child, he meets many people, a number of them in need—a young mother, a hungry transient. The kind and generous Panov cares for each person who crosses his path, all the time awaiting the exciting entry of Baby Jesus. As time passes, he begins to wonder, but that does not stop his generosity and kindness.

Then the day ends, and he goes to bed saddened. In his dream, though, the reality of the Christ child is revealed to him: "Just as you did it to one of the least of these who are members of my family, you did it to me" (Matt. 25:40).[4]

This call to look for Jesus around us is consistent with what's actually going on in Revelation, I think. Now we do need to pay attention to the crazy and at times overwhelming visions in Revelation. But we must not let them distract us from the basic message of the book. And we are given important clues to this message right away in the opening verses.

> The revelation of Jesus Christ, which God gave him to show his servants what must soon take place; he made it known by sending his angel to his servant John, who testified . . . to all that he saw. . . .
>
> John to the seven churches that are in Asia: Grace and peace from him who is and who was and who is to come, and from the seven spirits who are before his throne, and from Jesus Christ, the faithful witness, the firstborn of the dead, and the ruler of the kings of the earth. To him who loves us and freed us from our sins by his blood, and made us to be a kingdom of priests serving his God and Father, to him be glory and dominion forever and ever. Amen.

We are told at the get go that this book is "the revelation of *Jesus Christ.*" So, whatever else we think we see here, it all needs to be oriented back to this original point. How do these visions help reveal Jesus Christ?

Now, we could be like apocalyptic versions of Papa Panov, looking for visions of the all-conquering, overwhelmingly violent Christ coming in the clouds to dominate his enemies and reward his friends. Such visions often link with a sense that the best motivation for becoming Christ's friend is fear of eternal torture in the fires of hell. And fundamentalists like Hal Lindsey and skeptics like Jonathan Kirsch find plenty of supportive visions in Revelation for this view.

However, what if we look for something different, something that helps us love our neighbor and have confidence that such love goes with the grain of the universe and is worth suffering for? What will we then find?

Drop down to 1:5, our first description of Jesus. This is part of John's opening confession, "grace and peace" from the One who is, was, and is to come, from the seven spirits, and from Jesus Christ. Notice how Jesus is described: "the faithful witness, the firstborn of the dead, and the ruler of the kings of the earth," who "freed us by" his self-sacrifice. The term "faithful witness" could also be translated "faithful martyr." The Greek word is *matrys*; it has the clear sense of Jesus' faithful life embodying love of neighbor that led to his execution by the Romans. From the start, we have an image of the suffering servant, the faithful witness to God's love who came to care for others.

The victory that matters, the one affirmed at the start and, as it turns out, throughout the book, is won by Jesus' "blood." The victory is won by Jesus' willingness to remain faithful to the ways of love and compassion. He remained faithful even to the point of execution by a state that stood against such love and compassion when it challenged the state's status quo.

Revelation portrays two distinct kinds of "victory" or "conquering." John emphasizes this key theme throughout the book. Jesus "conquers" through self-sacrificial love. The Roman Empire, the powers-that-be of John's day, conquers through domination. Writers such as Hal Lindsey and Jonathan Kirsch, opposed to one another as they may be in terms of their own politics and religion, stand together in misinterpreting the meaning of the visions of violence and catastrophe in Revelation. Ultimately, these visions expose the evil of the Beast, the Roman Empire, all empires (including the American Empire). The wars and rumors of war reflect the *opposite* of God's will.

From start to finish, the "faithful servant" (the Lamb) takes the central role. Through his faithfulness, this "faithful servant" reveals authentic power and thereby is confessed as "ruler of the kings of the earth," the one who thus reveals God's will.

I will mention two visions of Jesus in Revelation that confirm that this book reveals Jesus the suffering servant, not Jesus the conquering avenger.

In Revelation 5, John weeps because he does not believe that anyone will be found who can open the scroll that contains the message of the consummation of history. He is told not to weep, someone has been found. So this is the key moment, really, of the entire book. Who is worthy to open the scroll? John *hears*, mighty, conquering king. But what does he *see* (again, the key element of sight, of revelation)? He sees a Lamb, standing (that is, resurrected) as if slaughtered (that is, executed by crucifixion). *This* Lamb, who conquered through persevering love, can open the scroll and therefore is worthy to be praised by all creation.

A second climactic moment comes in Revelation 19. For some time in the book, we read of anticipations of a great final battle, the "battle of Armageddon." All the armies of the powers-that-be gather for this battle. In the book-of-Revelation-as-violent reading, this is the key moment in the entire book. However, in the Revelation-as-revelation-of-Jesus reading, we see something different when we get to the "battle scene." The savior rides forth on a white horse, as if to battle. But he is armed only with a sword coming out of his mouth, the word of proclamation of the good news of God's love. And before he gets to the "battle," he is clothed in "a robe dipped in blood" (19:13)—that is, his blood has already been shed.

The act that frees us and wins the battle is Jesus' faithfulness to the point of execution, vindicated by God's raising him from the dead. And this has *already* happened. The "Battle of Armageddon" is simply a matter of the Powers of evil being gathered up and thrown into the lake of fire. And—a reference missed by the Revelation-as-violent interpreters—the kings of the earth (the paradigmatic enemies of God throughout the book) do not end up in the lake of fire but rather in the New Jerusalem itself (21:24). Jesus' victory—won by his love—results not in the punishment of human enemies but in their healing.

The book of Revelation has big hopes. It portrays the fall of Babylon. I understand this to be a dream of the end of systems of domination, of nations pouring their wealth (and their children) down the rathole of militarism, of economics that impoverish the billions and destroy the earth for the sake of further enriching the already rich. In hoping for the fall of Babylon, Revelation also hopes for the *healing* of Babylon's human apologists. The generals and capitalists and presidents who do the Beast's bidding are themselves in bondage to evil Powers. When those Powers are destroyed, their human servants are freed. The kings of the earth find healing. This is what Revelation hopes for.

And Revelation hopes for a transformed earth and a transformed heaven. There, drawing on other biblical imagery, the lamb and lion rest together; weapons of war are beat into tools for cultivating the earth; the boots of tramping warriors are burnt.

This message of hope is crucial in understanding the revelation of Jesus Christ that John reports in this book. But what truly matters for us is to recognize how these goals are attained. The *means* to these goals, the outcomes the book points to and all followers of the Lamb hope for, are all achieved through the self-sacrificial love of the Lamb. The "conquering" that achieves authentic victory throughout Revelation happens only through the power of consistent love. Jesus' faithful witness and God's nonviolent vindication through resurrection are what conquer.

Throughout the book, John's readers are exhorted in only one direction. They are not to fight the Beast's violence with violence of their own. They are not to seek to conquer the Beast using his methods. They have a very simple but extraordinarily challenging calling: Follow the Lamb wherever he goes.

John does not give us predictions about the future that stimulate us to pray for wars and rumors of war. John certainly does not intend to drive us to label our human enemies as subhuman in a way that justifies violence against them. John wants us to realize that we need each other and that human beings and our communities are the center of the action in the big drama he portrays.

God's answer to the chaos and violence the Powers have unleashed on earth is to form small peaceable communities that know God's love, experience it in their common life, and share this love throughout the world—with the ultimate outcome of the conversion of the kings of the earth (21:24) and the healing of the nations (22:2).

OUR END IN LIGHT OF JESUS

The distinctively Christian element of Christian eschatology is to be seen in it being centered on Jesus' life and teaching. Eschatology is best understood as the study of deep reality, of the ultimate nature and purpose of things—with the understanding that this includes both where we have come from and where we are going.

Christian eschatology asserts that history is best understood in terms of Jesus' way of love, compassion, openness, critique of power politics, and obedience to God. This way of Jesus is understood to be the purpose of human life.

For Christians, our understanding of the future is in full continuity with our understanding of the past. That is to say, we understand the meaning of deep reality by considering God's revelation in Jesus. Christians confess that God is *fully* revealed in Jesus in that there will be no new revelation that is in tension with God as revealed in Jesus.

Christian eschatology is "realized eschatology" in the sense that the Christ-event *has* shown God's victory. In Jesus' way of life, Jesus' faithfulness even to the death, God raising Jesus from death, God has shown the world the nature of God's will for human life. God's love is more powerful even than death.

Our hope, then, is founded on what God *has* done. Our hope is founded on who God has already been revealed to be. This point about the ultimacy of what God has already done is reflected in Jesus' story of "the rich man and Lazarus " (Luke 16:19-31). Jesus responds to the plea of the rich man that God send his brothers some new revelation to get them to turn from their unbelief. Jesus responds with a statement of realized eschatology—"they have Moses and the prophets." As Christians, we would add, "we also have Jesus," and that that is all we need. There will be no *new* bases for hope.

When the book of Revelation portrays the final "battle" between Jesus and the forces of evil, it turns out that there will actually *not* be a future battle. Jesus rides forth to battle in Revelation 19 having already shed his blood. There is no further battle; Jesus simply captures his enemies and throws them into the Lake of Fire. The only "battle" Jesus ever fought came during the final days of his life when his faithfulness to the death led to his being raised, winner of the battle of the ages.

Our hope is based ultimately on two points: (1) Do we trust that Jesus fully reveals God? (2) Do we trust that in raising Jesus from the dead, God insured that life and love continue victorious over death and evil?

The Bible's portrayal of eschatology as being present-oriented, not future-oriented, may also be seen in how "prophecy" is understood biblically. Primarily, prophecy in the Bible is a matter of the prophet receiving a message from God that provides insight into the *present* of the prophet.

When biblical prophets refer to the future, they do not make ironclad predictions so much as issue warnings that challenge their listeners in the present toward faithfulness. In general, these warnings take two forms—they can warn of negative consequences should the people not change their ways and turn from their unfaithfulness. Or, they can promise healing to come with the implicit warning that those who do not seek God will miss out on the healing.

The writer of Revelation names his treatise "prophecy." Revelation is best understood primarily as prophecy in the sense of challenging people of its own time to faithful living. For example, Revelation's readers are challenged to follow the Lamb wherever he goes and not to conform to the values of the Roman Empire (Babylon). Revelation is not best understood as prophecy in the sense of predicting the future in a way that would not have made sense to its writer or first readers.

The Bible's prophetic message does contain strong eschatological content in the sense of giving us necessary information about the ultimate meaning of reality. Jesus is Lord. We are to follow his way no matter what. Death cannot defeat those who trust in the Risen One as the definitive revelation of God. The eschatological message of the Bible affirms that God's faithfulness to God's ways of mercy and justice will continue. We can stake our lives on this. We do not know the time or day for the completion of God's healing work. We never will know this ahead of time. Our call simply is to be faithful all the time.

The content of biblical prophecy does "reveal" to us insights into the nature of reality. It helps us to discern our idolatries. It challenges us to make Jesus' values our values in all areas of life. biblical prophecy reveals to us that Jesus' way must shape all of our commitments.

Typically, discussions of eschatology consider issues related to "heaven," "hell," and "judgment." "Heaven," biblically, is best understood as the spiritual element of the world. Heaven is where God is known to be present. It is an element of historical reality, part of this world. Heaven is not atemporal, the realm of eternity in contrast to the finitude of everyday life.[5]

As part of this world, heaven, for the time being, does contain evil. This is reflected in various biblical stories that portray Satan in God's presence (such as Job). Heaven is the spiritual dimension of life—both for good and for evil. Revelation teaches that heaven will be transformed just as the rest of reality will be ("the new heaven and the new earth"). The spiritual forces of evil, abiding in heaven now, will be destroyed according to Revelation. When they are destroyed (thrown into the Lake of Fire, Rev. 20:10), according to the New Jerusalem vision in Rev. 21–22, the unity of heaven and earth will be fully seen.

In this understanding, "heavenly awareness" is the opposite of "otherworldliness." Rather, heavenly awareness means spiritual sensitivity concerning our present, historical existence. Heavenly awareness is seeing the unity of all life and the presence of God in everything—there is nowhere that God is not.

"Hell" is to be understood as existence apart from God. Hell is total alienation from the goodness of life. It is emptiness and lifelessness. As in heaven, hell is historical, the experience in life of deadness and separation from God. According to the vision in Revelation, the powers of evil will be "destroyed" with the coming of the New Heaven and New Earth. The newness is portrayed as the full revelation of reality as it is meant to be—without the alienation and brokenness that leads to hell on earth. Revelation 20 envisions a time when death and Hades and the Dragon, the Beast, and the False Prophet will be no more.

"Judgment" is part of the experience of human beings with God in the world. The Bible ultimately portrays God as loving everyone and desiring that each and every person be with God in heaven. According to the vision of the New Jerusalem in Revelation 21 and 22, the way to salvation, to joining with God, is always open to all ("the gates to the New Jerusalem are always open"). However, the Bible also clearly portrays this joining with God as something human beings must *choose*. The existence of hell is a necessary consequence of human beings having the power to make such a choice as a genuine choice. That is, human beings must have the power to choose "no."

What happens when the New Jerusalem "comes" and hell is "destroyed"? Logically, it would appear that those who have chosen against God would also be destroyed (an idea supported by Revelation 20:15). However, many Christians are uncomfortable with the idea that an all-loving God whose main power is persevering love would "give up" on particular human beings. Can human obstinacy outlast God's love? Is there a way to be a universalist without negating human freedom? Can God be loving toward a person and then destroy that person?

The practical issue for present-day Christians, it seems to me, is that our message must be one of God's love, not of fear of God's anger. Life with God is based on our "yes" to God, our trust, our turning from sinfulness and toward God, our acceptance of Jesus' way. Along with this affirmation also comes the awareness that there are natural consequences to saying "no."

In Luke 16, Jesus told the story of the rich man and Lazarus, at least in part to say that all his listeners need to know about what matters in life has already been revealed. They don't need some apocalyptic terror. They don't even need someone to return from the dead. In fact, if they don't learn from Moses and the prophets what matters most, they likely won't recognize any other revelation for what it is. What do Moses and the prophets teach? Love God and neighbor. That love is our true end. We can, we must, practice such love right now, in *this* life. It is as people living in history that God loves and heals us.

13

....

Do This and Live

[The Doctrine of the Christian Life (Ethics)]

W E BEGAN THIS BOOK ASKING THE QUESTION, What is theology? I have made the case that *theology* has to do with our hierarchy of values. What are the things that we believe are most important in life—and how are these priorities expressed in our actual lives? We have looked at the central themes of Christian theology to reflect carefully on how placing Jesus' life and teaching in the center might shape how we live (revealing what we actually believe).

If I were to try to boil my concerns down to one word, I would be hard pressed to think of a more important word than *integrity*. Doing theology as if Jesus matters challenges us to work very hard toward coherence between belief and practice, theology and ethics, faith and works. It is difficult to imagine anything that undermines the redemptive impact of Christian faith more than our lack of integrity when we say we believe one thing evem as our actions reveal a different set of values altogether.

FAITHFUL LIVING

In this final chapter, I want to revisit the theme of faithful living in light of the message of Jesus by returning once more to the classic story Jesus told in response to a lawyer asking him about eternal life in Luke 10.

Then a lawyer stood up to test Jesus. "Teacher," he said, "what must I do to inherit eternal?" [Jesus] said to him, "What is written in the law? What do you read there?" [The lawyer] answered, "You shall love the Lord your God with all your heart, and with all your soul, and with all your strength, and with all your mind; and your neighbor as yourself." And [Jesus] said to [the lawyer], "You have given the right answer; do this and you will live." (Luke 10:25-28)

The question the lawyer asks Jesus is our question, too. What must we do to inherit eternal life? What must we do to live? How do we live? How do we serve life?

In this book, I have defined "theology" as self-awareness about our basic values—understanding what matters most to us and articulating those priorities to others. If we also understand theology as "the study of God" (which is what the word literally means), we might say that when we do theology we are identifying our true god. Our hierarchy of values, the values that matter most to us, and what we choose and do and value are what reveal our actual god. Where does the rubber meet the road in our actual lives?

Christian theology, I believe, is theology in light of Jesus Christ. When our hierarchy of values and priorities are like Jesus' priorities, we will be worshiping the God Jesus claims is the true God. As we have seen above, these two names, "Jesus" and "Christ" are actually titles that underscore the importance of this person. "Jesus" means "savior," a term ancient Israel applied to their great leader with the same name, "Joshua." Romans during the first century thought of the emperor as their "savior." And "Christ" means "anointed one," "son of God," "messiah"—that is, literally it means "king."

To think of this person as Jesus and Christ (savior and king) is, for Christians, to confess that he embodies God. Jesus Christ shows us with clarity what God is like and what God wants from human beings. God is the merciful God of life who seeks to heal a hurting creation—and human beings have the vocation of joining God in this work.

If we confess Jesus as *our* savior and king, we are saying we want to align ourselves with his hierarchy of values. We are saying something definitive about our own identity. The task of theology is to help us understand and live with integrity with this identity. What do we value the most? What does shape what we do? To what do we devote our best energies and resources?

Our American money proclaims that "in God we trust." And of course, we do—but what "god"? We all have gods; we all trust in something; we all have something (a "god") at the top of our hierarchy of values. But who or what is the god in whom our nation trusts? Well, look at where our resources go.

In his book, *Great Plains*,[1] Ian Frazier gives a fascinating look at the western interior of North America. He highlights the extraction of untold natural wealth, generally with devastating consequences for the environment. He closes the book with a great, and deeply distressing irony. The bounty that has been taken from the ground in the Great Plains, worth billions of dollars, has been replaced with billions of dollars worth of buried nuclear weapons and their delivery systems. Quite a trade-off—irreplaceable natural beauty and life-systems replaced with systems whose only purpose is to destroy life. What does this exchange say about our nation's hierarchy of values?

It is now well known that our country devotes more money to military spending than do just about all the other countries in the world combined—amazing, given that we have no powerful enemies anywhere right now. In what god do we trust? Follow the money.

What does it say about a city's "god" when you see countless signs proclaiming, "We are open for business"? Where are the true houses of worship? How about the big box corporate mega-stores? As I write this the week after the Super Bowl, I'm reminded that we also might reflect on the god *Nike*, that is the god of victory. As the soul singer William Bell complained, all of us love winners, but if you're the unfortunate loser, "you lose alone."[2]

ALIGNING OUR VALUES WITH JESUS'

So, part of doing theology is self-awareness. The other part, for Christians, is trying to align our hierarchy of values with Jesus' values. As we better understand what our actual gods are, as we bring these gods to the surface, we then will be able to revise, adjust, and correct. By being more self-aware we will be able to transform our theology into the actual theology we want, that we believe will help us serve life.

This self-awareness should also include recognition that the various rival gods (redemptive violence, consumerism, the "free market") competing for our ultimate trust are not passive. The appropriate analogy is not searching a card catalogue in a library and having the comfortable space to decide without pressure which book we want to look at. Rather, the analogy is more the old county fair with the various barkers in the midway all vying for our attention, making promises, seeking more than anything to separate us from our money but to make us think we are happy about them doing so.

As Paul writes in Romans, these various principalities and powers actively seek to separate us from God (8:35-39). And they are pretty powerful in their allure. However, the Bible also tells us that the main power these idols have is deception. Once we see them for who or what they are—rivals to God, not God's servants as they claim—then their hold over us might be broken. Then we may be freed to model our theology (and our lives) after Jesus' theology and life.

WHAT DID JESUS TEACH?

So, let's look at Jesus' life and teaching. What do we find when we actually do our theology as if Jesus matters? As we have seen throughout this book, a passage from Luke's Gospel gives us about as much direction in just a few sentences as any place in the Bible.

Jesus faces a test when he is confronted by this lawyer, a recognized expert in Torah, the Law, the core of Israel's life and faith. The lawyer asks Jesus *the* question: What must we do to inherit eternal life? Don't let the word *eternal* distract you here. "Eternal life" for New Testament people was not focused on life in a different world, escaping from this world to go to "heaven." The lawyer is not asking, How can my soul end up living forever?

Eternal here has to do with quality. How do we live life as it is meant to be lived? How do we live in harmony with God and with God's intention for human beings? How do we fulfill our purpose? As human beings, as living creatures, we are all oriented to life—life's longing for itself. How do we best do this? That is the question.

Jesus makes like Socrates here. The lawyer asks, "What must I do to inherit life?" Jesus turns it back on him. What do *you* think? The lawyer is ready. He summarizes Torah in a nutshell. Love God with one's whole being and, as part of that love, love one's neighbor. Yes, Jesus says, you've got it right. Do this and live.

This answer the lawyer gives and Jesus affirms actually is a pretty rich and complicated statement. The issue here is life itself. The meaning of life, our place in life. The question about eternal life looms about as big and basic as any theological question a person could ask.

Jesus shows great respect for this lawyer. The lawyer turns directly to the law, to Torah, to the commands—the message God gave God's people about how to live together as God's people. Torah speaks to *life*, not just to legalistic rules and regulations about behavior. Torah is not mainly about an external toeing the line. Torah is about our very relationship with God. Torah is about the quality of life, our purposes and destiny. The writer of Psalm 119 captures this sense of Torah:

> Let your steadfast love come to me, O Lord, your salvation according to your promise. Then I shall have an answer for those who taunt me, for I trust in your word. Do not take the word of truth utterly out of my mouth, for my hope is in your ordinances. I will keep the law continually, forever and ever. I shall walk at liberty, for I have sought your precepts. I will also speak of your decrees before kings, and shall not be put to shame; I find my delight in your commandments, because I love them. I revere your commandments, which I love, and it will meditate on your statutes. (Ps. 119:41-48)

"I revere your commandments." And, from the start, Torah is about *love*. We too easily separate law and love—and with tragic consequences. We end up with loveless law and lawless love. Law becomes about power and retribution and has no soul. Love becomes about feelings and self-gratification and has no social embodiment. But Torah, in its truest meaning, speaks to hearts. Torah speaks a word of love. We see the centrality of love from the very beginning when the commandments are first given to Moses in Exodus 20. The first word in the commandments is "I am the Lord your God who delivered you from slavery and into freedom out of my mercy and love for you." The commands follow in response to God's love.

Leviticus 19 also emphasizes the centrality of love in portraying the law:

> You shall be holy, for I the Lord your God am holy. You shall each revere your mother and father, and you shall keep my sabbaths: I am the Lord your God. Do not turn to idols or make cast images for yourselves: I am the Lord your God. . . . You shall not hate in your heart anyone of your kin; you shall reprove your neighbor, or you will incur guilt yourself. You shall not take vengeance or bear a grudge against any of your people, but you shall love your neighbor as yourself: I am the Lord. (Lev. 19:1-4, 17-18)

The apostle Paul has often been characterized as reacting negatively against Torah. However, as with Jesus, we more accurately understand him as reacting against ways some of his contemporaries interpreted and applied Torah. In Romans 13, Paul embraces Torah—properly understood. Paul closely tracks the logic of Leviticus 19:

> Owe no one anything, except to love one another; for the one who loves another has fulfilled the law. The commandments, "You shall not commit adultery; You shall not murder; You shall not steal; You shall not covet; and any other commandment," are summed up in this word, "Love your neighbor as yourself." Love does no wrong to a neighbor; therefore, love is the fulfilling of the law. (Rom. 13:8-10)

The law brings life because it is grounded in and leads to love. But we can't *command* love, right? Certainly not in an external, coercive sense. Maybe we shouldn't command anything in an external, coercive sense.

As I write right now, I have just heard about recent events in the life of this little boy, about a year-and-a-half old—a boy I have a lot of interest in, my grandson Elias. I have heard some of what he's been learning. His mama is introducing him to the concept of "please." Well, Elias seems to understand: You say "please" when you are asking for something. However, he seems to understand something else, too. The "please" best comes from the heart, not from an external command. He'll say "please," alright—but only when it's his own idea, not when someone tells him to. . . . I agree!

We follow commands best when we want to, not when we feel forced. The commands in Torah are a response—we follow Torah because we have God's love, not to earn God's love. What could make the non-legalistic intentions of Torah more clear than how the lawyer (with Jesus' approval) summarizes the entire Law and Prophets: *love* God; *love* neighbor?

Love must come from the heart. We only know how to love because we have been loved. As Bruce Cockburn sings, "when you love love, love loves you too."[3] The way love works—wooing, not coercing—fits with the nature of creation as a whole. God has infused creation with God's Spirit, the Spirit of life. As Christians, we confess a unity among God the Creator, God the Spirit, and God incarnated in the human being, Jesus. God made what is out of love and continues to enliven it. And this love is defined by the message of Jesus.

Jesus and the lawyer are on the same page. Torah equals love which equals life. But then the lawyer presses on. He tests Jesus further. "And who is my neighbor?" Notice that the lawyer recognizes the direct link between love of God and love of neighbor. The lawyer recognizes that the clearest test of our love for God is our love for our neighbor.

We don't know how the lawyer himself would have answered this question. We don't know who the lawyer thought his neighbor was. Possibly, if the lawyer is like we are much of the time and if his culture was anything like ours, he would think of neighbor as limited to those inside his own circle of friends. The neighbor would be one like oneself—life and love are to be given to me and mine, alone.

When the lawyer asks who the neighbor is, Jesus makes another pedagogical move. Rather than a direct answer, he tells the story we have already examined from various angles, so let me this time pull it into the present. It's like I am back in Oregon, a University of Oregon grad with a sticker on my car to show it. I'm driving over to the coast and my car breaks down. After hours of dozens of cars speeding by heedless to my troubles someone finally stops. And it's an orange-and-black Hummer, driven by someone from Oregon State. A Beaver, for crying out loud!

Years ago, I heard a radio preacher talking about his car breaking down on the way to the airport. He had a hard time getting someone to stop, too, until finally a hippie van pulled over and helped him out. Ironically, the lesson the preacher drew from this experience wasn't about having his notion of neighbor shaken up, it was, well, you never know when you might get a chance to evangelize.

The Samaritans were the Jews' sworn enemies. And, in Jesus' story, the Samaritan is the hero! To his credit, the lawyer gets Jesus' point. The one who shows mercy is the neighbor. He is the one who shows what it takes to inherit eternal life, even if he is a Samaritan.

THEOLOGY AND HOW WE LIVE

So, in the end, theology is about how we live more than about our ideas or dogmas. Jesus takes the most theological question imaginable ("How do I inherit eternal life?") and answers it with a concrete directive. *Love* God; that is, *love* your neighbor; that is, act with transformative mercy toward anyone in need, most especially your enemies.

Jesus links this call to love enemies directly with God's own way of loving:

> Love your enemies, do good to those who hate you. . . . If you love those who love you, what credit is that to you? For even sinners love those who love them. If you do good to those who do good to you, what credit is that to you? For even sinners do the same. If you lend to those from whom you hope to receive, what credit is that to you? Even sinners lend to sinners, to receive as much again. But love your enemies, do good, and lend, expecting nothing in return. Your reward will be great, and you will be children of the Most High; for he is kind to the ungrateful and the wicked. Be merciful, just as your Father is merciful. (Luke 6:27, 32-36)

Paul reinforces this point in Romans 5 where he writes of God's love for us "in that while we were still sinners Christ died for us. . . . While we were enemies, we were reconciled to God through the death of his Son" (Rom. 5:8, 10). God's love serves as the basis for our being able to love others. God's mercy transforms us and empowers us. And God's mercy serves as our model.

Jesus is comprehensive in his definition of neighbor. In the Good Samaritan story the neighbor is the enemy. In his life, Jesus showed "neighbor love" not only to his friends and followers but also all kinds of other people. He showed neighbor love to religious leaders and outcast lepers, to the wealthy and the poor, to synagogue leaders, Roman soldiers, and revolutionaries. So when we reflect on the texts mentioned above such as Leviticus 19 and Romans 13 that call for love of "neighbor," if we see these in light of Jesus we recognize that "neighbor" means "fellow human being" and nothing less.

When Jesus began his public ministry, he affirmed the words of the prophet Isaiah. He claimed that these words were being fulfilled in his witness. We need to be attentive to the words Jesus proclaimed (Luke 4:14-21). His message of good news is directed at "the poor," "the captives," "the blind," and "the oppressed." We should resist spiritualizing these terms too much. Jesus showed in his ministry that he meant very literally that he brought a special message of hope and empowerment to those most vulnerable people.

Gustavo Gutiérrez, the great Peruvian liberation theologian, captured this central element of Jesus' message when he wrote of the travails of "non-persons" in our world today.[4] Too many people are pushed to the margins, dehumanized, trampled upon. These are precisely the people to whom Jesus reached out. In Luke's account we see an expression of a trinitarian unity. Jesus, the Son, speaks under the power of the Holy Spirit (4:18) and proclaims the "year of God's favor" (4:19). God is truly the source of this ministry of neighbor love, of neighbor restorative justice.

Jesus answers the lawyers question with an extraordinarily challenging command. "How do we gain eternal life?" By loving our fellow human beings—each one.

GO AND DO LIKEWISE

I will conclude by suggesting just how comprehensively this "go and do likewise" should be understood. Theology in light of Jesus concerns itself with neighborliness. And, as we have seen, this neighborliness has to do with serving life, the well-being of our fellow human beings.

We might think of this call to neighborliness in terms of three inter-locking circles. We are called to neighborliness in our faith communities, the locus of God's healing strategy. We are called to neighborliness in relation to the large social and political issues and policies in our society and the wider world. And we are called to neighborliness in relation to our geographical neighbors in our work of establishing and cultivating face-to-face communities in our workplaces, in our production and distribution of food, in our local economies.

The one circle includes our faith communities. "Go and do likewise" and create faith communities that embody the kind of face-to-face encouragement that Jesus had in mind in calling together his twelve disciples; that Paul had in mind when he wrote his powerful letters to congregations in Corinth, Rome, and Philippi; and that John had in mind in his messages to the seven congregations of Revelation 2 and 3.

In bringing together "Jews" and "Samaritans," people in need and people with excess, people with faith and people who doubt, people who are old and people who are young, Christian congregations model to the entire world God's ways of peace and healing.

Learn about love face to face in your common life. Find others who model Jesus' style of compassion—and accept the challenge to model such compassion yourselves. Nurture your children in healing environments. Worship together, exhorting one another to faithfulness. Provide a critical mass of those committed to genuine neighbor love that can sustain such love in a world hostile to worship of the true God.

The second circle includes working for genuine healing on a national and global scale. Go and do likewise and find ways to speak truth to power, to reform governmental structures toward genuine democracy, to seek to beat the swords of imperialist domination into plowshares that genuinely serve human well-being.

People of faith in North America have access to the decision-makers and policy setters, even if the people in power do not always (or often) welcome our influence.[5] Engagement in the political arena brings with it many temptations to waver from commitment to Jesus' message; however, that this message is needed may not be denied.

The third circle points more to work on a local level. Go and do likewise and create broader communities, alternatives to the corporate, profit-driven distribution of vital human resources. Food co-ops, credit unions, soup kitchens, farmers markets—these only scratch the surface of possibilities for human connection that may cultivate life in face of dehumanizing tendencies in our culture. Work to create economies that put human well-being ahead of shareholder dividends and CEO bonuses.

We should affirm *all* of these ways of responding to the words Jesus left the lawyer with. "Go and do likewise." Serve life on all levels—at least collectively, as we encourage one another to express our various gifts in response to the God that Jesus made visible among us.

Amen.

Responses

UNDERSCORING AND
DETOURING AROUND JESUS' LIFE

TED GRIMSRUD SEEKS TO REMEDY theology's "image problem" by engaging his readers in practical, down-to-earth, deliberate reflection about what matters most and what central values we live by. More specifically, he sets out to write a more accessible *Christian* theology that truly takes Jesus' life and teachings seriously.

Grimsrud accomplishes both goals well. He does a remarkable job of tackling the traditional Christian doctrines in a fresh way, consistently using Jesus' life and teaching as his starting point and interpretive norm. In the end, Grimsrud writes a compelling theology for those who claim to follow Jesus Christ. In fact, his theology challenges all Christians to truly practice Jesus' way of life and teaching in the world.

Effectively pointing out how the Nicean Creed and the Westminster Confession of Faith disregard Jesus' life and teaching, Grimsrud convincingly constructs a Christian theology arguing that what these traditional creeds leave out is precisely what matters most. Using the stories of Jesus' encounter with the lawyer from Luke 10:25-37 and Matt. 22:34-40, Grimsrud concludes that loving God and loving neighbor as oneself were Jesus' own highest values. Grimsrud's entire theology hinges on these love commands on which Jesus said all the law and the prophets hang.

While I agree with much of what Grimsrud asserts in this book and find his fresh articulation of traditional doctrines (salvation, sin, humanness, sacraments) to be worthy of consideration, it must be acknowledged that Grimsrud interprets Jesus' life and teaching giving particular stories and teaching from the Gospels priority. Jesus' story about the Prodigal Son recorded in Luke 10:11-32 is cited most frequently and functions as a primary story in Grimsrud's interpretation of Jesus' teaching. The stories of Jesus eating with sinners and of the lost sheep and the lost coins (Luke 10:1-10) are also central in Grimsrud's understanding of Jesus.

Grimsrud makes frequent reference to "the actual life and teaching" of Jesus but, in fact, some of Jesus' more difficult words or most troublesome teachings are not addressed in this book. One case in point: Grimsrud's use of Matthew 25:31-46 (p. 173) to argue for the importance of lived faith, without grappling with the fate of the goats and merely giving the readers a set of ellipses. Grimsrud's book would more fuller demonstrate the theological integrity for which he is reaching if he acknowledged the gospel accounts of Jesus' life and teaching that don't easily fit with the interpretive lens for Jesus that he is using here. What about Jesus' statements about gouging eyes out, hating father and mother, the outer darkness where there is weeping and gnashing of teeth or not giving the children's bread to the dogs, just to name a few?

Grimsrud's treatment of Jesus' life and teaching in this book leads the reader to believe that accessing Jesus' life and teaching from the Gospels is easy and creates one uniform picture of Jesus. If his first disciples often didn't grasp or misunderstood what Jesus was saying, maybe we should use greater humility in asserting a summary of his "actual teaching" and when determining which of Jesus' parables and teachings matter most.

As I was reading this manuscript, I kept hearing the critique of my former professor, Dr. Douglas Ottati, from Union Theological Seminary in Richmond, Virginia. In a class discussion on H. Richard Neibuhr's *Radical Monotheism and Western Culture*, Dr. Ottati chided Mennonites for giving Jesus greater priority than God. He noted that Jesus always pointed his listeners to God, not to himself. "Love *God* with your whole heart, soul, and mind. . . . " I wonder how Ted Grimsrud would re-spond to Dr. Ottati's critique, given that Grimsrud's whole the-ology rests on understanding "God *first of all* in terms of Jesus' life and teaching" (p. 33)? —*Brenda Martin Hurst, Pastor, Frazer Mennonite Church*

WHY WOULD JESUS MATTER?

TED GRIMSRUD IS CONCERNED TO SAY why Jesus matters for the-ology. In contrast to "abstract doctrines" about Jesus, he fo-cuses on Jesus' life and teachings so that we might *see* what kind of life God wants us to live and come to our *conclusion* about Jesus on that basis. Our christological confession is fi-nally our own act of perception and affirmation.

Even as there is much to affirm in insights Grimrsud draws from the aspects of Jesus' life, death, and teachings he high-lights, unfortunately his book reflects little of the great cosmic battle between the Father and Satan over Jesus' divine mes-sianic identity that is going on in the scene recorded in Matthew 16:13-23. In that battle Jesus blesses Peter because his conclusion, "You are the Messiah, the Son of the living God," if true, is *not his* (that is, based on his "flesh and blood" percep-tions) but is revealed ("apocalypsed"—*apekalypsen*) by the Fa-ther (16:17). Jesus curses Peter precisely because his conclusion *is his* (rooted in how Peter sees Jesus fulfilling current messianic expectations) and therefore Satan's (16:23).

Jesus renders judgment *against* the capacity of human per-ception to discern God's revelation in Jesus the Messiah. What the disciples *see* is insufficient. They need *God* to *act*; they need an *apocalypse* in which their distorted sight is crucified and res-urrected by divine power. If their confession that Jesus is God's Messiah is true, it is because God has *caused it to be so*, against their own best perceptions.

Grimsrud does not develop an account of the way in which *all humankind is enslaved* to cosmic and historical powers—Sin, Death, Satan, "principalities" and "authorities"—a desidera-tum found everywhere in Paul's writings and presupposed in the passion narratives of the canonical Gospels. Theological re-flection on Paul and the passion narratives is virtually absent in this book—it focuses almost exclusively on the gospel accounts *before* the confession of Peter at Caesarea Philippi.

Grimsrud thus fails to provide a doctrine of the atonement (a *Christus Victor* account) according to which humankind is enslaved to cosmic and historical powers and is wholly incapable of self-liberation. God alone, through the self-offering death and powerful resurrection of his son Jesus (himself divine and human, freely and fully participating in the event), delivers us from those enslaving powers, and through the Holy Spirit recreates us as new moral agents, activating our perception, confession, faith, and obedient action.

By limiting his attention almost exclusively to the accounts in the Gospels in which Jesus teaches and does deeds of mercy, Grimsrud finally achieves little more than a Jesusology, and that of the thinnest sort. He complains that in the traditional (Apostle's, Nicene) creedal definitions the "important elements [of Christology] (divinity, death, and resurrection) are delinked from their context in Jesus' life—and their meaning is thereby transformed. They become independent events rather than part of a single story that features Jesus' words and deeds" (p. 38). And yet, Grimsrud's construal in this complaint ironically undercuts the possibility of giving a reason why Jesus should matter at all. Jesus' life itself is not a "context" for anything. If we worry about the "delinking" of Nicene and Chalcedonian doctrines from Jesus' life and teachings, we should worry much more about the kind of "delinking" from those doctrines which Grimsrud encourages. Jesus' life and teachings easily dissolve into the social, cultural, political context of his time. It is only because Jesus was raised from the dead and ascended to the Father and sends the Spirit that anyone pays attention to his deeds and teachings.

Grimsrud of course affirms that the resurrection is God's vindication of Jesus' life and teachings. But the New Testament does not leave the matter there. Every New Testament document, *because of Jesus' resurrection*, places his deeds and teachings *within* the largest context possible—the context of *God's own decisive action*: the eternally existing divine Son becoming incarnate in Jesus of Nazareth, who dies, is raised, and ascends to the Father; the divine Holy Spirit arriving with power to create the church and to bring about the liberation, recreation, and transfiguration of the whole cosmos, the powers, and all humankind.

It is *that* theological "context" that makes the life of Jesus worthy of the attention Christians *must* give it if they are to live the kind of faithful lives that Grimsrud hopes they will and does, commendably, delineate. The creeds attest to the apocalyptic liberating action of the triune God. Their meaning stands a chance of being transformed by the life of Jesus only if the life of Jesus is first grasped, in the power of the Spirit, as in truth the very being and life of the Triune God among us. Only then does Jesus matter. —*Douglas Harink, Professor of Theology, King's University College*

AN ENGAGING INTRODUCTION
AND PERPLEXING PROBLEMS

IN THIS READABLE AND ENGAGING INTRODUCTION to central convictions of Christian faith, Ted Grimsrud takes as his starting point and lodestar the life story of Jesus in its totality—Jesus' death as inevitable outcome of what he stood for in life and his resurrection as God's confirmation that the priorities of Jesus expressed in his teaching and actions are God's priorities.

All Christian theology claims to make Jesus central in some sense, but so much of it devotes the better part of its energy to circumventing the biblical witness to what was central for Jesus. Not Grimsrud. His is an incarnational theology that wrestles with the implications for faith and practice of the biblical witness to Jesus as an expression of God's determination not to be God in splendid isolation but God in loving, other-seeking relationship with the whole of the created order, including humanity. The life story of Jesus witnesses to that divine determination but also draws people of faith into that story so as to continue that witness to God's love for the world.

In *Theology as if Jesus Matters*, Grimsrud returns again and again to Jesus' command to love both God and neighbor as the tuning fork for setting theological convictions in their proper key. Another central concern for Grimsrud is integrity, Christian practice being in sync with core Christian convictions and, indeed, giving perceptible practical expression to those convictions. In this way, his vision of theology is as much concerned with daily life as with belief, with how (and how well) Christians relate to the remainder of the created order as with what they profess or confess.

I am in basic agreement with Grimsrud's concern to do theology as if Jesus matters, and I share his pacifist convictions largely because of this shared premise. Thus, my comments below arise not so much from disagreement with Grimsrud as from agreement: Assuming the centrality of the life story of Jesus in its biblical wholeness, does Grimsrud's approach have integrity?

In two respects, I think Grimsrud's discussion might have been structured differently to cohere better with his central impulse. First, in view of what he says about "practice-first Christology," why separate discussion of salvation (chapter 8) from discussion of Jesus' identity (chapter 2)? This split is traditional, especially among theologians who think that the solution to humanity's plight is best seen in light of that plight rather than humanity's plight being best understood in light of God's restorative solution. But the split is not biblical and smacks of the creedal emphasis on doctrinal affirmations divorced from their context in the life story of Jesus.

And why postpone a discussion of ethics until the final chapter? If, taking its cue from Jesus, Christian theology is concerned with the God who is determined not to be God except in partnership with humanity, then ethics (loving neighbor) could well follow the early chapters on Jesus, God, and the Spirit of life. Would not a discussion of Christian ethics follow seamlessly from a discussion of the work of the Spirit?

There are two further points I am interested in pursuing with Grimsrud: first, interpretive difficulties associated with a Christology based on the Gospels; and second, his tendency to romanticize nature. It is not so straightforward to identify "the convictions Jesus had, Jesus' [own] hierarchy of values," since we do not have immediate access to Jesus. Moreover, not every gospel text contributes to a uniform perspective on Jesus. Interpretive choices must be made. I make the kind of interpretive choices Grimsrud makes, but some readers might find it difficult to appreciate why he gives priority to certain aspects of the fourfold biblical portrait of Jesus above others.

I am grateful to Grimsrud for trying to find coherence between what one says about God on the basis of the life story of Jesus found in the book of Scripture *and* on the basis of what we find in the book of nature. There is food for thought in his comments about projecting our violence onto nature, but if Grimsrud is correct that "for Christians, God is to be seen in all aspects of the created universe," that must include all the violent processes that have contributed to this cosmos being the way it is. Theology as if Jesus matters cannot avoid wrestling with this perplexing problem. To his credit, Grimsrud does so wrestle, but his remarks about nature take insufficient account of the violence that inheres in natural processes.
—*David Neville, School of Theology, Charles Sturt University, Australia*

HIGHLIGHTS AND WRINKLES
OF A JESUS-CENTERED THEOLOGY

I ENTHUSIASTICALLY SUPPORT TED GRIMSRUD'S claim that Jesus' life and teaching must be central to how we think theologically as Christians. For Grimsrud the Spirit of Christ is the core conviction that undergirds and shapes the values and concrete practices of an earthy, engaged life within a broken world that yearns for healing.

Grimsrud rightly criticizes the creeds for jumping from Jesus' birth to his death and ignoring Jesus' life and teaching. The creeds turn Jesus into a Divine Being at the expense of Jesus' humanity. Though the creeds affirm that Jesus is fully human, by saying nothing about his life and teachings as a guide for our lives, they make Jesus' humanity basically irrelevant for the core convictions of many Christians.

Theologies of the atonement turn the cross into a metaphysical transaction to secure our salvation for the life to come rather than the cross as a model for faithful discipleship. Thus it is not surprising that many Christians think the Christian life is about believing the right things so we can gain eternal life, rather than a set of values that shapes practices to address the care of creation, justice for the poor and marginalized, and nonviolence as an alternative to the myth of redemptive violence.

Theology as if Jesus matters also significantly alters how we relate to people of other religious faiths. Rather than seeking to convert people to believing the right things so that they receive eternal life, we would be in dialogue with others about those values and practices embodied in the Spirit of Jesus that bring healing and wholeness to the world. The concrete and practical transforming initiatives taught by Jesus in the Sermon on the Mount on peacemaking and doing justice is a fruitful framework for conversation and joint action as we engage people of both secular and other faith traditions. (This is illuminated in the scholarly work of Glen Stassen which I would add to Grimsrud's bibliography, *Just Peacemaking: Transforming Initiatives for Justice and Peace,* Westminster/John Knox Press, 1992. See especially chapter 2, "Turning toward the Sermon on the Mount," and chapter 3, "Transforming Initiatives in the New Testament," pp. 53-88.)

One important issue that needs to be addressed is Grimsrud's methodology for developing a picture of Jesus. He draws from the four Gospels, as if there were *one* composite view of Jesus in the Bible instead of attending to the four portraits of Jesus. The story of Jesus is, I believe, richer when we pay more attention to the variety of ways Jesus' life and teachings are narrated by the different gospel writers. We benefit from a comparative literary reading of the four Gospels to help us see more vividly the particular emphases and nuances as each gospel addresses a variety of issues and audiences in different contexts. Such a reading enriches the contemporary imagination as we discern the meaning of Jesus for our own time and place.

Does Grimsrud intend to imply that the story of Jesus can fully encompass everything we would want to say about God? If by "God" we mean the ultimate or foundational reality for interpreting the whole of creation, would not God also include an interpretation of powerful cosmic forces like earthquakes and volcanos? Though these forces result in the majesty and beauty of mountains that we proclaim "declare the glory of God," at the same time such forces are indifferent to and sometimes downright destructive of human life. The forces of weather that sustain life on the Great Plains are the same forces that produce tornados. I find Rudolf Otto's phrase, "mysterium tremendum," helpful to describe powers of "God" that are both beautiful and terrifying. Are the forces that express God's creative power in the universe in tension with Grimsrud's statement that "God created life in such a way that faithfulness to God leads to happiness, contentment, and joy" (p. 57)?

Finally, I have a concern about Grimsrud's uncritical reference to "dominion" in the Genesis 1 creation story and his composite interpretation of the two stories of creation as if the human relationship to the natural order were the same in both stories. Attention to each story would empower us to see a tension in Genesis in how we humans are to relate to the natural order that is profoundly relevant to how we address creation care today.

We have space only to summarize Old Testament scholar Ted Hiebert, who says the priestly story of Genesis 1 views God as a Sovereign Lord in the universe. Humans are made in God's image to have dominion and subdue the earth. In the farmer's story of creation of Genesis 2, humans are earthlings who belong to the earth community, come from the ground, and are called to take care of and "serve" the earth. We need to avoid the anthropocentric emphasis reflected in the language of dominion over nature. An ethic of creation care seeks a balance between humans as members *of* the earth community (Gen. 2) and as moral agents accountable to God *for* the earth (Gen. 1). (See Ted Hiebert, "Creation, Fall, and Humanity's Role in the Creation," in Calvin Redekop, ed., *Creation and Environment: An Anabaptist Perspective on a Sustainable World,* The Johns Hopkins University Press, 2000.)

The issues and concerns I have raised should not detract from my support for Grimsrud's Jesus-centered theology. Theology as if Jesus matters is a much needed corrective to the weakness of the Christian theological tradition. We will, however, get our theology right not primarily because we have gotten our ideas right, but because the Spirit of Jesus has become embodied in a way of living that brings healing to the world.
—*Duane Friesen, Edmund G. Kaufman Professor Emeritus of Bible and Religion, Bethel College (Kan.).*

THE AUTHOR RESPONDS TO RESPONDENTS

I DEEPLY APPRECIATE THE STIMULATING thoughtfulness displayed by the four respondents. A few brief reflections:

Brenda Martin Hurst expresses concern that I did not focus on "Jesus' more difficult words or most troublesome teachings." My intent is to focus on the heart of his message—love of God and neighbor. This isn't a book surveying everything Jesus said. Is Hurst suggesting that if we took into account the "more difficult words" that would change how we understand the heart of his message? I don't think it would.

She wonders if I give Jesus higher priority than God. Absolutely not. I argue for sharing *Jesus'* hierarchy of values and portrayal of God. He provides *the* lens through which we understand the God we worship. A great deal of mischief results when Christians imagine we can add other lenses that operate independently from the vision we get from Jesus.

I am especially grateful for Doug Harink's response for illustrating the kind of theology I seek to articulate an alternative to.

I confess that I don't know what he means by "the great cosmic battle between the Father and Satan"—except that it seems to place some theological construct between us and the story of Jesus' way of love and its normativity for our faith.

Harink seems more interested in using Matthew 16:17 for his "apocalyptic" agenda than taking seriously its role in the story of Jesus' ministry. Peter's problem seems to be that he can't accept the vulnerability of a suffering Christ. I fear Harink also has trouble accepting the vulnerability of a story-based Christology. As John Howard Yoder points out, part of the power of the gospel itself is its vulnerability, in that it may be either accepted or rejected and must be embodied in persevering love to be experienced as true.

David Neville, affirming what I do as "an incarnational theology" that centers on "God's determination . . . to be . . . God in loving, other-seeking relationship with the whole of the created order," reads me as I want to be read.

His questions are good challenges—I separated discussion of Jesus' identity from salvation as a practical decision due to wanting to discuss anthropology before soteriology, not meaning to imply that salvation is somehow distinct from the story of Jesus. My chapter on ethics is meant to be a coda on the book that is from start to finish about ethics.

I grant that my view of "nature" is optimistic. (I resist calling it "romantic.") However, I am basing it on a reading of the biblical portrayal ("the earth is full of the steadfast love of God," Ps. 33). I think in our present cultural moment we too easily marginalize that portrayal in our quickness to use human moral language ("violence") to describe natural processes.

Duane Friesen raises an excellent question: "Does . . . the story of Jesus . . . fully encompass everything we would want to say about God?" I would say the story of Jesus gives us our interpretive lens for all data we consider concerning God. Much more than what we learn directly from the story of Jesus needs to factor in—but we still need to interpret it all, to filter it in some way.

I believe that we should give the benefit of the doubt to interpretations of this "much more" that cohere with what we know about Jesus. Colossians 1:15-23 affirms that "in [Jesus] all things in heaven and on earth were created," implying that we may expect to see coherence between the data we draw on concerning God from the story of Jesus and other data.

I tend to be suspicious about tendencies to draw inferences about *God* from nature or elsewhere that move in a different trajectory than the story of Jesus. —*Ted Grimsrud*

Notes

CHAPTER ONE

1. Robert M. Pirsig, *Zen and the Art of Motorcycle Maintenance: An Inquiry into Values* (New York: Bantam Books, 1984).

2. Walter Wink, *Engaging the Powers: Discernment and Resistance in a World of Domination* (Minneapolis: Fortress Press, 1992) and *The Powers That Be: Theology For a New Millennium* (New York: Doubleday, 1998).

3. I get this phrase *embedded theology* (along with "deliberative theology," used of the process of deliberating more self-consciously about our convictions) from Howard W. Stone and James O. Duke, *How to Think Theologically* (Minneapolis: Fortress Press, 1996), especially chapter one ("Faith, Understanding, and Reflection").

4. John Prine, "Your Flag Decal Won't Get You Into Heaven Anymore," from the record *John Prine* (Atlantic Records, 1971).

5. William James, *The Principles of Psychology* (Cambridge, Mass.: Harvard University Press, 1981 [1890]), 462.

6. John H. Leith, ed., *Creeds of the Churches: A Reader in Christian Doctrine from the Bible to the Present* 3rd. ed. (Louisville: John Knox Press, 1983), 24.

CHAPTER 2

1. A writer who has influenced me a great deal and who self-consciously begins his constructive theology with Christology is C. Norman Kraus. See *God Our Savior: Theology in a Christological Mode* (Scottdale, Pa.: Herald Press, 1991).

2. See John Howard Yoder, *Christian Attitudes to War, Peace, and Revolution* (Grand Rapids, Mich.: Brazos, 2009).

3. See James Carroll, *Constantine's Sword: The Church and the Jews* (Boston: Houghton-Mifflin Books, 2001), especially Part Three: "Constantine, Augustine, and the Jews."

4. See John Howard Yoder, *The Politics of Jesus*, 2nd. edition (Grand Rapids, Mich.: Eerdmans, 1994), especially chapters 6 ("Trial Balance") and 7 ("The Disciple of Christ and the Way of Jesus").

5. John H. Leith, ed., *Creeds of the Churches: A Reader in Christian Doctrine, from the Bible to the Present*, 3rd. ed. (Louisville: Westminster John Knox, 1983), 30-31.

6. Leith, ed., *Creeds of the Churches*. 203.

CHAPTER 3

1. See my essay on this point, "Whither Contemporary Anabaptist Theology?" in Ted Grimsrud, *Embodying the Way of Jesus: Anabaptist Convictions for the Twenty-First Century* (Eugene, Ore.: Wipf and Stock, 2007), 23-36.

2. John H. Leith, ed., *Creeds of the Churches: A Reader in Christian Doctrine from the Bible to the Present*, 3rd. ed. (Louisville: John Knox Press, 1983), 197.

3. See William D. Miller, *A Harsh and Dreadful Love: Dorothy Day and the Catholic Worker Movement* (New York: Image Books, 1973). This edition of the book has Eichenberg's woodcut on its front cover.

4. Studs Terkel, *American Dreams: Lost and Found* (New York: Pantheon Books, 1980), 222-33.

5. Steve Earle, "Nothing But a Child," from the record *Copperhead Road* (MCA, 1988).

6. See Ted Grimsrud, *Triumph of the Lamb: A Self-Study Guide to the Book of Revelation* (Scottdale, Pa.: Herald Press, 1987; reprinted by Wipf and Stock), 66-70.

CHAPTER 4

1. A. James Reimer wrote in 1987: "A Trinitarian understanding of God and his ways with the world is more than simply an approach; it is in some sense the content of truth itself," "Response to Glenn Brubacher," *Conrad Grebel Review* 5.1 (Winter 1987), 74.

2. One important detailed theological treatment of the doctrine of the Holy Spirit, by German theologian Jürgen Moltmann, was called, in English translation, *The Spirit of Life*. See Jürgen Moltman, *The Spirit of Life: A Universal Affirmation* (Minneapolis: Fortress Press, 1992). For a more popular-level supplementary volume, see Jürgen Moltmann, *The Source of Life: The Holy Spirit and the Theology of Life* (Minneapolis: Fortress Press, 1997).

3. The translation, "the spirit of God," is listed in a footnote to the NRSV as an alternative translation to "a wind from God." I have added the upper case "S" to "spirit" to make the point that we may legitimately see here a reference to the Holy Spirit.

4. Richard Tarnas, *The Passion of the Western Mind: Understanding the Ideas That Have Shaped Our World View* (New York: Ballantine Books, 1991), 432.

5. Again, I have added the upper case "S" to "spirit" to make the point about God's direct involvement in the creation of life.

6. As in Genesis 1:2, the word is *ruach*—translated as "breath" in the NRSV. I render it "Spirit" to emphasize God's direct involvement in the creation of human life.

7. Wendell Berry, "Is Life a Miracle?" in *Citizenship Papers* (Washington, D.C.: Shoemaker and Hoard Publishers, 2003), 182-83.

8. Again, I add an upper case "S" to the NRSV's "spirit."

CHAPTER 5

1. In his epilogue to the 1994 edition of his most widely read book, *The Politics of Jesus*, Yoder writes briefly about this issue, focusing on questions about political involvement and effectiveness. "In Jesus we have a clue to which kinds of causation, which kinds of community-building, which kinds of conflict management, go with the grain of the cosmos, of which we know, as Caesar does not, that Jesus is both the Word (the inner logic of things) and the Lord ('sitting at the right hand'). It is not that we begin with a mechanistic universe and then look for cracks and chinks where a little creative freedom might sneak in (for which we would then give God credit): it is that we confess the deterministic world to be enclosed within, smaller than, the sovereignty of the God of the Resurrection and Ascension. 'He's got the whole world in his hands' is a post-ascension testimony. The difference it makes for political behavior is more than merely poetic or motivational." *The Politics Of Jesus*, 2nd. ed. (Grand Rapids, Mich.: Eerdmans, 1994), 246-47.

2. This paper was published as "A Pacifist Critique of the Modern Western Worldview" in *Transforming the Powers: Peace, Justice, and the Domination System*, ed. Ray Gingerich and Ted Grimsrud (Minneapolis: Fortress Press, 2006), 53-64.

3. W. H. Auden, "September 1939."

4. See Ted Grimsrud and Howard Zehr, "Rethinking God, Justice, and the Treatment of Offenders," *Journal of Offender Rehabilitation* 35 (2002), 253-79.

5. See Ted Grimsrud, "Healing Justice: The Prophet Amos and a 'New' Theology of Justice," in *Peace and Justice Shall Embrace: Power and Theopolitics in the Bible*, ed. Ted Grimsrud and Loren L. Johns (Telford, Pa.: Pandora Press U.S., 2000), 64-85.

6. Mary E. Clark, *In Search of Human Nature* (New York: Routledge, 2002).

7. Clark, *In Search*, 7.

8. Clark, *In Search*, 10.

9. Clark, *In Search*, 102.

10. See James C. Scott's discussion of the fate of Germany's Black Forest in *Seeing Like a State: How Certain Schemes to Improve the Human Conditions Have Failed* (New Haven, Conn.: Yale University Press, 1998).

11. Monty Roberts, *The Man Who Listened to Horses* (New York: Random House, 1997).

12. Bruce Cockburn, "Where the Death Squad Lives," from the album *Big Circumstance* (True North Records, 1988).

13. Gerard Manley Hopkins, "God's Grandeur."

14. Gabriel Horn, *Contemplations of a Primal Mind* (Novato, Calif.: New World Library, 1996), 28.

15. Horn, *Contemplations*, 28-29.

16. Albert Borgmann, *Crossing the Postmodern Divide* (Chicago: University of Chicago Press, 1992), 110-47.

17. Richard Tarnas, *The Passion of the Western Mind: Understanding the Ideas that Have Shaped Our World View* (New York: Ballantine Books, 1992), 432.

18. Martin Buber, *I and Thou*, trans. Walter Kaufmann (New York: Scribners, 1970), 143.

CHAPTER 6

1. Key writings for me included: John Howard Yoder, *The Original Revolution: Essays on Christian Pacifism* (Scottdale, Pa.: Herald Press, 1971); Yoder, *The Politics of Jesus* (Grand Rapids, Mich.: Eerdmans, 1972; rev. ed. 1994); Guy F. Hershberger, *The Way of the Cross in Human Relations* (Scottdale, Pa.: Herald Press, 1957; reprinted Eugene, Ore.: Wipf and Stock Publishers, 2001); and Millard C. Lind, "The Theology of Warfare in Ancient Israel" (Ph.D. dissertation, Pittsburgh Theological Seminary, 1963); a revised version was published as *Yahweh is a Warrior: The Theology of Warfare in the Old Testament* (Scottdale, Pa.: Herald Press, 1980).

2. Harold Lindsell, *The Battle for the Bible* (Grand Rapids, Mich.: Zondervan, 1976).

3. For a helpful discussion of the various historical views on these issues among Christians and guidance for how best to understand the Bible in relation to such issues see Willard M. Swartley, *Slavery, Sabbath, War, and Women: Case Issues in Biblical Interpretation* (Scottdale, Pa.: Herald Press, 1983).

4. Gabriel Josipovici, *The Book of God* (New Haven, Conn.: Yale University Press), 234.

CHAPTER 7

1. Abraham Joshua Heschel, *Who Is Man?* (Stanford, Calif.: Stanford University Press, 1965), 27.

2. See Mary Clark, *In Search of Human Nature* (New York: Routledge, 2002) for a thorough examination of contemporary understandings of human nature.

3. I learned this term from Donald Kraybill, *The Upside-Down Kingdom*, 3rd. ed. (Scottdale, Pa.: Herald Press, 2003), a helpful account of Jesus' way of being human.

4. This term comes from Gordon D. Kaufman, *In Face of Mystery: A*

Constructive Theology (Cambridge, Mass.: Harvard University Press, 1993).

5. See Ted Grimsrud, "A Pacifist Critique of the Modern Worldview," in *Transforming the Powers: Peace, Justice, and the Domination System,* ed. Ray Gingerich and Ted Grimsrud (Minneapolis: Fortress Press, 2006).

6. See Ernest Becker, *The Denial of Death* (New York: Macmillan, 1973); and Daniel Liechty, *Reflecting on Faith in a Post-Christian Time* (Telford, Pa.: Cascadia Publishing House, 2003).

7. See Ashley Montagu's many writings, including, most directly relevant, *The Nature of Human Aggression* (New York: Oxford University Press, 1976).

8. See James Gilligan, *Violence: Our Deadly Epidemic and Its Causes* (New York: Putnam, 1996). Gilligan, while not at all writing from a theological perspective, provides an illustration how a particularly problematic sinful behavior (violence) may fruitfully be analyzed as a public health issue.

CHAPTER 8

1. John Donahue, *The Gospel in Parable: Metaphor, Narrative, and Theology in the Synoptic Gospels* (Minneapolis: Fortress Press, 1988).

2. Timothy Gorringe, *God's Just Vengeance: Crime, Violence, and the Rhetoric of Salvation* (New York: Cambridge University Press, 1996).

3. For a fuller discussion, see Ted Grimsrud and Howard Zehr, "Rethinking God, Justice, and the Treatment of Offenders," *Journal of Offender Rehabilitation* 35 (2002), 253-79. This essay was also republished in *Religion, Community, and the Rehabilitation of Criminal Offenders,* ed. Thomas P. O'Connor and Nathaniel Pallone (New York: Haworth Press, 2002), 259-86.

4. James Gilligan, *Violence: Our Deadly Epidemic and Its Causes* (New York: Putnam, 1996), 185.

5. Gilligan, *Violence,* 23-24.

6. Gilligan, *Violence,* 155.

7. Gilligan, *Violence,* 25.

8. James Gilligan, *Preventing Violence* (New York: Thames and Hidson, 2001), 20.

9. See Walter Wink's profound analysis of the Powers and Jesus victory in *Engaging the Powers: Discernment and Resistance in a World of Domination* (Minneapolis: Fortress Press, 1992).

10. I learned this term from Wink, *Engaging.*

CHAPTER 9

1. See Willard M. Swartley, *Slavery, Sabbath, Women, and War: Case Studies in Biblical Interpretation* (Scottdale, Pa.: Herald Press, 1983).

2. See Harry Potter, *Hanging in Judgment: Religion and the Death Penalty in England* (New York: Continuum, 1993).

3. See Alfred W. McCoy, *A Question of Torture: CIA Interrogation, From the Cold War to the War on Terror* (New York: Metropolitan Books, 2006).

4. This term is central to Walter Wink's analysis in his book *Engaging the Powers: Discernment and Resistance in a World of Domination* (Minneapolis: Fortress Press, 1992).

5. See David Kratz Mathies, "'Holding Fast' to Principles or Drawing Boundaries of Exclusion? The Use and Misuse of the *Confession of Faith in a Mennonite Perspective*," *Conrad Grebel Review* 25.3 (2007), 68-85.

6. See, for example, Stephen Toulmin, *Cosmopolis: The Hidden Agenda of Modernity* (Chicago: University of Chicago Press, 1992).

CHAPTER 10

1. James Wm. McClendon Jr., in his trilogy on constructive theology, coined the use of the term *baptist* with a lower case "b" to describe the Christian tradition that has emphasized ethics and discipleship and believers baptism (this would include Mennonites and other self-consciously Anabaptist groups, but also Baptists, Disciples of Christ, and many other similar traditions). For his discussion of this term, see James Wm. McClendon, Jr., *Ethics: Systematic Theology*, vol. 1, 2nd. ed. (Nashville: Abingdon Press, 2002).

2. Sara Miles, *Take This Bread: A Radical Conversion* (New York: Ballantine Books, 2007).

3. Abraham J. Heschel, *God in Search of Man: A Philosophy of Judaism* (New York: Farrar, Straus, and Giroux, 1956), quoted by Maurice Friedman in his review of Heschel's book, *The Journal of Religion* 37.1 (Jan. 1957), 53.

4. Miles, *Take This Bread*, 240.

CHAPTER 11

1. John Howard Yoder, *Body Politics: Five Practices of the Christian Community Before the Watching World* (Scottdale, Pa.: Herald Press, 1992).

2. I want to be clear about the interpretive moves I am making here. I am not so much trying to propose a reading of John 14:6 on its own terms as reflect on the general New Testament sense of Jesus as the "way." Lamar Williamson, Jr., in his commentary on John, suggests "in canonical context and in light of Jesus' final command to Peter, 'Follow me' (John 21:19), readers may rightly understand Jesus' claim as an invitation to follow his way" (*Preaching the Gospel of John: Proclaiming the Living Word* [Louisville, Ky.: Westminster John Knox Press, 2004], 180).

CHAPTER 12

1. Hal Lindsey, *The Late, Great Planet Earth* (Grand Rapids, Mich.: Zondervan, 1970).

2. Jonathan Kirsch, *A History of the End of the World: How the Most Controversial Book in the Bible Changed the Course of Western Civilization* (San

Francisco: HarperSanFrancisco, 2006), 18.

3. When I was in graduate school, I wrote a popular-level commentary on Revelation: *The Triumph of the Lamb: A Self-Study Guide to the Book of Revelation* (Scottdale, Pa.: Herald Press, 1987; reprinted by Eugene, Ore.: Wipf and Stock Publishers, 1998). While I have learned much since then and would write the book quite differently today, it contains a great deal that I still affirm and is reflected in my comments here.

4. One version of this story is retold in Meg Holder, *Papa Panov's Special Day* (Wheaton, Ill.: Tyndale House Publishers, 2002).

5. See N.T. Wright, *Surprised by Hope: Rethinking Heaven, the Resurrection, and the Mission of the Church* (New York: HarperOne, 2008).

CHAPTER 13

1. Ian Frazier, *Great Plains* (New York: Farrar, Straus, and Giroux, 1989).

2. William Bell, "Everybody Love a Winner," from the record *The Soul of a Bell* (Stax Records, 1967).

3. Bruce Cockburn, "Love Loves You Too," from the record *Dart To the Heart* (Columbia, 1994).

4. The classic text from Gutiérrez is *A Theology of Liberation: History, Politics, and Salvation* (Maryknoll, N.Y.: Orbis Books, 1973). A focused reflection on the travail on "non-persons" may be found in Gustavo Gutierrez, *On Job: God-Talk and the Suffering of the Innocent* (Maryknoll, N.Y.: Orbis Books, 1987).

5. For detailed reflections on the role of Christian pacifists in North American democratic processes, see Ted Grimsrud, "Anabaptist Faith and American Democracy," *Mennonite Quarterly Review* 78.3 (July 2004), 341-62. Reprinted in Ted Grimsrud, *Embodying the Way of Jesus: Anabaptist Convictions for the Twenty-First Century* (Eugene, Ore.: Wipf and Stock Publishers, 2007), 141-59.

Suggestions for Further Reading

What follow are suggestions of materials that I believe readers of this book will find stimulating and accessible. I disagree with a lot of what many of these books say, but I have found all of the books useful in moving toward clarity in my own convictions.

1. WHAT DO WE DO WITH THEOLOGY?

Ted Grimsrud. *Embodying the Way of Jesus: Anabaptist Convictions for the Twenty-First Century.* Eugene, Oregon: Wipf and Stock Publishers, 2007.

C. Norman Kraus. *God Our Savior: Theology in a Christological Mode.* Scottdale, Pa.: Herald Press, 1991.

Howard W. Stone and James O. Duke. *How to Think Theologically.* Minneapolis, Fortress Press, 1996.

2. THE PERSON OF CHRIST

Marcus Borg. *Jesus: Uncovering the Life, Teachings, and Relevance of a Religious Revolutionary.* San Francisco: HarperSanFrancisco, 2006.

Shane Claiborne and Chris Haw. *Jesus for President: Politics for Ordinary Radicals.* Grand Rapids: Zondervan, 2008.

John Howard Yoder. *The Politics of Jesus.* 2nd. ed. Grand Rapids, Mich.: Eerdmans, 1994.

3. GOD

Michael J. Gorman. *Inhabiting the Cruciform God: Kenosis, Justification, and Theosis in Paul's Narrative Soteriology.* Grand Rapids, Mich.: Eerdmans, 2009.

Gordon Kaufman. *God—Mystery—Diversity: Christian Theology in a Pluralistic World.* Minneapolis: Fortress Press, 1996.

Sallie McFague. *Models of God: Theology for an Ecological, Nuclear Age.* Minneapolis: Fortress Press, 1987.

4. THE HOLY SPIRIT

Wendell Berry. *Life is a Miracle: An Essay Against Modern Superstition.* Washington, D.C.: Counterpoint, 2001.

Martin Buber. *I and Thou.* Trans. Walter Kaufmann. New York: Scribner's, 1970.

Jürgen Moltmann. *The Source of Life: The Holy Spirit and the Theology of Life.* Minneapolis: Fortress Press, 1997.

5. CREATION

Wendell Berry. *The Gift of Good Land: Further Essays Cultural and Agricultural.* San Francisco: North Point Press, 1981.

Terence Fretheim. *God and World in the Old Testament: A Relational Theology of Creation.* Nashville: Abingdon Press, 2005.

Calvin Redekop, ed. *Creation and Environment: An Anabaptist Perspective on a Sustainable World.* Baltimore: Johns Hopkins University Press, 2000.

6. REVELATION

Walter Brueggemann. *The Bible Makes Sense.* Winona, Minn.: St. Mary's Press, 1977.

Ted Grimsrud. *God's Healing Strategy: An Introduction to the Main Themes of the Bible.* 2nd. ed. Telford, Pa.: Cascadia Publishing House, 2009.

Willard M. Swartley. *Send Forth Your Light: A Vision for Peace, Mission, and Worship.* Scottdale, Pa.: Herald Press, 2007.

7. HUMANITY

Mary E. Clark. *In Search of Human Nature.* New York: Routledge, 2002.

Abraham Heschel. *Who is Man?* Stanford, Calif.: Stanford University Press, 1965.

Richard Middleton. *The Liberating Image: The Imago Dei in Genesis One.* Grand Rapids, Mich.: Brazos Press, 2005.

8. THE WORK OF CHRIST

Rita Nakashima Brock and Rebecca Parker. *Proverbs of Ashes: Violence, Redemptive Suffering, and the Search for What Saves Us.* Boston: Beacon Press, 2001.

Terrence J. Rynne. *Gandhi & Jesus: The Saving Power of Nonviolence.* Maryknoll, N.Y.: Orbis Books, 2008.

J. Denny Weaver. *The Nonviolent Atonement.* Grand Rapids, Mich.: Eerdmans, 2001.

9. THE CHURCH

David Augsburger. *Dissident Discipleship: A Spirituality of Self-Surrender, Love of God, and Love of Neighbor.* Grand Rapids, Mich.: Brazos Press, 2006.

Gerhard Lohfink. *Does God Need the Church? Toward a Theology of the People of God.* Collegeville, Minn.: Michael Glazier Books, 1999.

Brian D. McLaren. *Everything Must Change: Jesus, Global Crises, and a Revolution of Hope.* Nashville: Thomas Nelson, 2007.

10. THE SACRAMENTS

William T. Cavanaugh. *Torture and Eucharist: Theology, Politics, and the body of Christ.* Blackwell, 1991.

Sara Miles. *Take This Bread: A Radical Conversion.* New York: Ballantine Books, 2007.

John Howard Yoder. *Body Politics: Five Practices of the Christian Community Before the Watching World.* Scottdale, Pa.: Herald Press, 1991.

11. THE RELIGIONS

John D. Caputo. *On Religion.* New York: Routledge, 2001.

Daniel Liechty. *Reflecting on Faith in a Post-Christian Time.* Telford, Pa.: Cascadia Publishing House, 2003.

Dennis L. Ockholm and Timothy R. Phillips, eds. *Four Views on Salvation in a Pluralistic World.* Grand Rapids, Mich.: Zondervan,

12.THE END TIMES

Ted Grimsrud. *Triumph of the Lamb: A Self-Study Guide to the Book of Revelation*. Scottdale, Pa.: Herald Press, 1987.

Michael Northcott. *An Angel Directs the Storm: Apocalyptic Religion and American Empire*. New York: I. B. Tauris, 2004.

N. T. Wright. *Surprised by Hope: Rethinking Heaven, the Resurrection, and the Mission of the Church*. San Francisco, HarperOne, 2008.

13. ETHICS

Denise Breton and Stephen Lehman. *The Mystic Heart of Justice: Restoring Wholeness in a Broken World*. West Chester, Pa.: Chrysalis Books, 2001.

David C. Korten. *The Great Turning: From Empire to Earth Community*. San Francisco: Berrett-Koehler Publishers, 2006.

Walter Wink. *Engaging the Powers: Discernment and Resistance in a World of Domination*. Minneapolis: Fortress Press, 1992.

The Author

Ted Grimsrud is a pastor and theologian living in Harrisonburg, Virginia. He served ten years in congregational ministry and since 1996 has been a member of the faculty at Eastern Mennonite University, where he is currently Professor of Theology and Peace Studies.

Ted was born in Eugene, Oregon, and raised in rural Elkton, Oregon. A graduate of the University of Oregon, he and his wife Kathleen Temple joined the Mennonite Church after attending Associated Mennonite Biblical Seminary, from which he received an M.A. in Peace Studies. His Ph.D. was received from the Graduate Theological Union, Berkeley, California, in Christian Ethics, with an emphasis on the ethics of peacemaking.

Ted has published numerous books, scholarly, and popular articles. His most recent books are *Embodying the Way of Jesus: Anabaptist Convictions for the Twenty-First Century* (2007) and *Reasoning Together: A Conversation on Homosexuality,* co-authored with Mark Thiessen Nation (2008).

Ted and Kathleen have one son, Johan Grimsrud, one daughter-in-law, Jill Humphrey, and one grandson, Elias. They are members of Shalom Mennonite Congregation.